SAN MATEO CITY PUBLIC LIBRARY
3 9047 02647413 6

D0933859

FROM THE LIBR
Gilbert G. Wayn
Donated to t
San Mateo Public

THE POEMS OF JOHN GREENLEAF

WHITTIER

THE AMERICAN POETS
EDITED BY LOUIS UNTERMEYER FOR
THE HERITAGE PRESS

JOHN GREENLEAF WHITTIER

From the portrait by Wyatt Eaton, 1878; as engraved by Timothy Cole

THE POEMS OF JOHN GREENLEAF

WHITTIER

SELECTED AND EDITED, WITH A COMMENTARY,

BY *LOUIS UNTERMEYER;* ILLUSTRATED WITH

PENCIL DRAWINGS BY *R. J. HOLDEN*

THE HERITAGE PRESS, NEW YORK

The Editor's Introduction

I

Say "John Greenleaf Whittier" — and most of us immediately picture a pleasant old man who wrote about barefoot boys and fading, half-forgotten landscapes; a bearded New England patriarch who mumbled morals for textbooks; a chill spirit whose element was winter, "a granite boulder sheeted in snow."

But it is an incomplete, if not wholly misshapen, portrait. Except during the twilight of his life, Whittier was a creature of heat and fervor, a headlong spirit of revolt, a fearless and magnificently fighting Quaker. In *A Fable for Critics,* James Russell Lowell put aside the barb of satire to praise that spirit:

> There is Whittier, whose swelling and vehement heart
> Strains the strait-breasted drab of the Quaker apart,
> And reveals the live Man, still supreme and erect,
> Underneath the bemummying wrappers of sect;
> There was ne'er a man born who had more of the swing
> Of the true lyric bard and all that kind of thing;
> And his failures arise (though he seem not to know it)
> From the very same cause that has made him a poet, —
> A fervor of mind which knows no separation
> 'Twixt simple excitement and pure inspiration;
> Let his mind once get head in its favorite direction
> And the torrent of verse bursts the dams of reflection.

It was not a cold or congealing mind, but a hammering heart that beat out the best of American ballads, the withering "Ichabod," the fiery "Expostulation" and other anti-slavery poems, classics of courage and indignation.

II

He was a worker from the beginning. Unlike most of his genteel contemporaries, Whittier was reared neither as a gentleman nor a scholar. His forebears had been farmers, weavers, hard-working orthodox Quakers. Born on a farm at Haverhill, Massachusetts, December 17, 1807, he spent the first eighteen years of his life plowing and planting, attending to the livestock, and milking seven cows as a small part of the daily chores.

He was not a precocious genius. As Whitman Bennett points out in his *Whittier: Bard of Freedom,* "Bryant, writing 'Thanatopsis' and 'To a Waterfowl' when scarcely more than an adolescent and never greatly surpassing them in later years, is the exact antithesis of Whittier, who came into his full glory with the writing of 'Snow-Bound' at fifty-eight."

Whittier's was literally a barefoot boyhood; scantily educated, he dreamed of the classroom not with the proverbial disdain of youth, but with desire. A juvenile verse is significant in its half-pathetic, half-humorous longing:

> And must I always swing the flail
> And help to fill the milking pail?
> I wish to go away to school;
> I do not wish to be a fool.

He was nineteen before his boyhood ambition was fulfilled. Whittier's father eked out a living for the family by peddling small goods. During the winter the boy earned extra money by making slippers (eight cents a pair), and was able to attend Haverhill Academy for two terms. Samuel T. Pickard, Whittier's first biographer, tells us that young Whittier "calculated so closely every item of expense that he knew before the beginning of the term he would have twenty-five cents to spare at its close, and he actually had."

The home library was small; besides the Bible, there were some thirty volumes by and about eminent Quakers. Whittier had rhymed his way through childhood, but the full-throated voice of poetry came to him through a casual visitor who "after eating his bread and cheese and drinking his mug of cider, gave us 'Bonnie Doon,' 'Highland Mary,' and 'Auld Lang Syne.' " Joshua Coffin, the boy's schoolteacher, gave him a popular selection of Burns's *Poems*, and the little volume was so deeply cherished that it remained with the poet for the rest of his life. The immature versifier could scarcely appreciate the simple but skillful music of Burns's lyrics, but the young Yankee farm hand intuitively responded to the spirit of the Scottish plowboy.

At eighteen Whittier's first published poem appeared in William Lloyd Garrison's *Free Press*. The young editor, only three years older than Whittier, wrote a laudatory paragraph and was so interested in his discovery that he drove to Haverhill to meet his contributor. The result was a friendship of the greatest importance to both men. Whittier was not only intellectually stimulated by his ardent new friend but was quickened to creation. Between the ages of eighteen and twenty-one the poet published more than one hundred and forty poems. The verses were too rapidly written to achieve excellence; many of them were haphazard, many were merely facile. But there was a forthrightness behind them which, struggling through stereotyped phrases and stock situations, was as eager as it was sincere.

At twenty-one Whittier was again confronted with the necessity of earning a living. Abijah Thayer, editor of the small Haverhill *Gazette*, came to his aid and helped him to secure work on the *American Manufacturer*. This took Whittier to Boston, where he somehow combined poetry with hack-work for a trade journal; but before the year was out, his father's health failed and he went back to the farm. Before he was twenty-three, the elder Whittier died, leaving his son to take care of himself, his mother, his aunt, and his younger sister. Fortunately he was offered another editorial position, and the summer of 1830 found him established in Hartford. Here, except for brief intervals of travel, he remained until he was twenty-five, when a breakdown forced him to resign his post as editor.

In *Quaker Militant* Albert Mordell considers this sickness a psychic collapse, a significant phase of sexual repression and neurotic bachelorhood. But Whittier, as though to anticipate the analysts, maintained that he was overworked and that his illness was "as real as the nose on my face." Whitman Bennett, Whittier's most recent champion, came to the poet's defense and wrote "he had lived and saved money on a pittance. Throughout the period he had published almost a poem a week and must have written prose enough to fill a sizable volume. With his fragile physique, the wonder is that he stood the grind so long."

At twenty-five, Whittier was again living at home. This was in 1832, the year of the publication of *Moll Pitcher*, his first long poem to appear in book form. It was not a good poem, and although Whittier salvaged pieces of it, he did not allow it to be printed as a whole in his *Collected Poems*. Nevertheless, Whittier had now entered the arena as a public poet.

III

In November, 1831, Whittier published his tribute "To William Lloyd Garrison," the man who in the first issue of *The Liberator* nailed up his slogan: "I am in earnest. I will not equivocate — I will not excuse — I will not retreat a single inch — and I will be heard." It was the turning point of Whittier's career. The first verse announced his credo:

> Champion of those who groan beneath
> Oppression's iron hand;
> In view of penury, hate, and death,
> I see thee fearless stand.

The die was cast. At the age of twenty-six Whittier became a crusader; he dedicated himself to the cause of Justice and Freedom. Although many bucolic and even sentimental poems were to flow from his pen, Whittier sternly faced an issue which many of his contemporaries feared.

His Quaker convictions were confirmed by Garrison; his Quaker blood had always risen at the sight of men enslaved by men, for the Quakers were against slavery from the beginning. Garrison's abolitionist writings stirred Whittier to a fever of indignation. In 1833 the poet published, at his own expense, a pamphlet entitled *Justice and Expediency* and became one of the founders of the American Anti-Slavery Society. He spoke now not only with the accents of the exalted bard, but with the intrepid voice of conscience. It is impossible for us to realize how much daring was required for what seemed an act not only of fearlessness but foolhardiness. Even the courageous Emerson disapproved; he ranked the abolitionists with "madmen, madwomen, Dunkards, Muggletonians, Come-Outers, Groaners, Seventh Day Baptists, Calvinists," and other eccentrics.

When Whittier became the poet-politician of the anti-slavery cause, he opposed not only the *status quo* but the structure of complacent society; he challenged an economy founded on injustice, sanctioned by law and blessed by the clergy: a system erected on the exploitation of slave labor and "held together by cotton." Whittier did not underrate the forces arrayed against him, but he was not abashed by them. His was a vigorous voice at the anti-slavery conventions; he helped guide the course of the movement; he wrote fighting editorials. Only his poor health stopped him from taking an active part in the legislature to which he was sent in his twenty-eighth year.

In 1838 Whittier went to Philadelphia, became editor of the *Pennsylvania Freeman*, and moved his office to Pennsylvania Hall, a partly completed structure which was being consecrated as a Temple of Liberty for the Anti-Slavery Society. The Hall was inaugurated on May 14, 1838. Three days after the official opening, an organized pro-slavery mob, with the endorsement of the Philadelphia Mayor, ransacked Whittier's office and set the building on fire. (See the poem "Pennsylvania Hall" on page 231.) The crowd was triumphant and threatening; Whittier's life was in danger. But the morning after the catastrophe, Whittier concluded a challenging editorial with these lines: "Let the abhorred deed speak for itself. Let all men see by what a frail tenure they hold property and life in a land overshadowed by the curse of slavery."

IV

After thirty Whittier struggled against physical handicaps. The Philadelphia outrage brought on another collapse, this time more severe than the Hartford breakdown. Bursts of energy were followed by periods of prolonged exhaustion, and, though Whittier lived into his mid-eighties, most of his life was spent as an invalid. A friendship begun in his thirties with a minor poetess, Elizabeth Lloyd, seemed about to ripen into love, but the documents in *Whittier's Unknown Romance* show that the poet was more pursued than pursuing. The "romance" flared up again after fifteen years. Miss Lloyd had become Mrs. Howell, a widow, and Whittier, still unmarried, was over fifty.

But, although Mrs. Howell was still ardent and Whittier believed himself to be in love, he was not sufficiently eager. His fervor lapsed again into friendship, his letters became polite instead of passionate, and he remained a bachelor.

Suffering from insomnia, from pains in the head and his "old complaint of palpitation," it is possible that Whittier may have exaggerated his physical ailments — Emerson twitted him because he "bragged of bad health" — the more so since he outlived most of his colleagues. But the attacks were real, and that Whittier survived them is not a proof of hypochondria but of stubborn determination.

His protests against slavery grew in pitch and power. Articles, poems, and pamphlets denounced the evil with renewed intensity. He was responsible for the election of the abolitionist Charles Sumner to the Senate. He became the laureate of protest.

A new spirit energized the verse. It vibrated through the volume issued in 1863, *In War Time and Other Poems;* it still uplifts the ringing "Laus Deo" and pounds through "Barbara Frietchie" with the strength of marching feet.

V

Snow-Bound, which combines a series of portraits in an immortal idyl, was published in 1866. It was sensationally successful. Praised by the erudite few, it was read by the multitudes; Whittier's first royalties were about ten thousand dollars. *The Tent on the Beach*, published a year after *Snow-Bound*, was an even greater success than its immediate predecessor. The barefoot boy who had made slippers at eight cents a pair was suddenly affluent.

Whittier was now sixty, already a legendary figure. He sank into old age with dignity and relief; he enjoyed the lingering twilight. His verse became increasingly devotional. Hymns and such deeply religious poems as "The Eternal Goodness" became his major occupation for twenty years. His seventieth and eightieth birthdays were celebrated as national events. The militant poet was now an honored patriarch.

On September 3, 1892 the aging poet knew he was dying. An apoplectic stroke paralyzed his right side. He did not lose consciousness, but three days later the nurse saw that the end had come. She started to pull down the shades. But the poet wanted light to the last. With an effort he raised his left hand in protest. "No — no," he said, and died. Had he lived two more months he would have been eighty-five.

VI

Whittier's sincerity was surpassed only by his energy. During his lifetime he published some forty volumes which included work in almost every genre. The writing is as uneven in style as it is varied in subject. Whittier confessed that he was unworthy to stand among the singers he admired. Yet, though there is truth as well as modesty in his disavowal, Whittier's Quaker meekness has a glory of its own. In the stanzas written as an introduction to the first general collection of his poems, he acknowledges Milton's divinity, Marvell's grace, Spenser's melodiousness, and Sidney's silvery phrases, "sprinkling our noon of time with freshest morning dew." But he declares himself undeserving of their high company:

> The rigor of a frozen clime,
> The harshness of an untaught ear,
> The jarring words of one whose rhyme
> Beat often Labor's hurried time,
> Or Duty's rugged march through storm and strife, are here.

Nevertheless, the almost apologetic proem ends on a note that, though modest, is confident. "O Freedom!" Whittier concludes, "if to me belong nor mighty Milton's gift divine nor Marvell's wit, still with a love as deep and strong as theirs, I lay, like them, my best gifts on thy shrine."

This pure devotion to Freedom sometimes resulted in impure poetry, in haphazard rhymes, faulty grammar, and ungainly repetitions. The intense faith in God, the ardent hope in Justice found expressions in lines that were not expected to survive the occasions that inspired them; they were spontaneous, not carefully measured, protests, "alarm signals, trumpet calls to action, words wrung from the writer's heart, forged at white heat." If they were harsh or intemperate, the world's heart beat faster and the pulse of humanity was quickened by them.

But, although the partisan poetry has survived by virtue of its moral fervor, the less vociferous verses are not only the most endearing but the most enduring. The rural Muse speaks to us intimately and with appropriate naïveté in "Telling the Bees," "The Trailing Arbutus," "Sweet Fern," "The Barefoot Boy," and "Maud Muller," redolent of hay and sunny clover. "Skipper Ireson's Ride," "Cassandra Southwick," and "Barbara Frietchie" have become historic American ballads. "Snow-Bound" is a rustic idyl accomplished with all the graphic details of a Dutch portrait painter; "if one who had been brought up in a New England village should be stricken blind," wrote John Macy, "'Snow-Bound' would give him eyes again for all that Whittier describes."

Such poems are as sure of their permanent place as of their popularity. Woven of country homespun, the materials may not be richly styled, but they are rugged. They have worn well; it will be a long time before they are worn out.

The Table of Contents

II

SNOW-BOUND

III

OF PLACES AND PEOPLE

IV

THE TENT ON THE BEACH

V

WAR AND ANTI-SLAVERY

VI

REMINISCENCE AND REFORM

VII

THE ETERNAL GOODNESS

A List of the Drawings

Proem

I love the old melodious lays
Which softly melt the ages through,
The songs of Spenser's golden days,
Arcadian Sidney's silvery phrase,
Sprinkling our noon of time with freshest morning dew.

Yet, vainly in my quiet hours
To breathe their marvellous notes I try;
I feel them, as the leaves and flowers
In silence feel the dewy showers,
And drink with glad, still lips the blessing of the sky.

The rigor of a frozen clime,
The harshness of an untaught ear,
The jarring words of one whose rhyme
Beat often Labor's hurried time,
Or Duty's rugged march through storm and strife, are here.

Of mystic beauty, dreamy grace,
No rounded art the lack supplies;
Unskilled the subtle lines to trace,
Or softer shades of Nature's face,
I view her common forms with unanointed eyes.

Nor mine the seer-like power to show
The secrets of the heart and mind;
To drop the plummet-line below
Our common world of joy and woe,
A more intense despair or brighter hope to find.

Yet here at least an earnest sense
Of human right and weal is shown;
A hate of tyranny intense,
And hearty in its vehemence,
As if my brother's pain and sorrow were my own.

O Freedom! if to me belong
Nor mighty Milton's gift divine,
Nor Marvell's wit and graceful song,
Still with a love as deep and strong
As theirs, I lay, like them, my best gifts on thy shrine.

THE WHITTIER HOME AT AMESBURY

The Poems of John Greenleaf Whittier

I

BALLADS AND LEGENDS

The Editor's Commentary

WHITTIER ROAMED over two continents and several centuries for his narrative and legendary poems. But he was most at ease in the ballads which drew their inspiration as well as their inflection from native sources. "Cassandra Southwick" is a melodrama firmly rooted in New England soil; "Maud Muller" is forthright and indigenous to the core; "Skipper Ireson's Ride" is enlivened by the actual Yankee twang.

"Maud Muller," unlike most of the other ballads, had no foundation in fact. Whittier remembered stopping beside a hayfield and talking to a pretty country girl who "strove to hide her bare feet by raking hay over them, blushing as she did so, through the tan of her cheek and neck." The trivial incident still speaks to us in all its naïveté; innocuous, even sententious, the story is obviously invented, but the lines are their own appraisal as household words.

"Cassandra Southwick" and "Skipper Ireson's Ride" reveal the moralizing Quaker joined with the exploring poet. History has exonerated the skipper of Whittier's ballad; it has been established that the crew refused to go to the aid of the disabled vessel and shielded themselves by blaming the captain. But Whittier was ignorant of the facts when he wrote his hard-hitting rhymes and their grim refrain — and the reader may be grateful for a fiction that is not only stranger than truth but (at least for the poet's purpose) better.

"Pentucket," a little known poem, is even closer to Whittier's heart. Pentucket was Haverhill, Whittier's home; and the farm-boy often followed the plow-horse in furrowed ground once bloody with massacre.

The settings change; the open fields become crowded streets; the names are forgotten. But the emotions do not fade, and the words that revive them are as fresh and illuminating today as when, almost a hundred years ago, they brightened the eyes of their first readers.

Maud Muller

Maud Muller on a summer's day
Raked the meadow sweet with hay.

Beneath her torn hat glowed the wealth
Of simple beauty and rustic health.

Singing, she wrought, and her merry glee
The mock-bird echoed from his tree.

But when she glanced to the far-off town,
White from its hill-slope looking down,

The sweet song died, and a vague unrest
And a nameless longing filled her breast, —

A wish that she hardly dared to own,
For something better than she had known.

The Judge rode slowly down the lane,
Smoothing his horse's chestnut mane.

He drew his bridle in the shade
Of the apple-trees, to greet the maid,

And asked a draught from the spring that flowed
Through the meadow across the road.

She stooped where the cool spring bubbled up,
And filled for him her small tin cup,

And blushed as she gave it, looking down
On her feet so bare, and her tattered gown.

"Thanks!" said the Judge; "a sweeter draught
From a fairer hand was never quaffed."

He spoke of the grass and flowers and trees,
Of the singing birds and the humming bees;

Then talked of the haying, and wondered whether
The cloud in the west would bring foul weather.

And Maud forgot her brier-torn gown,
And her graceful ankles bare and brown;

And listened, while a pleased surprise
Looked from her long-lashed hazel eyes.

At last, like one who for delay
Seeks a vain excuse, he rode away.

Maud Muller looked and sighed: "Ah me!
That I the Judge's bride might be!

"He would dress me up in silks so fine,
And praise and toast me at his wine.

"My father should wear a broadcloth coat;
My brother should sail a painted boat.

"I'd dress my mother so grand and gay,
And the baby should have a new toy each day.

"And I'd feed the hungry and clothe the poor,
And all should bless me who left our door."

The Judge looked back as he climbed the hill,
And saw Maud Muller standing still.

"A form more fair, a face more sweet,
Ne'er hath it been my lot to meet.

"And her modest answer and graceful air
Show her wise and good as she is fair.

"Would she were mine, and I to-day,
Like her, a harvester of hay;

"No doubtful balance of rights and wrongs,
Nor weary lawyers with endless tongues,

"But low of cattle and song of birds,
And health and quiet and loving words."

But he thought of his sisters, proud and cold,
And his mother, vain of her rank and gold.

So, closing his heart, the Judge rode on,
And Maud was left in the field alone.

MAUD MULLER

He drew his bridle in the shade. . .
And asked a draft from the spring

But the lawyers smiled that afternoon,
When he hummed in court an old love-tune;

And the young girl mused beside the well
Till the rain on the unraked clover fell.

He wedded a wife of richest dower,
Who lived for fashion, as he for power.

Yet oft, in his marble hearth's bright glow,
He watched a picture come and go;

And sweet Maud Muller's hazel eyes
Looked out in their innocent surprise.

Oft, when the wine in his glass was red,
He longed for the wayside well instead;

And closed his eyes on his garnished rooms
To dream of meadows and clover-blooms.

And the proud man sighed, with a secret pain,
"Ah, that I were free again!

"Free as when I rode that day,
Where the barefoot maiden raked her hay."

She wedded a man unlearned and poor,
And many children played round her door.

But care and sorrow, and childbirth pain,
Left their traces on heart and brain.

And oft, when the summer sun shone hot
On the new-mown hay in the meadow lot,

And she heard the little spring brook fall
Over the roadside, through the wall,

In the shade of the apple-tree again
She saw a rider draw his rein;

And, gazing down with timid grace,
She felt his pleased eyes read her face.

Sometimes her narrow kitchen walls
Stretched away into stately halls;

The weary wheel to a spinnet turned,
The tallow candle an astral burned,

And for him who sat by the chimney lug,
Dozing and grumbling o'er pipe and mug,

A manly form at her side she saw,
And joy was duty and love was law.

Then she took up her burden of life again,
Saying only, "It might have been."

Alas for maiden, alas for Judge,
For rich repiner and household drudge!

God pity them both! and pity us all,
Who vainly the dreams of youth recall.

For of all sad words of tongue or pen,
The saddest are these: "It might have been!"

Ah, well! for us all some sweet hope lies
Deeply buried from human eyes;

And, in the hereafter, angels may
Roll the stone from its grave away!

Cassandra Southwick

In 1658 two young persons, son and daughter of Lawrence Southwick of Salem, who had himself been imprisoned and deprived of nearly all his property for having entertained Quakers at his house, were fined for non-attendance at church. They being unable to pay the fine, the General Court issued an order empowering "the Treasurer of the County to sell the said persons to any of the English nation of *Virginia* or *Barbadoes,* to answer said fines." An attempt was made to carry this order into execution, but no shipmaster was found willing to convey them to the West Indies.

To the God of all sure mercies let my blessing rise to-day,
From the scoffer and the cruel He hath plucked the spoil away;
Yea, He who cooled the furnace around the faithful three,
And tamed the Chaldean lions, hath set His handmaid free!

Last night I saw the sunset melt through my prison bars,
Last night across my damp earth-floor fell the pale gleam of stars;
In the coldness and the darkness all through the long night-time,
My grated casement whitened with autumn's early rime.

Alone, in that dark sorrow, hour after hour crept by;
Star after star looked palely in and sank adown the sky;
No sound amid night's stillness, save that which seemed to be
The dull and heavy beating of the pulses of the sea;

All night I sat unsleeping, for I knew that on the morrow
The ruler and the cruel priest would mock me in my sorrow,
Dragged to their place of market, and bargained for and sold,
Like a lamb before the shambles, like a heifer from the fold!

Oh, the weakness of the flesh was there, — the shrinking and the shame;
And the low voice of the Tempter like whispers to me came:
"Why sit'st thou thus forlornly," the wicked murmur said,
"Damp walls thy bower of beauty, cold earth thy maiden bed?

"Where be the smiling faces, and voices soft and sweet,
Seen in thy father's dwelling, heard in the pleasant street?
Where be the youths whose glances, the summer Sabbath through,
Turned tenderly and timidly unto thy father's pew?

"Why sit'st thou here, Cassandra? — Bethink thee with what mirth
Thy happy schoolmates gather around the warm, bright hearth;
How the crimson shadows tremble on foreheads white and fair,
On eyes of merry girlhood, half hid in golden hair.

"Not for thee the hearth-fire brightens, not for thee kind words are spoken,
Not for thee the nuts of Wenham woods by laughing boys are broken;
No first-fruits of the orchard within thy lap are laid,
For thee no flowers of autumn the youthful hunters braid.

"O weak, deluded maiden! — by crazy fancies led,
With wild and raving railers an evil path to tread;
To leave a wholesome worship, and teaching pure and sound,
And mate with maniac women, loose-haired and sackcloth bound, —

"Mad scoffers of the priesthood, who mock at things divine,
Who rail against the pulpit, and holy bread and wine;

Sore from their cart-tail scourgings, and from the pillory lame,
Rejoicing in their wretchedness, and glorying in their shame.

"And what a fate awaits thee! — a sadly toiling slave,
Dragging the slowly lengthening chain of bondage to the grave!
Think of thy woman's nature, subdued in hopeless thrall,
The easy prey of any, the scoff and scorn of all!"

Oh, ever as the Tempter spoke, and feeble Nature's fears
Wrung drop by drop the scalding flow of unavailing tears,
I wrestled down the evil thoughts, and strove in silent prayer,
To feel, O Helper of the weak! that Thou indeed wert there!

I thought of Paul and Silas, within Philippi's cell,
And how from Peter's sleeping limbs the prison shackles fell,
Till I seemed to hear the trailing of an angel's robe of white,
And to feel a blessed presence invisible to sight.

Bless the Lord for all his mercies! — for the peace and love I felt,
Like dew of Hermon's holy hill, upon my spirit melt;
When "Get behind me, Satan!" was the language of my heart,
And I felt the Evil Tempter with all his doubts depart.

Slow broke the gray cold morning; again the sunshine fell,
Flecked with the shade of bar and grate within my lonely cell;
The hoar-frost melted on the wall, and upward from the street
Came careless laugh and idle word, and tread of passing feet.

At length the heavy bolts fell back, my door was open cast,
And slowly at the sheriff's side, up the long street I passed;
I heard the murmur round me, and felt, but dared not see,
How, from every door and window, the people gazed on me.

And doubt and fear fell on me, shame burned upon my cheek,
Swam earth and sky around me, my trembling limbs grew weak:
"O Lord! support thy handmaid; and from her soul cast out
The fear of man, which brings a snare, the weakness and the doubt."

Then the dreary shadows scattered, like a cloud in morning's breeze,
And a low deep voice within me seemed whispering words like these:
"Though thy earth be as the iron, and thy heaven a brazen wall,
Trust still His loving-kindness whose power is over all."

We paused at length, where at my feet the sunlit waters broke

On glaring reach of shining beach, and shingly wall of rock;
The merchant-ships lay idly there, in hard clear lines on high,
Tracing with rope and slender spar their network on the sky.

And there were ancient citizens, cloak-wrapped and grave and cold,
And grim and stout sea-captains with faces bronzed and old,
And on his horse, with Rawson, his cruel clerk at hand,
Sat dark and haughty Endicott, the ruler of the land.

And poisoning with his evil words the ruler's ready ear,
The priest leaned o'er his saddle, with laugh and scoff and jeer;
It stirred my soul, and from my lips the seal of silence broke,
As if through woman's weakness a warning spirit spoke

I cried, "The Lord rebuke thee, thou smiter of the meek,
Thou robber of the righteous, thou trampler of the weak!
Go light the dark, cold hearth-stones, — go turn the prison lock
Of the poor hearts thou hast hunted, thou wolf amid the flock!"

Dark lowered the brows of Endicott, and with a deeper red
O'er Rawson's wine-empurpled cheek the flush of anger spread;
"Good people," quoth the white-lipped priest, "heed not her words so
wild,
Her Master speaks within her, — the Devil owns his child!"

But gray heads shook, and young brows knit, the while the sheriff read
That law the wicked rulers against the poor have made,
Who to their house of Rimmon and idol priesthood bring
No bended knee of worship, nor gainful offering.

Then to the stout sea-captains the sheriff, turning, said, —
"Which of ye, worthy seamen, will take this Quaker maid?
In the Isle of fair Barbadoes, or on Virginia's shore,
You may hold her at a higher price than Indian girl or Moor."

Grim and silent stood the captains; and when again he cried,
"Speak out, my worthy seamen!" — no voice, no sign replied;
But I felt a hard hand press my own, and kind words met my ear, —
"God bless thee, and preserve thee, my gentle girl and dear!"

A weight seemed lifted from my heart, a pitying friend was nigh, —
I felt it in his hard, rough hand, and saw it in his eye;
And when again the sheriff spoke, that voice, so kind to me,
Growled back its stormy answer like the roaring of the sea, —

"Pile my ship with bars of silver, pack with coins of Spanish gold,
From keel-piece up to deck-plank, the roomage of her hold,
By the living God who made me! — I would sooner in your bay
Sink ship and crew and cargo, than bear this child away!"

"Well answered, worthy captain, shame on their cruel laws!"
Ran through the crowd in murmurs loud the people's just applause.
"Like the herdsman of Tekoa, in Israel of old,
Shall we see the poor and righteous again for silver sold?"

I looked on haughty Endicott; with weapon half-way drawn,
Swept round the throng his lion glare of bitter hate and scorn;
Fiercely he drew his bridle-rein, and turned in silence back,
And sneering priest and baffled clerk rode murmuring in his track.

Hard after them the sheriff looked, in bitterness of soul;
Thrice smote his staff upon the ground, and crushed his parchment roll.
"Good friends," he said, "since both have fled, the ruler and the priest,
Judge ye, if from their further work I be not well released."

Loud was the cheer which, full and clear, swept round the silent bay,
As, with kind words and kinder looks, he bade me go my way;
For He who turns the courses of the streamlet of the glen,
And the river of great waters, had turned the hearts of men.

Oh, at that hour the very earth seemed changed beneath my eye,
A holier wonder round me rose the blue walls of the sky,
A lovelier light on rock and hill and stream and woodland lay,
And softer lapsed on sunnier sands the waters of the bay.

Thanksgiving to the Lord of life! to Him all praises be,
Who from the hands of evil men hath set his handmaid free;
All praise to Him before whose power the mighty are afraid,
Who takes the crafty in the snare which for the poor is laid!

Sing, O my soul, rejoicingly, on evening's twilight calm
Uplift the loud thanksgiving, pour forth the grateful psalm;
Let all dear hearts with me rejoice, as did the saints of old,
When of the Lord's good angel the rescued Peter told.

And weep and howl, ye evil priests and mighty men of wrong,
The Lord shall smite the proud, and lay His hand upon the strong.
Woe to the wicked rulers in His avenging hour!
Woe to the wolves who seek the flocks to raven and devour!

But let the humble ones arise, the poor in heart be glad,
And let the mourning ones again with robes of praise be clad.
For He who cooled the furnace, and smoothed the stormy wave,
And tamed the Chaldean lions, is mighty still to save!

The New Wife and the Old

The following ballad is founded upon one of the marvellous legends connected with the famous General M——, of Hampton, New Hampshire, who was regarded by his neighbors as a Yankee Faust, in league with the adversary. I give the story, as I heard it when a child, from a venerable family visitant.

Dark the halls, and cold the feast,
Gone the bridemaids, gone the priest.
All is over, all is done,
Twain of yesterday are one!
Blooming girl and manhood gray,
Autumn in the arms of May!

Hushed within and hushed without,
Dancing feet and wrestlers' shout;
Dies the bonfire on the hill;
All is dark and all is still,
Save the starlight, save the breeze
Moaning through the graveyard trees;
And the great sea-waves below,
Pulse of the midnight beating slow.

From the brief dream of a bride
She hath wakened, at his side.
With half-uttered shriek and start, —
Feels she not his beating heart?
And the pressure of his arm,
And his breathing near and warm?

Lightly from the bridal bed
Springs that fair dishevelled head,
And a feeling, new, intense,
Half of shame, half innocence,
Maiden fear and wonder speaks
Through her lips and changing cheeks.

From the oaken mantel glowing,
Faintest light the lamp is throwing

On the mirror's antique mould,
High-backed chair, and wainscot old,
And, through faded curtains stealing,
His dark sleeping face revealing.

Listless lies the strong man there,
Silver-streaked his careless hair;
Lips of love have left no trace
On that hard and haughty face;
And that forehead's knitted thought
Love's soft hand hath not unwrought.

"Yet," she sighs, "he loves me well,
More than these calm lips will tell.
Stooping to my lowly state,
He hath made me rich and great,
And I bless him, though he be
Hard and stern to all save me!"

While she speaketh, falls the light
O'er her fingers small and white;
Gold and gem, and costly ring
Back the timid lustre fling, —
Love's selectest gifts, and rare,
His proud hand had fastened there.

Gratefully she marks the glow
From those tapering lines of snow;
Fondly o'er the sleeper bending,
His black hair with golden blending,
In her soft and light caress,
Cheek and lip together press.

Ha! — that start of horror! why
That wild stare and wilder cry,
Full of terror, full of pain?
Is there madness in her brain?
Hark! that gasping, hoarse and low,
"Spare me, — spare me, — let me go!"

God have mercy! — icy cold
Spectral hands her own enfold,
Drawing silently from them
Love's fair gifts of gold and gem.

"Waken! save me!" still as death
At her side he slumbereth.

Ring and bracelet all are gone,
And that ice-cold hand withdrawn;
But she hears a murmur low,
Full of sweetness, full of woe,
Half a sigh and half a moan:
"Fear not! give the dead her own!"

Ah! — the dead wife's voice she knows!
That cold hand whose pressure froze,
Once in warmest life had borne
Gem and band her own hath worn.
"Wake thee! wake thee!" Lo, his eyes
Open with a dull surprise.

In his arms the strong man folds her,
Closer to his breast he holds her;
Trembling limbs his own are meeting,
And he feels her heart's quick beating:
"Nay, my dearest, why this fear?"
"Hush!" she saith, "the dead is here!"

"Nay, a dream, — an idle dream."
But before the lamp's pale gleam
Tremblingly her hand she raises.
There no more the diamond blazes,
Clasp of pearl, or ring of gold, —
"Ah!" she sighs, "her hand was cold!"

Broken words of cheer he saith,
But his dark lip quivereth,
And as o'er the past he thinketh,
From his young wife's arms he shrinketh;
Can those soft arms round him lie,
Underneath his dead wife's eye?

She her fair young head can rest
Soothed and childlike on his breast,
And in trustful innocence
Draw new strength and courage thence;
He, the proud man, feels within
But the cowardice of sin!

She can murmur in her thought
Simple prayers her mother taught,
And His blessed angels call,
Whose great love is over all;
He, alone, in prayerless pride,
Meets the dark Past at her side!

One, who living shrank with dread
From his look, or word, or tread,
Unto whom her early grave
Was as freedom to the slave,
Moves him at this midnight hour,
With the dead's unconscious power!

Ah, the dead, the unforgot!
From their solemn homes of thought,
Where the cypress shadows blend
Darkly over foe and friend,
Or in love or sad rebuke,
Back upon the living look.

And the tenderest ones and weakest,
Who their wrongs have borne the meekest,
Lifting from those dark, still places,
Sweet and sad-remembered faces,
O'er the guilty hearts behind
An unwitting triumph find.

The Swan Song of Parson Avery

When the reaper's task was ended, and the summer wearing late,
Parson Avery sailed from Newbury, with his wife and children eight,
Dropping down the river-harbor in the shallop "Watch and Wait."

Pleasantly lay the clearings in the mellow summer-morn,
With the newly planted orchards dropping their fruits first-born,
And the home-roofs like brown islands amid a sea of corn.

Broad meadows reached out seaward the tided creeks between,
And hills rolled wave-like inland, with oaks and walnuts green; —
A fairer home, a goodlier land, his eyes had never seen.

Yet away sailed Parson Avery, away where duty led,

And the voice of God seemed calling, to break the living bread
To the souls of fishers starving on the rocks of Marblehead.

All day they sailed: at nightfall the pleasant land-breeze died,
The blackening sky, at midnight, its starry lights denied,
And far and low the thunder of tempest prophesied!

Blotted out were all the coast-lines, gone were rock, and wood, and
sand;
Grimly anxious stood the skipper with the rudder in his hand,
And questioned of the darkness what was sea and what was land.

And the preacher heard his dear ones, nestled round him, weeping
sore:
"Never heed, my little children! Christ is walking on before
To the pleasant land of heaven, where the sea shall be no more."

All at once the great cloud parted, like a curtain drawn aside,
To let down the torch of lightning on the terror far and wide;
And the thunder and the whirlwind together smote the tide.

There was wailing in the shallop, woman's wail and man's despair,
A crash of breaking timbers on the rocks so sharp and bare,
And, through it all, the murmur of Father Avery's prayer.

From his struggle in the darkness with the wild waves and the blast,
On a rock, where every billow broke above him as it passed,
Alone, of all his household, the man of God was cast.

There a comrade heard him praying, in the pause of wave and wind:
"All my own have gone before me, and I linger just behind:
Not for life I ask, but only for the rest Thy ransomed find!

"In this night of death I challenge the promise of Thy word! —
Let me see the great salvation of which mine ears have heard! —
Let me pass from hence forgiven, through the grace of Christ, our
Lord!

"In the baptism of these waters wash white my every sin,
And let me follow up to Thee my household and my kin!
Open the sea-gate of Thy heaven, and let me enter in!"

When the Christian sings his death-song, all the listening heavens
draw near,
And the angels, leaning over the walls of crystal, hear

How the notes so faint and broken swell to music in God's ear.

The ear of God was open to His servant's last request;
As the strong wave swept him downward the sweet hymn upward
pressed,
And the soul of Father Avery went, singing, to its rest.

There was wailing on the mainland, from the rocks of Marblehead;
In the stricken church of Newbury the notes of prayer were read;
And long, by board and hearthstone, the living mourned the dead.

And still the fishers outbound, or scudding from the squall,
With grave and reverent faces, the ancient tale recall,
When they see the white waves breaking on the Rock of Avery's Fall!

Pentucket

The village of Haverhill, on the Merrimac, called by the Indians Pentucket, was for nearly seventeen years a frontier town, and during thirty years endured all the horrors of savage warfare. In the year 1708, a combined body of French and Indians, under the command of De Chaillons, and Hertel de Rouville, the infamous and bloody sacker of Deerfield, made an attack upon the village, which at that time contained only thirty houses. Sixteen of the villagers were massacred, and a still larger number made prisoners. About thirty of the enemy also fell, and among them Hertel de Rouville. The minister of the place, Benjamin Rolfe, was killed by a shot through his own door.

How sweetly on the wood-girt town
The mellow light of sunset shone!
Each small, bright lake, whose waters still
Mirror the forest and the hill,
Reflected from its waveless breast
The beauty of a cloudless west,
Glorious as if a glimpse were given
Within the western gates of heaven,
Left, by the spirit of the star
Of sunset's holy hour, ajar!

Beside the river's tranquil flood
The dark and low-walled dwellings stood,
Where many a rood of open land
Stretched up and down on either hand,
With corn-leaves waving freshly green
The thick and blackened stumps between.
Behind, unbroken, deep and dread,
The wild, untravelled forest spread,

Back to those mountains, white and cold,
Of which the Indian trapper told,
Upon whose summits never yet
Was mortal foot in safety set.

Quiet and calm without a fear
Of danger darkly lurking near,
The weary laborer left his plough,
The milkmaid carolled by her cow;
From cottage door and household hearth
Rose songs of praise, or tones of mirth.
At length the murmur died away,
And silence on that village lay.
— So slept Pompeii, tower and hall,
Ere the quick earthquake swallowed all,
Undreaming of the fiery fate
Which made its dwellings desolate!

Hours passed away. By moonlight sped
The Merrimac along his bed.
Bathed in the pallid lustre, stood
Dark cottage-wall and rock and wood,
Silent, beneath that tranquil beam,
As the hushed grouping of a dream.
Yet on the still air crept a sound,
No bark of fox, nor rabbit's bound,
Nor stir of wings, nor waters flowing,
Nor leaves in midnight breezes blowing.

Was that the tread of many feet,
Which downward from the hillside beat?
What forms were those which darkly stood
Just on the margin of the wood?
Charred tree-stumps in the moonlight dim,
Or paling rude, or leafless limb?
No, — through the trees fierce eyeballs glowed,
Dark human forms in moonshine showed,
Wild from their native wilderness,
With painted limbs and battle-dress!

A yell the dead might wake to hear
Swelled on the night air, far and clear;
Then smote the Indian tomahawk
On crashing door and shattering lock;

Then rang the rifle-shot, and then
The shrill death-scream of stricken men, —
Sank the red axe in woman's brain,
And childhood's cry arose in vain.
Bursting through roof and window came,
Red, fast, and fierce, the kindled flame,
And blended fire and moonlight glared
On still dead men and scalp-knives bared.

The morning sun looked brightly through
The river willows, wet with dew.
No sound of combat filled the air,
No shout was heard, nor gunshot there;
Yet still the thick and sullen smoke
From smouldering ruins slowly broke;
And on the greensward many a stain,
And, here and there, the mangled slain,
Told how that midnight bolt had sped
Pentucket, on thy fated head!

Even now the villager can tell
Where Rolfe beside his hearthstone fell,
Still show the door of wasting oak,
Through which the fatal death-shot broke,
And point the curious stranger where
De Rouville's corse lay grim and bare;
Whose hideous head, in death still feared,
Bore not a trace of hair or beard;
And still, within the churchyard ground,
Heaves darkly up the ancient mound,
Whose grass-grown surface overlies
The victims of that sacrifice.

Skipper Ireson's Ride

Of all the rides since the birth of time,
Told in story or sung in rhyme, —
On Apuleius's Golden Ass,
Or one-eyed Calender's horse of brass,
Witch astride of a human back,
Islam's prophet on Al-Borák, —
The strangest ride that ever was sped
Was Ireson's, out from Marblehead!

Old Floyd Ireson, for his hard heart,
Tarred and feathered and carried in a cart
By the women of Marblehead!

Body of turkey, head of owl,
Wings a-droop like a rained-on fowl,
Feathered and ruffled in every part,
Skipper Ireson stood in the cart.
Scores of women, old and young,
Strong of muscle, and glib of tongue,
Pushed and pulled up the rocky lane,
Shouting and singing the shrill refrain:
"Here's Flud Oirson, fur his horrd horrt,
Torr'd an' futherr'd an' corr'd in a corrt
By the women o' Morble'ead!"

Wrinkled scolds with hands on hips,
Girls in bloom of cheek and lips,
Wild-eyed, free-limbed, such as chase
Bacchus round some antique vase,
Brief of skirt, with ankles bare,
Loose of kerchief and loose of hair,
With conch-shells blowing and fish-horns' twang,
Over and over the Mænads sang:
"Here's Flud Oirson, fur his horrd horrt,
Torr'd an' futherr'd an' corr'd in a corrt
By the women o' Morble'ead!"

Small pity for him! — He sailed away
From a leaking ship in Chaleur Bay, —
Sailed away from a sinking wreck,
With his own town's-people on her deck!
"Lay by! lay by!" they called to him.
Back he answered, "Sink or swim!
Brag of your catch of fish again!"
And off he sailed through the fog and rain!
Old Floyd Ireson, for his hard heart,
Tarred and feathered and carried in a cart
By the women of Marblehead!

Fathoms deep in dark Chaleur
That wreck shall lie forevermore.
Mother and sister, wife and maid,
Looked from the rocks of Marblehead

Over the moaning and rainy sea, —
Looked for the coming that might not be!
What did the winds and the sea-birds say
Of the cruel captain who sailed away? —
  Old Floyd Ireson, for his hard heart,
  Tarred and feathered and carried in a cart
    By the women of Marblehead!

Through the street, on either side,
Up flew windows, doors swung wide;
Sharp-tongued spinsters, old wives gray,
Treble lent the fish-horn's bray.
Sea-worn grandsires, cripple-bound,
Hulks of old sailors run aground,
Shook head, and fist, and hat, and cane,
And cracked with curses the hoarse refrain:
  "Here's Flud Oirson, fur his horrd horrt,
  Torr'd an' futherr'd an' corr'd in a corrt
    By the women o' Morble'ead!"

Sweetly along the Salem road
Bloom of orchard and lilac showed.
Little the wicked skipper knew
Of the fields so green and the sky so blue.
Riding there in his sorry trim,
Like an Indian idol glum and grim,
Scarcely he seemed the sound to hear
Of voices shouting, far and near:
  "Here's Flud Oirson, fur his horrd horrt,
  Torr'd an' futherr'd an' corr'd in a corrt
    By the women o' Morble'ead!"

"Hear me, neighbors!" at last he cried, —
"What to me is this noisy ride?
What is the shame that clothes the skin
To the nameless horror that lives within?
Waking or sleeping, I see a wreck,
And hear a cry from a reeling deck!
Hate me and curse me, — I only dread
The hand of God and the face of the dead!"
  Said old Floyd Ireson, for his hard heart,
  Tarred and feathered and carried in a cart
    By the women of Marblehead!

SKIPPER IRESON'S RIDE

Old Floyd Ireson, for his hard heart,
Tarred and feathered and carried in a cart

Then the wife of the skipper lost at sea
Said, "God has touched him! why should we!"
Said an old wife mourning her only son,
"Cut the rogue's tether and let him run!"
So with soft relentings and rude excuse,
Half scorn, half pity, they cut him loose,
And gave him a cloak to hide him in,
And left him alone with his shame and sin.
Poor Floyd Ireson, for his hard heart,
Tarred and feathered and carried in a cart
By the women of Marblehead!

The Norsemen

In the early part of the present century, a fragment of a statue, rudely chiselled from dark gray stone, was found in the town of Bradford, on the Merrimac. Its origin must be left entirely to conjecture. The fact that the ancient Northmen visited the northeast coast of North America and probably New England, some centuries before the discovery of the western world by Columbus, is now very generally admitted.

Gift from the cold and silent Past!
A relic to the present cast,
Left on the ever-changing strand
Of shifting and unstable sand,
Which wastes beneath the steady chime
And beating of the waves of Time!
Who from its bed of primal rock
First wrenched thy dark, unshapely block?
Whose hand, of curious skill untaught,
Thy rude and savage outline wrought?

The waters of my native stream
Are glancing in the sun's warm beam;
From sail-urged keel and flashing oar
The circles widen to its shore:
And cultured field and peopled town
Slope to its willowed margin down.
Yet, while this morning breeze is bringing
The home-life sound of school-bells ringing,
And rolling wheel, and rapid jar
Of the fire-winged and steedless car,
And voices from the wayside near
Come quick and blended on my ear, —

A spell is in this old gray stone,
My thoughts are with the Past alone!

A change! — The steepled town no more
Stretches along the sail-thronged shore;
Like palace-domes in sunset's cloud,
Fade sun-gilt spire and mansion proud:
Spectrally rising where they stood,
I see the old, primeval wood;
Dark, shadow-like, on either hand
I see its solemn waste expand;
It climbs the green and cultured hill,
It arches o'er the valley's rill,
And leans from cliff and crag to throw
Its wild arms o'er the stream below.
Unchanged, alone, the same bright river
Flows on, as it will flow forever!
I listen, and I hear the low
Soft ripple where its waters go;
I hear behind the panther's cry,
The wild-bird's scream goes thrilling by,
And shyly on the river's brink
The deer is stooping down to drink.

But hark! — from wood and rock flung back,
What sound comes up the Merrimac?
What sea-worn barks are those which throw
The light spray from each rushing prow?
Have they not in the North Sea's blast
Bowed to the waves the straining mast?
Their frozen sails the low, pale sun
Of Thulë's night has shone upon;
Flapped by the sea-wind's gusty sweep
Round icy drift, and headland steep.
Wild Jutland's wives and Lochlin's daughters
Have watched them fading o'er the waters,
Lessening through driving mist and spray,
Like white-winged sea-birds on their way!

Onward they glide, — and now I view
Their iron-armed and stalwart crew;
Joy glistens in each wild blue eye,
Turned to green earth and summer sky.
Each broad, seamed breast has cast aside

Its cumbering vest of shaggy hide;
Bared to the sun and soft warm air,
Streams back the Northmen's yellow hair.
I see the gleam of axe and spear,
A sound of smitten shields I hear,
Keeping a harsh and fitting time
To Saga's chant, and Runic rhyme;
Such lays as Zetland's Scald has sung,
His gay and naked isles among;
Or muttered low at midnight hour
Round Odin's mossy stone of power.
The wolf beneath the Arctic moon
Has answered to that startling rune;
The Gael has heard its stormy swell,
The light Frank knows its summons well;
Iona's sable-stoled Culdee
Has heard it sounding o'er the sea,
And swept, with hoary beard and hair,
His altar's foot in trembling prayer!

'T is past, — the 'wildering vision dies
In darkness on my dreaming eyes!
The forest vanishes in air,
Hill-slope and vale lie starkly bare;
I hear the common tread of men,
And hum of work-day life again;
The mystic relic seems alone
A broken mass of common stone;
And if it be the chiselled limb
Of Berserker or idol grim,
A fragment of Valhalla's Thor,
The stormy Viking's god of War,
Or Praga of the Runic lay,
Or love-awakening Siona,
I know not, — for no graven line,
Nor Druid mark, nor Runic sign,
Is left me here, by which to trace
Its name, or origin, or place.
Yet, for this vision of the Past,
This glance upon its darkness cast,
My spirit bows in gratitude
Before the Giver of all good,
Who fashioned so the human mind,
That, from the waste of Time behind,

A simple stone, or mound of earth,
Can summon the departed forth;
Quicken the Past to life again,
The Present lose in what hath been,
And in their primal freshness show
The buried forms of long ago.
As if a portion of that Thought
By which the Eternal will is wrought,
Whose impulse fills anew with breath
The frozen solitude of Death,
To mortal mind were sometimes lent,
To mortal musings sometimes sent,
To whisper — even when it seems
But Memory's fantasy of dreams —
Through the mind's waste of woe and sin,
Of an immortal origin!

Telling the Bees

A remarkable custom, brought from the Old Country, formerly prevailed in the rural districts of New England. On the death of a member of the family, the bees were at once informed of the event, and their hives dressed in mourning. This ceremonial was supposed to be necessary to prevent the swarms from leaving their hives and seeking a new home. The scene is minutely that of the Whittier homestead.

Here is the place; right over the hill
Runs the path I took;
You can see the gap in the old wall still,
And the stepping-stones in the shallow brook.

There is the house, with the gate red-barred,
And the poplars tall;
And the barn's brown length, and the cattle-yard,
And the white horns tossing above the wall.

There are the beehives ranged in the sun;
And down by the brink
Of the brook are her poor flowers, weed-o'errun,
Pansy and daffodil, rose and pink.

A year has gone, as the tortoise goes,
Heavy and slow;
And the same rose blows, and the same sun glows,
And the same brook sings of a year ago.

TELLING THE BEES

. . . went drearily singing the chore-girl small,
Draping each line with a shred of black

There's the same sweet clover-smell in the breeze;
And the June sun warm
Tangles his wings of fire in the trees,
Setting, as then, over Fernside farm.

I mind me how with a lover's care
From my Sunday coat
I brushed off the burrs, and smoothed my hair,
And cooled at the brookside my brow and throat.

Since we parted, a month had passed, —
To love, a year;
Down through the beeches I looked at last
On the little red gate and the well-sweep near.

I can see it all now, — the slantwise rain
Of light through the leaves,
The sundown's blaze on her window-pane,
The bloom of her roses under the eaves.

Just the same as a month before, —
The house and the trees,
The barn's brown gable, the vine by the door, —
Nothing changed but the hives of bees.

Before them, under the garden wall,
Forward and back,
Went drearily singing the chore-girl small,
Draping each hive with a shred of black.

Trembling, I listened: the summer sun
Had the chill of snow;
For I knew she was telling the bees of one
Gone on the journey we all must go!

Then I said to myself, "My Mary weeps
For the dead to-day:
Haply her blind old grandsire sleeps
The fret and the pain of his age away."

But her dog whined low; on the doorway sill,
With his cane to his chin,
The old man sat; and the chore-girl still
Sung to the bees stealing out and in.

And the song she was singing ever since
In my ear sounds on: —
"Stay at home, pretty bees, fly not hence!
Mistress Mary is dead and gone!"

Barclay of Ury

Among the earliest converts to the doctrines of Friends in Scotland was Barclay of Ury, an old and distinguished soldier, who had fought under Gustavus Adolphus, in Germany. As a Quaker, he became the object of persecution and abuse at the hands of the magistrates and the populace. None bore the indignities of the mob with greater patience and nobleness of soul than this once proud gentleman and soldier. One of his friends, on an occasion of uncommon rudeness, lamented that he should be treated so harshly in his old age who had been so honored before. "I find more satisfaction," said Barclay, "as well as honor, in being thus insulted for my religious principles, than when, a few years ago, it was usual for the magistrates, as I passed the city of Aberdeen, to meet me on the road and conduct me to public entertainment in their hall, and then escort me out again, to gain my favor."

Up the streets of Aberdeen,
By the kirk and college green,
Rode the Laird of Ury;
Close behind him, close beside,
Foul of mouth and evil-eyed,
Pressed the mob in fury.

Flouted him the drunken churl,
Jeered at him the serving-girl,
Prompt to please her master;
And the begging carlin, late
Fed and clothed at Ury's gate,
Cursed him as he passed her.

Yet, with calm and stately mien,
Up the streets of Aberdeen
Came he slowly riding;
And, to all he saw and heard,
Answering not with bitter word,
Turning not for chiding.

Came a troop with broadswords swinging,
Bits and bridles sharply ringing,
Loose and free and froward;
Quoth the foremost, "Ride him down!
Push him! prick him! through the town
Drive the Quaker coward!"

But from out the thickening crowd
Cried a sudden voice and loud:
    "Barclay! Ho! a Barclay!"
And the old man at his side
Saw a comrade, battle tried,
    Scarred and sunburned darkly;

Who with ready weapon bare,
Fronting to the troopers there,
    Cried aloud: "God save us,
Call ye coward him who stood
Ankle deep in Lützen's blood,
    With the brave Gustavus?"

"Nay, I do not need thy sword,
Comrade mine," said Ury's lord;
    "Put it up, I pray thee:
Passive to His holy will,
Trust I in my Master still,
    Even though He slay me.

"Pledges of thy love and faith,
Proved on many a field of death,
    Not by me are needed."
Marvelled much that henchman bold,
That his laird, so stout of old,
    Now so meekly pleaded.

"Woe's the day!" he sadly said,
With a slowly shaking head,
    And a look of pity;
"Ury's honest lord reviled,
Mock of knave and sport of child,
    In his own good city!

"Speak the word, and, master mine,
As we charged on Tilly's line,
    And his Walloon lancers,
Smiting through their midst we'll teach
Civil look and decent speech
    To these boyish prancers!"

"Marvel not, mine ancient friend,
Like beginning, like the end,"

Quoth the Laird of Ury;
"Is the sinful servant more
Than his gracious Lord who bore
Bonds and stripes in Jewry?

"Give me joy that in His name
I can bear, with patient frame,
All these vain ones offer;
While for them He suffereth long,
Shall I answer wrong with wrong,
Scoffing with the scoffer?

"Happier I, with loss of all,
Hunted, outlawed, held in thrall,
With few friends to greet me,
Than when reeve and squire were seen,
Riding out from Aberdeen,
With bared heads to meet me.

"When each goodwife, o'er and o'er,
Blessed me as I passed her door;
And the snooded daughter,
Through her casement glancing down,
Smiled on him who bore renown
From red fields of slaughter.

"Hard to feel the stranger's scoff,
Hard the old friend's falling off,
Hard to learn forgiving;
But the Lord His own rewards,
And His love with theirs accords,
Warm and fresh and living.

"Through this dark and stormy night
Faith beholds a feeble light
Up the blackness streaking;
Knowing God's own time is best,
In a patient hope I rest
For the full day-breaking!"

So the Laird of Ury said,
Turning slow his horse's head
Towards the Tolbooth prison,
Where, through iron gates, he heard

Poor disciples of the Word
Preach of Christ arisen!

Not in vain, Confessor old,
Unto us the tale is told
Of thy day of trial;
Every age on him who strays
From its broad and beaten ways
Pours its seven-fold vial.

Happy he whose inward ear
Angel comfortings can hear,
O'er the rabble's laughter;
And while Hatred's fagots burn,
Glimpses through the smoke discern
Of the good hereafter.

Knowing this, that never yet
Share of Truth was vainly set
In the world's wide fallow;
After hands shall sow the seed,
After hands from hill and mead
Reap the harvests yellow.

Thus, with somewhat of the Seer,
Must the moral pioneer
From the Future borrow;
Clothe the waste with dreams of grain,
And, on midnight's sky of rain,
Paint the golden morrow!

The Angels of Buena Vista

A letter-writer from Mexico during the Mexican war, when detailing some of the incidents at the terrible fight of Buena Vista, mentioned that Mexican women were seen hovering near the field of death, for the purpose of giving aid and succor to the wounded. One poor woman was found surrounded by the maimed and suffering of both armies, ministering to the wants of Americans as well as Mexicans with impartial tenderness.

Speak and tell us, our Ximena, looking northward far away,
O'er the camp of the invaders, o'er the Mexican array,
Who is losing? who is winning? are they far or come they near?
Look abroad, and tell us, sister, whither rolls the storm we hear.

"Down the hills of Angostura still the storm of battle rolls;
Blood is flowing, men are dying; God have mercy on their souls!"
Who is losing? who is winning? "Over hill and over plain,
I see but smoke of cannon clouding through the mountain rain."

Holy Mother! keep our brothers! Look, Ximena, look once more.
"Still I see the fearful whirlwind rolling darkly as before,
Bearing on, in strange confusion, friend and foeman, foot and horse,
Like some wild and troubled torrent sweeping down its mountain
course."

Look forth once more, Ximena! "Ah! the smoke has rolled away;
And I see the Northern rifles gleaming down the ranks of gray.
Hark! that sudden blast of bugles! there the troop of Minon wheels;
There the Northern horses thunder, with the cannon at their heels.

"Jesu, pity! how it thickens! now retreat and now advance!
Right against the blazing cannon shivers Puebla's charging lance!
Down they go, the brave young riders; horse and foot together fall;
Like a ploughshare in the fallow, through them ploughs the Northern
ball."

Nearer came the storm and nearer, rolling fast and frightful on!
Speak, Ximena, speak and tell us, who has lost, and who has won?
"Alas! alas! I know not; friend and foe together fall,
O'er the dying rush the living: pray, my sisters, for them all!

"Lo! the wind the smoke is lifting. Blessed Mother, save my brain!
I can see the wounded crawling slowly out from heaps of slain.
Now they stagger, blind and bleeding; now they fall, and strive to rise;
Hasten, sisters, haste and save them, lest they die before our eyes!

"O my heart's love! O my dear one! lay thy poor head on my knee;
Dost thou know the lips that kiss thee? Canst thou hear me? canst thou
see?
O my husband, brave and gentle! O my Bernal, look once more
On the blessed cross before thee! Mercy! mercy! all is o'er!"

Dry thy tears, my poor Ximena; lay thy dear one down to rest;
Let his hands be meekly folded, lay the cross upon his breast;
Let his dirge be sung hereafter, and his funeral masses said;
To-day, thou poor bereaved one, the living ask thy aid.

Close beside her, faintly moaning, fair and young, a soldier lay,
Torn with shot and pierced with lances, bleeding slow his life away;
But, as tenderly before him the lorn Ximena knelt,
She saw the Northern eagle shining on his pistol-belt.

With a stifled cry of horror straight she turned away her head;
With a sad and bitter feeling looked she back upon her dead;
But she heard the youth's low moaning, and his struggling breath of
pain,
And she raised the cooling water to his parching lips again.

Whispered low the dying soldier, pressed her hand and faintly smiled;
Was that pitying face his mother's? did she watch beside her child?
All his stranger words with meaning her woman's heart supplied;
With her kiss upon his forehead, "Mother!" murmured he, and died!

"A bitter curse upon them, poor boy, who led thee forth,
From some gentle, sad-eyed mother, weeping, lonely, in the North!"
Spake the mournful Mexic woman, as she laid him with her dead,
And turned to soothe the living, and bind the wounds which bled.

Look forth once more, Ximena! "Like a cloud before the wind
Rolls the battle down the mountains, leaving blood and death behind;
Ah! they plead in vain for mercy; in the dust the wounded strive;
Hide your faces, holy angels! O thou Christ of God, forgive!"

Sing, O Night, among thy mountains! let the cool, gray shadows fall;
Dying brothers, fighting demons, drop thy curtain over all!
Through the thickening winter twilight, wide apart the battle rolled,
In its sheath the sabre rested, and the cannon's lips grew cold.

But the noble Mexic women still their holy task pursued,
Through that long, dark night of sorrow, worn and faint and lacking
food.
Over weak and suffering brothers, with a tender care they hung,
And the dying foeman blessed them in a strange and Northern tongue.

Not wholly lost, O Father! is this evil world of ours;
Upward, through its blood and ashes, spring afresh the Eden flowers;
From its smoking hell of battle, Love and Pity send their prayer,
And still thy white-winged angels hover dimly in our air!

Mabel Martin: A Harvest Idyl

Susanna Martin, an aged woman of Amesbury, Mass., was tried and executed for the alleged crime of witchcraft. Her home was in what is now known as Pleasant Valley on the Merrimac, a little above the old Ferry way, where, tradition says, an attempt was made to assassinate Sir Edmund Andros on his way to Falmouth (afterward Portland) and Pemaquid, which was frustrated by a warning timely given. Goody Martin was the only woman hanged on the north side of the Merrimac during the dreadful delusion. The aged wife of Judge Bradbury, who lived on the other side of the Powow River, was imprisoned and would have been put to death but for the collapse of the hideous persecution.

PROEM

I call the old time back: I bring my lay
In tender memory of the summer day
When, where our native river lapsed away,

We dreamed it over, while the thrushes made
Songs of their own, and the great pine-trees laid
On warm noonlights the masses of their shade.

And *she* was with us, living o'er again
Her life in ours, despite of years and pain, —
The Autumn's brightness after latter rain.

Beautiful in her holy peace as one
Who stands, at evening, when the work is done,
Glorified in the setting of the sun!

Her memory makes our common landscape seem
Fairer than any of which painters dream;
Lights the brown hills and sings in every stream;

For she whose speech was always truth's pure gold
Heard, not unpleased, its simple legends told,
And loved with us the beautiful and old.

I. THE RIVER VALLEY

Across the level tableland,
A grassy, rarely trodden way,
With thinnest skirt of birchen spray

And stunted growth of cedar, leads
To where you see the dull plain fall
Sheer off, steep-slanted, ploughed by all

THE WITCH'S DAUGHTER

For Mabel Martin sat apart. . .
She sat apart, as one forbid

The seasons' rainfalls. On its brink
  The over-leaning harebells swing,
  With roots half bare the pine-trees cling;

And, through the shadow looking west,
  You see the wavering river flow
  Along a vale, that far below

Holds to the sun, the sheltering hills
  And glimmering water-line between,
  Broad fields of corn and meadows green,

And fruit-bent orchards grouped around
  The low brown roofs and painted eaves,
  And chimney-tops half hid in leaves.

No warmer valley hides behind
  Yon wind-scourged sand-dunes, cold and bleak;
  No fairer river comes to seek

The wave-sung welcome of the sea,
  Or mark the northmost border line
  Of sun-loved growths of nut and vine.

Here, ground-fast in their native fields,
  Untempted by the city's gain,
  The quiet farmer folk remain

Who bear the pleasant name of Friends,
  And keep their fathers' gentle ways
  And simple speech of Bible days;

In whose neat homesteads woman holds
  With modest ease her equal place,
  And wears upon her tranquil face

The look of one who, merging not
  Her self-hood in another's will,
  Is love's and duty's handmaid still.

Pass with me down the path that winds
  Through birches to the open land,
  Where, close upon the river strand

You mark a cellar, vine o'errun,
Above whose wall of loosened stones
The sumach lifts its reddening cones,

And the black nightshade's berries shine,
And broad, unsightly burdocks fold
The household ruin, century-old.

Here, in the dim colonial time
Of sterner lives and gloomier faith,
A woman lived, tradition saith,

Who wrought her neighbors foul annoy,
And witched and plagued the countryside,
Till at the hangman's hand she died.

Sit with me while the westering day,
Falls slantwise down the quiet vale,
And, haply ere yon loitering sail,

That rounds the upper headland, falls
Below Deer Island's pines, or sees
Behind it Hawkswood's belt of trees

Rise black against the sinking sun,
My idyl of its days of old,
The valley's legend, shall be told.

II. THE HUSKING

It was the pleasant harvest-time,
When cellar-bins are closely stowed,
And garrets bend beneath their load,

And the old swallow-haunted barns, —
Brown-gabled, long, and full of seams
Through which the moted sunlight streams,

And winds blow freshly in, to shake
The red plumes of the roosted cocks,
And the loose hay-mow's scented locks, —

Are filled with summer's ripened stores,
Its odorous grass and barley sheaves,
From their low scaffolds to their eaves.

On Esek Harden's oaken floor,
With many an autumn threshing worn,
Lay the heaped ears of unhusked corn.

And thither came young men and maids,
Beneath a moon that, large and low,
Lit that sweet eve of long ago.

They took their places; some by chance,
And others by a merry voice
Or sweet smile guided to their choice.

How pleasantly the rising moon,
Between the shadow of the mows,
Looked on them through the great elm-boughs!

On sturdy boyhood, sun-embrowned,
On girlhood with its solid curves
Of healthful strength and painless nerves!

And jests went round, and laughs that made
The house-dog answer with his howl,
And kept astir the barn-yard fowl;

And quaint old songs their fathers sung
In Derby dales and Yorkshire moors,
Ere Norman William trod their shores;

And tales, whose merry license shook
The fat sides of the Saxon thane,
Forgetful of the hovering Dane, —

Rude plays to Celt and Cimbri known,
The charms and riddles that beguiled
On Oxus' banks the young world's child, —

That primal picture-speech wherein
Have youth and maid the story told,
So new in each, so dateless old,

Recalling pastoral Ruth in her
Who waited, blushing and demure,
The red-ear's kiss of forfeiture.

III. THE WITCH'S DAUGHTER

But still the sweetest voice was mute
That river-valley ever heard
From lips of maid or throat of bird;

For Mabel Martin sat apart,
And let the hay-mow's shadow fall
Upon the loveliest face of all.

She sat apart, as one forbid,
Who knew that none would condescend
To own the Witch-wife's child a friend.

The seasons scarce had gone their round,
Since curious thousands thronged to see
Her mother at the gallows-tree;

And mocked the prison-palsied limbs
That faltered on the fatal stairs,
And wan lip trembling with its prayers!

Few questioned of the sorrowing child,
Or, when they saw the mother die,
Dreamed of the daughter's agony.

They went up to their homes that day,
As men and Christians justified:
God willed it, and the wretch had died!

Dear God and Father of us all,
Forgive our faith in cruel lies, —
Forgive the blindness that denies!

Forgive thy creature when he takes,
For the all-perfect love Thou art,
Some grim creation of his heart.

Cast down our idols, overturn
Our bloody altars; let us see
Thyself in Thy humanity!

Young Mabel from her mother's grave
Crept to her desolate hearth-stone,
And wrestled with her fate alone;

With love, and anger, and despair,
The phantoms of disordered sense,
The awful doubts of Providence!

Oh, dreary broke the winter days,
And dreary fell the winter nights
When, one by one, the neighboring lights

Went out, and human sounds grew still,
And all the phantom-peopled dark
Closed round her hearth-fire's dying spark.

And summer days were sad and long,
And sad the uncompanioned eves,
And sadder sunset-tinted leaves,

And Indian Summer's airs of balm;
She scarcely felt the soft caress,
The beauty died of loneliness!

The school-boys jeered her as they passed,
And, when she sought the house of prayer,
Her mother's curse pursued her there.

And still o'er many a neighboring door
She saw the horseshoe's curvëd charm,
To guard against her mother's harm:

That mother, poor and sick and lame,
Who daily, by the old arm-chair,
Folded her withered hands in prayer; —

Who turned, in Salem's dreary jail,
Her worn old Bible o'er and o'er,
When her dim eyes could read no more!

Sore tried and pained, the poor girl kept
Her faith, and trusted that her way,
So dark, would somewhere meet the day.

And still her weary wheel went round
Day after day, with no relief:
Small leisure have the poor for grief.

IV. THE CHAMPION

So in the shadow Mabel sits;
  Untouched by mirth she sees and hears,
  Her smile is sadder than her tears.

But cruel eyes have found her out,
  And cruel lips repeat her name,
  And taunt her with her mother's shame.

She answered not with railing words,
  But drew her apron o'er her face,
  And, sobbing, glided from the place.

And only pausing at the door,
  Her sad eyes met the troubled gaze
  Of one who, in her better days,

Had been her warm and steady friend,
  Ere yet her mother's doom had made
  Even Esek Harden half afraid.

He felt that mute appeal of tears,
  And, starting, with an angry frown,
  Hushed all the wicked murmurs down.

"Good neighbors mine," he sternly said,
  "This passes harmless mirth or jest;
  I brook no insult to my guest.

"She is indeed her mother's child,
  But God's sweet pity ministers
  Unto no whiter soul than hers.

"Let Goody Martin rest in peace;
  I never knew her harm a fly,
  And witch or not, God knows — not I.

"I know who swore her life away;
  And as God lives, I'd not condemn
  An Indian dog on word of them."

The broadest lands in all the town,
  The skill to guide, the power to awe,
  Were Harden's; and his word was law.

None dared withstand him to his face,
But one sly maiden spake aside:
"The little witch is evil-eyed!

"Her mother only killed a cow,
Or witched a churn or dairy-pan;
But she, forsooth, must charm a man!"

V. IN THE SHADOW

Poor Mabel, homeward turning, passed
The nameless terrors of the wood,
And saw, as if a ghost pursued,

Her shadow gliding in the moon;
The soft breath of the west-wind gave
A chill as from her mother's grave.

How dreary seemed the silent house!
Wide in the moonbeams' ghastly glare
Its windows had a dead man's stare!

And, like a gaunt and spectral hand,
The tremulous shadow of a birch
Reached out and touched the door's low porch,

As if to lift its latch; hard by,
A sudden warning call she heard,
The night-cry of a boding bird.

She leaned against the door; her face,
So fair, so young, so full of pain,
White in the moonlight's silver rain.

The river, on its pebbled rim,
Made music such as childhood knew;
The door-yard tree was whispered through

By voices such as childhood's ear
Had heard in moonlights long ago;
And through the willow-boughs below

She saw the rippled waters shine;
Beyond, in waves of shade and light,
The hills rolled off into the night.

She saw and heard, but over all
A sense of some transforming spell,
The shadow of her sick heart fell.

And still across the wooded space
The harvest lights of Harden shone,
And song and jest and laugh went on.

And he, so gentle, true, and strong,
Of men the bravest and the best,
Had he, too, scorned her with the rest?

She strove to drown her sense of wrong,
And, in her old and simple way,
To teach her bitter heart to pray.

Poor child! the prayer, begun in faith,
Grew to a low, despairing cry
Of utter misery: "Let me die!

"Oh! take me from the scornful eyes,
And hide me where the cruel speech
And mocking finger may not reach!

"I dare not breathe my mother's name:
A daughter's right I dare not crave
To weep above her unblest grave!

"Let me not live until my heart,
With few to pity, and with none
To love me, hardens into stone.

"O God! have mercy on Thy child,
Whose faith in Thee grows weak and small,
And take me ere I lose it all!"

A shadow on the moonlight fell,
And murmuring wind and wave became
A voice whose burden was her name.

VI. THE BETROTHAL

Had then God heard her? Had He sent
His angel down? In flesh and blood,
Before her Esek Harden stood!

He laid his hand upon her arm:
"Dear Mabel, this no more shall be;
Who scoffs at you must scoff at me.

"You know rough Esek Harden well;
And if he seems no suitor gay,
And if his hair is touched with gray,

"The maiden grown shall never find
His heart less warm than when she smiled,
Upon his knees a little child!"

Her tears of grief were tears of joy,
As, folded in his strong embrace,
She looked in Esek Harden's face.

"O truest friend of all!" she said,
"God bless you for your kindly thought,
And make me worthy of my lot!"

He led her forth, and, blent in one,
Beside their happy pathway ran
The shadows of the maid and man.

He led her through his dewy fields,
To where the swinging lanterns glowed,
And through the doors the huskers showed.

"Good friends and neighbors!" Esek said:
"I'm weary of this lonely life;
In Mabel see my chosen wife!

"She greets you kindly, one and all;
The past is past, and all offence
Falls harmless from her innocence.

"Henceforth she stands no more alone;
You know what Esek Harden is; —
He brooks no wrong to him or his.

"Now let the merriest tales be told,
And let the sweetest songs be sung
That ever made the old heart young!

"For now the lost has found a home;
And a lone hearth shall brighter burn,
As all the household joys return!"

Oh, pleasantly the harvest-moon,
Between the shadow of the mows,
Looked on them through the great elm-boughs!

On Mabel's curls of golden hair,
On Esek's shaggy strength it fell;
And the wind whispered, "It is well!"

The Legend of St. Mark

The day is closing dark and cold,
With roaring blast and sleety showers;
And through the dusk the lilacs wear
The bloom of snow, instead of flowers.

I turn me from the gloom without,
To ponder o'er a tale of old;
A legend of the age of Faith,
By dreaming monk or abbess told.

On Tintoretto's canvas lives
That fancy of a loving heart,
In graceful lines and shapes of power,
And hues immortal as his art.

In Provence (so the story runs)
There lived a lord, to whom, as slave,
A peasant-boy of tender years
The chance of trade or conquest gave.

Forth-looking from the castle tower,
Beyond the hills with almonds dark,
The straining eye could scarce discern
The chapel of the good St. Mark.

And there, when bitter word or fare
The service of the youth repaid,
By stealth, before that holy shrine,
For grace to bear his wrong, he prayed.

The steed stamped at the castle gate,
The boar-hunt sounded on the hill;
Why stayed the Baron from the chase,
With looks so stern, and words so ill?

"Go, bind yon slave! and let him learn,
By scath of fire and strain of cord,
How ill they speed who give dead saints
The homage due their living lord!"

They bound him on the fearful rack,
When, through the dungeon's vaulted dark,
He saw the light of shining robes,
And knew the face of good St. Mark.

Then sank the iron rack apart,
The cords released their cruel clasp,
The pincers, with their teeth of fire,
Fell broken from the torturer's grasp.

And lo! before the Youth and Saint,
Barred door and wall of stone gave way;
And up from bondage and the night
They passed to freedom and the day!

O dreaming monk! thy tale is true;
O painter! true thy pencil's art;
In tones of hope and prophecy,
Ye whisper to my listening heart!

Unheard no burdened heart's appeal
Moans up to God's inclining ear;
Unheeded by his tender eye,
Falls to the earth no sufferer's tear.

For still the Lord alone is God!
The pomp and power of tyrant man
Are scattered at his lightest breath,
Like chaff before the winnower's fan.

Not always shall the slave uplift
His heavy hands to Heaven in vain.
God's angel, like the good St. Mark,
Comes shining down to break his chain!

O weary ones! ye may not see
Your helpers in their downward flight;
Nor hear the sound of silver wings
Slow beating through the hush of night!

But not the less gray Dothan shone,
With sunbright watchers bending low
That Fear's dim eye beheld alone
The spear-heads of the Syrian foe.

There are, who, like the Seer of old,
Can see the helpers God has sent,
And how life's rugged mountain-side
Is white with many an angel tent!

They hear the heralds whom our Lord
Sends down his pathway to prepare;
And light, from others hidden, shines
On their high place of faith and prayer.

Let such, for earth's despairing ones,
Hopeless, yet longing to be free,
Breathe once again the Prophet's prayer:
"Lord, ope their eyes, that they may see!"

The Double-Headed Snake of Newbury

Far away in the twilight time
Of every people, in every clime,
Dragons and griffins and monsters dire,
Born of water, and air, and fire,
Or nursed, like the Python, in the mud
And ooze of the old Deucalion flood,
Crawl and wriggle and foam with rage,
Through dusk tradition and ballad age.
So from the childhood of Newbury town
And its time of fable the tale comes down
Of a terror which haunted bush and brake,
The Amphisbæna, the Double Snake!

Thou who makest the tale thy mirth,
Consider that strip of Christian earth
On the desolate shore of a sailless sea,

Full of terror and mystery,
Half redeemed from the evil hold
Of the wood so dreary, and dark, and old,
Which drank with its lips of leaves the dew
When Time was young, and the world was new,
And wove its shadows with sun and moon,
Ere the stones of Cheops were squared and hewn.
Think of the sea's dread monotone,
Of the mournful wail from the pine-wood blown,
Of the strange, vast splendors that lit the North,
Of the troubled throes of the quaking earth,
And the dismal tales the Indian told,
Till the settler's heart at his hearth grew cold,
And he shrank from the tawny wizard boasts,
And the hovering shadows seemed full of ghosts,
And above, below, and on every side,
The fear of his creed seemed verified;—
And think, if his lot were now thine own,
To grope with terrors nor named nor known,
How laxer muscle and weaker nerve
And a feebler faith thy need might serve;
And own to thyself the wonder more
That the snake had two heads, and not a score!

Whether he lurked in the Oldtown fen
Or the gray earth-flax of the Devil's Den,
Or swam in the wooded Artichoke,
Or coiled by the Northman's Written Rock,
Nothing on record is left to show;
Only the fact that he lived, we know,
And left the cast of a double head
In the scaly mask which he yearly shed.
For he carried a head where his tail should be,
And the two, of course, could never agree,
But wriggled about with main and might,
Now to the left and now to the right;
Pulling and twisting this way and that,
Neither knew what the other was at.

A snake with two heads, lurking so near!
Judge of the wonder, guess at the fear!
Think what ancient gossips might say,
Shaking their heads in their dreary way,
Between the meetings on Sabbath-day!

How urchins, searching at day's decline
The Common Pasture for sheep or kine,
The terrible double-ganger heard
In leafy rustle or whir of bird!
Think what a zest it gave to the sport,
In berry-time, of the younger sort,
As over pastures blackberry-twined,
Reuben and Dorothy lagged behind,
And closer and closer, for fear of harm,
The maiden clung to her lover's arm;
And how the spark, who was forced to stay,
By his sweetheart's fears, till the break of day,
Thanked the snake for the fond delay!

Far and wide the tale was told,
Like a snowball growing while it rolled.
The nurse hushed with it the baby's cry;
And it served, in the worthy minister's eye,
To paint the primitive serpent by.
Cotton Mather came galloping down
All the way to Newbury town,
With his eyes agog and his ears set wide,
And his marvellous inkhorn at his side;
Stirring the while in the shallow pool
Of his brains for the lore he learned at school,
To garnish the story, with here a streak
Of Latin and there another of Greek:
And the tales he heard and the notes he took,
Behold! are they not in his Wonder-Book?

Stories, like dragons, are hard to kill.
If the snake does not, the tale runs still
In Byfield Meadows, on Pipestave Hill.
And still, whenever husband and wife
Publish the shame of their daily strife,
And, with mad cross-purpose, tug and strain
At either end of the marriage-chain,
The gossips say with a knowing shake
Of their gray heads, "Look at the Double Snake!
One in body and two in will,
The Amphisbæna is living still!"

Kathleen

O Norah, lay your basket down,
  And rest your weary hand,
And come and hear me sing a song
  Of our old Ireland.

There was a lord of Galaway,
  A mighty lord was he;
And he did wed a second wife,
  A maid of low degree.

But he was old, and she was young,
  And so, in evil spite,
She baked the black bread for his kin,
  And fed her own with white.

She whipped the maids and starved the kern,
  And drove away the poor;
"Ah, woe is me!" the old lord said,
  "I rue my bargain sore!"

This lord he had a daughter fair,
  Beloved of old and young,
And nightly round the shealing-fires
  Of her the gleeman sung.

"As sweet and good is young Kathleen
  As Eve before her fall";
So sang the harper at the fair,
  So harped he in the hall.

"Oh, come to me, my daughter dear!
  Come sit upon my knee,
For looking in your face, Kathleen,
  Your mother's own I see!"

He smoothed and smoothed her hair away,
  He kissed her forehead fair;
"It is my darling Mary's brow,
  It is my darling's hair!"

Oh, then spake up the angry dame,
  "Get up, get up," quoth she,
"I'll sell ye over Ireland,
  I'll sell ye o'er the sea!"

She clipped her glossy hair away,
That none her rank might know,
She took away her gown of silk,
And gave her one of tow,

And sent her down to Limerick town
And to a seaman sold
This daughter of an Irish lord
For ten good pounds in gold.

The lord he smote upon his breast,
And tore his beard so gray;
But he was old, and she was young,
And so she had her way.

Sure that same night the Banshee howled
To fright the evil dame,
And fairy folks, who loved Kathleen,
With funeral torches came.

She watched them glancing through the trees,
And glimmering down the hill;
They crept before the dead-vault door,
And there they all stood still!

"Get up, old man! the wake-lights shine!"
"Ye murthering witch," quoth he,
"So I'm rid of your tongue, I little care
If they shine for you or me."

"Oh, whoso brings my daughter back,
My gold and land shall have!"
Oh, then spake up his handsome page,
"No gold nor land I crave!

"But give to me your daughter dear,
Give sweet Kathleen to me,
Be she on sea or be she on land,
I'll bring her back to thee."

"My daughter is a lady born,
And you of low degree,
But she shall be your bride the day
You bring her back to me."

He sailëd east, he sailëd west,
And far and long sailed he,
Until he came to Boston town,
Across the great salt sea.

"Oh, have ye seen the young Kathleen,
The flower of Ireland?
Ye'll know her by her eyes so blue,
And by her snow-white hand!"

Out spake an ancient man, "I know
The maiden whom ye mean;
I bought her of a Limerick man,
And she is called Kathleen.

"No skill hath she in household work,
Her hands are soft and white,
Yet well by loving looks and ways
She doth her cost requite."

So up they walked through Boston town,
And met a maiden fair,
A little basket on her arm
So snowy-white and bare.

"Come hither, child, and say hast thou
This young man ever seen?"
They wept within each other's arms,
The page and young Kathleen.

"Oh give to me this darling child,
And take my purse of gold."
"Nay, not by me," her master said,
"Shall sweet Kathleen be sold.

"We loved her in the place of one
The Lord hath early ta'en;
But, since her heart's in Ireland,
We give her back again!"

Oh, for that same the saints in heaven
For his poor soul shall pray,
And Mary Mother wash with tears
His heresies away.

Sure now they dwell in Ireland;
As you go up Claremore
Ye'll see their castle looking down
The pleasant Galway shore.

And the old lord's wife is dead and gone,
And a happy man is he,
For he sits beside his own Kathleen,
With her darling on his knee.

The Well of Loch Maree

Calm on the breast of Loch Maree
A little isle reposes;
A shadow woven of the oak
And willow o'er it closes.

Within, a Druid's mound is seen,
Set round with stony warders;
A fountain, gushing through the turf,
Flows o'er its grassy borders.

And whoso bathes therein his brow,
With care or madness burning,
Feels once again his healthful thought
And sense of peace returning.

O restless heart and fevered brain,
Unquiet and unstable,
That holy well of Loch Maree
Is more than idle fable!

Life's changes vex, its discords stun,
Its glaring sunshine blindeth,
And blest is he who on his way
That fount of healing findeth!

The shadows of a humbled will
And contrite heart are o'er it;
Go read its legend, "TRUST IN GOD,"
On Faith's white stones before it.

The Pipes at Lucknow

Pipes of the misty moorlands,
  Voice of the glens and hills;
The droning of the torrents,
  The treble of the rills!
Not the braes of bloom and heather,
  Nor the mountains dark with rain,
Nor maiden bower, nor border tower,
  Have heard your sweetest strain!

Dear to the Lowland reaper,
  And plaided mountaineer, —
To the cottage and the castle
  The Scottish pipes are dear; —
Sweet sounds the ancient pibroch
  O'er mountain, loch, and glade;
But the sweetest of all music
  The pipes at Lucknow played.

Day by day the Indian tiger
  Louder yelled, and nearer crept;
Round and round the jungle-serpent
  Near and nearer circles swept.
"Pray for rescue, wives and mothers, —
  Pray to-day!" the soldier said;
"To-morrow, death's between us
  And the wrong and shame we dread."

Oh, they listened, looked, and waited,
  Till their hope became despair;
And the sobs of low bewailing
  Filled the pauses of their prayer.
Then up spake a Scottish maiden,
  With her ear unto the ground:
"Dinna ye hear it? — dinna ye hear it?
  The pipes o' Havelock sound!"

Hushed the wounded man his groaning;
  Hushed the wife her little ones;
Alone they heard the drum-roll
  And the roar of Sepoy guns.
But to sounds of home and childhood
  The Highland ear was true; —
As her mother's cradle-crooning
  The mountain pipes she knew.

Like the march of soundless music
  Through the vision of the seer,
More of feeling than of hearing,
  Of the heart than of the ear,
She knew the droning pibroch,
  She knew the Campbell's call:
"Hark! hear ye no MacGregor's,
  The grandest o' them all!"

Oh, they listened, dumb and breathless,
  And they caught the sound at last;
Faint and far beyond the Goomtee
  Rose and fell the piper's blast!
Then a burst of wild thanksgiving
  Mingled woman's voice and man's;
"God be praised! — the march of Havelock!
  The piping of the clans!"

Louder, nearer, fierce as vengeance,
  Sharp and shrill as swords at strife,
Came the wild MacGregor's clan-call,
  Stinging all the air to life.
But when the far-off dust-cloud
  To plaided legions grew,
Full tenderly and blithesomely
  The pipes of rescue blew!

Round the silver domes of Lucknow,
  Moslem mosque and Pagan shrine,
Breathed the air to Britons dearest,
  The air of Auld Lang Syne.
O'er the cruel roll of war-drums
  Rose that sweet and homelike strain;
And the tartan clove the turban,
  As the Goomtee cleaves the plain

Dear to the corn-land reaper
  And plaided mountaineer, —
To the cottage and the castle
  The piper's song is dear.
Sweet sounds the Gaelic pibroch
  O'er mountain, glen, and glade;
But the sweetest of all music
  The Pipes at Lucknow played!

MY PLAYMATE

The sweetest and the saddest day
It seemed of all the year

My Playmate

The pines were dark on Ramoth hill,
  Their song was soft and low;
The blossoms in the sweet May wind
  Were falling like the snow.

The blossoms drifted at our feet,
  The orchard birds sang clear;
The sweetest and the saddest day
  It seemed of all the year.

For, more to me than birds or flowers,
  My playmate left her home,
And took with her the laughing spring,
  The music and the bloom.

She kissed the lips of kith and kin,
  She laid her hand in mine:
What more could ask the bashful boy
  Who fed her father's kine?

She left us in the bloom of May:
  The constant years told o'er
Their seasons with as sweet May morns,
  But she came back no more.

I walk, with noiseless feet, the round
  Of uneventful years;
Still o'er and o'er I sow the spring
  And reap the autumn ears.

She lives where all the golden year
  Her summer roses blow;
The dusky children of the sun
  Before her come and go.

There haply with her jewelled hands
  She smooths her silken gown, —
No more the homespun lap wherein
  I shook the walnuts down.

The wild grapes wait us by the brook,
  The brown nuts on the hill,
And still the May-day flowers make sweet
  The woods of Follymill.

The lilies blossom in the pond,
The bird builds in the tree,
The dark pines sing on Ramoth hill
The slow song of the sea.

I wonder if she thinks of them,
And how the old time seems, —
If ever the pines of Ramoth wood
Are sounding in her dreams.

I see her face, I hear her voice;
Does she remember mine?
And what to her is now the boy
Who fed her father's kine?

What cares she that the orioles build
For other eyes than ours, —
That other hands with nuts are filled,
And other laps with flowers?

O playmate in the golden time!
Our mossy seat is green,
Its fringing violets blossom yet,
The old trees o'er it lean.

The winds so sweet with birch and fern
A sweeter memory blow;
And there in spring the veeries sing
The song of long ago.

And still the pines of Ramoth wood
Are moaning like the sea, —
The moaning of the sea of change
Between myself and thee!

Cobbler Keezar's Vision

The beaver cut his timber
With patient teeth that day,
The minks were fish-wards, and the crows
Surveyors of highway, —

When Keezar sat on the hillside
  Upon his cobbler's form,
With a pan of coals on either hand
  To keep his waxed-ends warm.

And there, in the golden weather,
  He stitched and hammered and sung;
In the brook he moistened his leather,
  In the pewter mug his tongue.

Well knew the tough old Teuton
  Who brewed the stoutest ale,
And he paid the goodwife's reckoning
  In the coin of song and tale.

The songs they still are singing
  Who dress the hills of vine,
The tales that haunt the Brocken
  And whisper down the Rhine.

Woodsy and wild and lonesome,
  The swift stream wound away,
Through birches and scarlet maples
  Flashing in foam and spray, —

Down on the sharp-horned ledges
  Plunging in steep cascade,
Tossing its white-maned waters
  Against the hemlock's shade.

Woodsy and wild and lonesome,
  East and west and north and south;
Only the village of fishers
  Down at the river's mouth;

Only here and there a clearing,
  With its farm-house rude and new,
And tree-stumps, swart as Indians,
  Where the scanty harvest grew.

No shout of home-bound reapers,
  No vintage-song he heard,
And on the green no dancing feet
  The merry violin stirred.

"Why should folk be glum," said Keezar,
"When Nature herself is glad,
And the painted woods are laughing
At the faces so sour and sad?"

Small heed had the careless cobbler
What sorrow of heart was theirs
Who travailed in pain with the births of God,
And planted a state with prayers, —

Hunting of witches and warlocks,
Smiting the heathen horde, —
One hand on the mason's trowel,
And one on the soldier's sword!

But give him his ale and cider,
Give him his pipe and song,
Little he cared for Church or State,
Or the balance of right and wrong.

" 'Tis work, work, work," he muttered, —
"And for rest a snuffle of psalms!"
He smote on his leathern apron
With his brown and waxen palms.

"Oh for the purple harvests
Of the days when I was young!
For the merry grape-stained maidens,
And the pleasant songs they sung!

"Oh for the breath of vineyards,
Of apples and nuts and wine!
For an oar to row and a breeze to blow
Down the grand old river Rhine!"

A tear in his blue eye glistened,
And dropped on his beard so gray.
"Old, old am I," said Keezar,
"And the Rhine flows far away!"

But a cunning man was the cobbler;
He could call the birds from the trees,
Charm the black snake out of the ledges,
And bring back the swarming bees.

All the virtues of herbs and metals,
  All the lore of the woods, he knew,
And the arts of the Old World mingled
  With the marvels of the New.

Well he knew the tricks of magic,
  And the lapstone on his knee
Had the gift of the Mormon's goggles
  Or the stone of Doctor Dee.

For the mighty master Agrippa
  Wrought it with spell and rhyme
From a fragment of mystic moonstone
  In the tower of Nettesheim.

To a cobbler Minnesinger
  The marvellous stone gave he, —
And he gave it, in turn, to Keezar,
  Who brought it over the sea.

He held up that mystic lapstone,
  He held it up like a lens,
And he counted the long years coming
  By twenties and by tens.

"One hundred years," quoth Keezar,
  "And fifty have I told:
Now open the new before me,
  And shut me out the old!"

Like a cloud of mist, the blackness
  Rolled from the magic stone,
And a marvellous picture mingled
  The unknown and the known.

Still ran the stream to the river,
  And river and ocean joined;
And there were the bluffs and the blue sea-line,
  And cold north hills behind.

But the mighty forest was broken
  By many a steepled town,
By many a white-walled farm-house,
  And many a garner brown.

Turning a score of mill-wheels,
  The stream no more ran free;
White sails on the winding river,
  White sails on the far-off sea.

Below in the noisy village
  The flags were floating gay,
And shone on a thousand faces
  The light of a holiday.

Swiftly the rival ploughmen
  Turned the brown earth from their shares;
Here were the farmer's treasures,
  There were the craftsman's wares.

Golden the goodwife's butter,
  Ruby her currant-wine;
Grand were the strutting turkeys,
  Fat were the beeves and swine.

Yellow and red were the apples,
  And the ripe pears russet-brown,
And the peaches had stolen blushes
  From the girls who shook them down.

And with blooms of hill and wildwood,
  That shame the toil of art,
Mingled the gorgeous blossoms
  Of the garden's tropic heart.

"What is it I see?" said Keezar:
  "Am I here, or am I there?
Is it a fête at Bingen?
  Do I look on Frankfort fair?

"But where are the clowns and puppets,
  And imps with horns and tail?
And where are the Rhenish flagons?
  And where is the foaming ale?

"Strange things, I know, will happen, —
  Strange things the Lord permits;
But that droughty folk should be jolly
  Puzzles my poor old wits.

"Here are smiling manly faces,
  And the maiden's step is gay;
Nor sad by thinking, nor mad by drinking,
  Nor mopes, nor fools, are they.

"Here's pleasure without regretting,
  And good without abuse,
The holiday and the bridal
  Of beauty and of use.

"Here's a priest and there is a Quaker,
  Do the cat and dog agree?
Have they burned the stocks for ovenwood?
  Have they cut down the gallows-tree?

"Would the old folk know their children?
  Would they own the graceless town,
With never a ranter to worry
  And never a witch to drown?"

Loud laughed the cobbler Keezar,
  Laughed like a school-boy gay;
Tossing his arms above him,
  The lapstone rolled away.

It rolled down the rugged hillside,
  It spun like a wheel bewitched,
It plunged through the leaning willows,
  And into the river pitched.

There, in the deep, dark water,
  The magic stone lies still,
Under the leaning willows
  In the shadow of the hill.

But oft the idle fisher
  Sits on the shadowy bank,
And his dreams make marvellous pictures
  Where the wizard's lapstone sank.

And still, in the summer twilights,
  When the river seems to run
Out from the inner glory,
  Warm with the melted sun,

The weary mill-girl lingers
  Beside the charmëd stream,
And the sky and the golden water
  Shape and color her dream.

Fair wave the sunset gardens,
  The rosy signals fly;
Her homestead beckons from the cloud,
  And love goes sailing by.

The Two Rabbins

The Rabbi Nathan twoscore years and ten
Walked blameless through the evil world, and then,
Just as the almond blossomed in his hair,
Met a temptation all too strong to bear,
And miserably sinned. So, adding not
Falsehood to guilt, he left his seat, and taught
No more among the elders, but went out
From the great congregation girt about
With sackcloth, and with ashes on his head,
Making his gray locks grayer. Long he prayed,
Smiting his breast; then, as the Book he laid
Open before him for the Bath-Col's choice,
Pausing to hear that Daughter of a Voice,
Behold the royal preacher's words: "A friend
Loveth at all times, yea, unto the end;
And for the evil day thy brother lives."
Marvelling, he said: "It is the Lord who gives
Counsel in need. At Ecbatana dwells
Rabbi Ben Isaac, who all men excels
In righteousness and wisdom, as the trees
Of Lebanon the small weeds that the bees
Bow with their weight. I will arise, and lay
My sins before him."

And he went his way
Barefooted, fasting long, with many prayers;
But even as one who, followed unawares,
Suddenly in the darkness feels a hand
Thrill with its touch his own, and his cheek fanned
By odors subtly sweet, and whispers near
Of words he loathes, yet cannot choose but hear,

So, while the Rabbi journeyed, chanting low
The wail of David's penitential woe,
Before him still the old temptation came,
And mocked him with the motion and the shame
Of such desires that, shuddering, he abhorred
Himself; and, crying mightily to the Lord
To free his soul and cast the demon out,
Smote with his staff the blankness round about.

At length, in the low light of a spent day,
The towers of Ecbatana far away
Rose on the desert's rim; and Nathan, faint
And footsore, pausing where for some dead saint
The faith of Islam reared a domëd tomb,
Saw some one kneeling in the shadow, whom
He greeted kindly: "May the Holy One
Answer thy prayers, O stranger!" Whereupon
The shape stood up with a loud cry, and then,
Clasped in each other's arms, the two gray men
Wept, praising Him whose gracious providence
Made their paths one. But straightway, as the sense
Of his transgression smote him, Nathan tore
Himself away: "O friend beloved, no more
Worthy am I to touch thee, for I came,
Foul from my sins, to tell thee all my shame.
Haply thy prayers, since naught availeth mine,
May purge my soul, and make it white like thine.
Pity me, O Ben Isaac, I have sinned!"

Awestruck Ben Isaac stood. The desert wind
Blew his long mantle backward, laying bare
The mournful secret of his shirt of hair.
"I too, O friend, if not in act," he said,
"In thought have verily sinned. Hast thou not read,
'Better the eye should see than that desire
Should wander?' Burning with a hidden fire
That tears and prayers quench not, I come to thee
For pity and for help, as thou to me.
Pray for me, O my friend!" But Nathan cried,
"Pray thou for me, Ben Isaac!"

Side by side
In the low sunshine by the turban stone
They knelt; each made his brother's woe his own,

Forgetting, in the agony and stress
Of pitying love, his claim of selfishness;
Peace, for his friend besought, his own became;
His prayers were answered in another's name;
And, when at last they rose up to embrace,
Each saw God's pardon in his brother's face!

Long after, when his headstone gathered moss,
Traced on the targum-marge of Onkelos
In Rabbi Nathan's hand these words were read:

"Hope not the cure of sin till Self is dead;
Forget it in love's service, and the debt
Thou canst not pay the angels shall forget;
Heaven's gate is shut to him who comes alone;
Save thou a soul, and it shall save thy own!"

Norembega

Norembega, or Norimbegue, is the name given by early French fishermen and explorers to a fabulous country south of Cape Breton, first discovered by Verrazzani in 1524. It was supposed to have a magnificent city of the same name on a great river, probably the Penobscot. The site of this barbaric city is laid down on a map published at Antwerp in 1570. In 1604 Champlain sailed in search of the Northern Eldorado, twenty-two leagues up the Penobscot from the Isle Haute. He supposed the river to be that of Norembega, but wisely came to the conclusion that those travellers who told of the great city had never seen it. He saw no evidences of anything like civilization, but mentions the finding of a cross, very old and mossy, in the woods.

The winding way the serpent takes
  The mystic water took,
From where, to count its beaded lakes,
  The forest sped its brook.

A narrow space 'twixt shore and shore,
  For sun or stars to fall,
While evermore, behind, before,
  Closed in the forest wall.

The dim wood hiding underneath
  Wan flowers without a name;
Life tangled with decay and death,
  League after league the same.

Unbroken over swamp and hill
The rounding shadow lay,
Save where the river cut at will
A pathway to the day.

Beside that track of air and light,
Weak as a child unweaned,
At shut of day a Christian knight
Upon his henchman leaned.

The embers of the sunset's fires
Along the clouds burned down;
"I see," he said, "the domes and spires
Of Norembega town."

"Alack! the domes, O master mine,
Are golden clouds on high;
Yon spire is but the branchless pine
That cuts the evening sky."

"Oh, hush and hark! What sounds are these
But chants and holy hymns?"
"Thou hear'st the breeze that stirs the trees
Through all their leafy limbs."

"Is it a chapel bell that fills
The air with its low tone?"
"Thou hear'st the tinkle of the rills,
The insect's vesper drone."

"The Christ be praised! — He sets for me
A blessed cross in sight!"
"Now, nay, 'tis but yon blasted tree
With two gaunt arms outright!"

"Be it wind so sad or tree so stark,
It mattereth not, my knave;
Methinks to funeral hymns I hark,
The cross is for my grave!

"My life is sped; I shall not see
My home-set sails again;
The sweetest eyes of Normandie
Shall watch for me in vain.

"Yet onward still to ear and eye
The baffling marvel calls;
I fain would look before I die
On Norembega's walls.

"So, haply, it shall be thy part
At Christian feet to lay
The mystery of the desert's heart
My dead hand plucked away.

"Leave me an hour of rest; go thou
And look from yonder heights;
Perchance the valley even now
Is starred with city lights."

The henchman climbed the nearest hill,
He saw nor tower nor town,
But, through the drear woods, lone and still,
The river rolling down.

He heard the stealthy feet of things
Whose shapes he could not see,
A flutter as of evil wings,
The fall of a dead tree.

The pines stood black against the moon,
A sword of fire beyond;
He heard the wolf howl, and the loon
Laugh from his reedy pond.

He turned him back: "O master dear,
We are but men misled;
And thou hast sought a city here
To find a grave instead."

"As God shall will! what matters where
A true man's cross may stand,
So Heaven be o'er it here as there
In pleasant Norman land?

"These woods, perchance, no secret hide
Of lordly tower and hall;
Yon river in its wanderings wide
Has washed no city wall;

"Yet mirrored in the sullen stream
 The holy stars are given:
Is Norembega, then, a dream
 Whose waking is in Heaven?

"No builded wonder of these lands
 My weary eyes shall see;
A city never made with hands
 Alone awaiteth me —

" '*Urbs Syon mystica*'; I see
 Its mansions passing fair,
'*Condita cælo*'; let me be,
 Dear Lord, a dweller there!"

Above the dying exile hung
 The vision of the bard,
As faltered on his failing tongue
 The song of good Bernard.

The henchman dug at dawn a grave
 Beneath the hemlocks brown,
And to the desert's keeping gave
 The lord of fief and town.

Years after, when the Sieur Champlain
 Sailed up the unknown stream,
And Norembega proved again
 A shadow and a dream,

He found the Norman's nameless grave
 Within the hemlock's shade,
And, stretching wide its arms to save,
 The sign that God had made,

The cross-boughed tree that marked the spot
 And made it holy ground:
He needs the earthly city not
 Who hath the heavenly found.

The Sisters

Annie and Rhoda, sisters twain,
Woke in the night to the sound of rain,

The rush of wind, the ramp and roar
Of great waves climbing a rocky shore.

Annie rose up in her bed-gown white,
And looked out into the storm and night.

"Hush, and hearken!" she cried in fear,
"Hearest thou nothing, sister dear?"

"I hear the sea, and the plash of rain,
And roar of the northeast hurricane.

"Get thee back to the bed so warm,
No good comes of watching a storm.

"What is it to thee, I fain would know,
That waves are roaring and wild winds blow?

"No lover of thine's afloat to miss
The harbor-lights on a night like this."

"But I heard a voice cry out my name,
Up from the sea on the wind it came!

"Twice and thrice have I heard it call,
And the voice is the voice of Estwick Hall!"

On her pillow the sister tossed her head.
"Hall of the Heron is safe," she said.

"In the tautest schooner that ever swam
He rides at anchor in Annisquam.

"And, if in peril from swamping sea
Or lee shore rocks, would he call on thee?"

But the girl heard only the wind and tide,
And wringing her small white hands she cried:

"O sister Rhoda, there's something wrong;
I hear it again, so loud and long.

" 'Annie! Annie!' I hear it call,
And the voice is the voice of Estwick Hall!"

Up sprang the elder, with eyes aflame,
"Thou liest! He never would call thy name!

"If he did, I would pray the wind and sea
To keep him forever from thee and me!"

Then out of the sea blew a dreadful blast;
Like the cry of a dying man it passed.

The young girl hushed on her lips a groan,
But through her tears a strange light shone, —

The solemn joy of her heart's release
To own and cherish its love in peace.

"Dearest!" she whispered, under breath,
"Life was a lie, but true is death.

"The love I hid from myself away
Shall crown me now in the light of day.

"My ears shall never to wooer list,
Never by lover my lips be kissed.

"Sacred to thee am I henceforth,
Thou in heaven and I on earth!"

She came and stood by her sister's bed:
"Hall of the Heron is dead!" she said.

"The wind and the waves their work have done,
We shall see him no more beneath the sun.

"Little will reck that heart of thine;
It loved him not with a love like mine.

"I, for his sake, were he but here,
Could hem and 'broider thy bridal gear,

"Though hands should tremble and eyes be wet,
And stitch for stitch in my heart be set.

"But now my soul with his soul I wed;
Thine the living, and mine the dead!"

The Homestead

Against the wooded hills it stands,
Ghost of a dead home, staring through
Its broken lights on wasted lands
Where old-time harvests grew.

Unploughed, unsown, by scythe unshorn,
The poor, forsaken farm-fields lie,
Once rich and rife with golden corn
And pale green breadths of rye.

Of healthful herb and flower bereft,
The garden plot no housewife keeps;
Through weeds and tangle only left,
The snake, its tenant, creeps.

A lilac spray, still blossom-clad,
Sways slow before the empty rooms;
Beside the roofless porch a sad
Pathetic red rose blooms.

His track, in mould and dust of drouth,
On floor and hearth the squirrel leaves,
And in the fireless chimney's mouth
His web the spider weaves.

The leaning barn, about to fall,
Resounds no more on husking eves;
No cattle low in yard or stall,
No thresher beats his sheaves.

So sad, so drear! It seems almost
Some haunting Presence makes its sign;
That down yon shadowy lane some ghost
Might drive his spectral kine!

O home so desolate and lorn!
Did all thy memories die with thee?
Were any wed, were any born,
Beneath this low roof-tree?

Whose axe the wall of forest broke,
And let the waiting sunshine through?
What goodwife sent the earliest smoke
Up the great chimney flue?

THE HOMESTEAD

Ghost of a dead home, staring through
Its broken lights on wasted lands

Did rustic lovers hither come?
  Did maidens, swaying back and forth
In rhythmic grace, at wheel and loom,
  Make light their toil with mirth?

Did child feet patter on the stair?
  Did boyhood frolic in the snow?
Did gray age, in her elbow chair,
  Knit, rocking to and fro?

The murmuring brook, the sighing breeze,
  The pine's slow whisper, cannot tell;
Low mounds beneath the hemlock-trees
  Keep the home secrets well.

Cease, mother-land, to fondly boast
  Of sons far off who strive and thrive,
Forgetful that each swarming host
  Must leave an emptier hive!

O wanderers from ancestral soil,
  Leave noisome mill and chaffering store:
Gird up your loins for sturdier toil,
  And build the home once more!

Come back to bayberry-scented slopes,
  And fragrant fern, and ground-nut vine;
Breathe airs blown over holt and copse
  Sweet with black birch and pine.

What matter if the gains are small
  That life's essential wants supply?
Your homestead's title gives you all
  That idle wealth can buy.

All that the many-dollared crave,
  The brick-walled slaves of 'Change and mart,
Lawns, trees, fresh air, and flowers, you have,
  More dear for lack of art.

Your own sole masters, freedom-willed,
  With none to bid you go or stay,
Till the old fields your fathers tilled,
  As manly men as they!

With skill that spares your toiling hands,
And chemic aid that science brings,
Reclaim the waste and outworn lands,
And reign thereon as kings!

The Three Bells

Beneath the low-hung night cloud
That raked her splintering mast
The good ship settled slowly,
The cruel leak gained fast.

Over the awful ocean
Her signal guns pealed out.
Dear God! was that Thy answer
From the horror round about?

A voice came down the wild wind,
"Ho! ship ahoy!" its cry:
"Our stout Three Bells of Glasgow
Shall lay till daylight by!"

Hour after hour crept slowly,
Yet on the heaving swells
Tossed up and down the ship-lights,
The lights of the Three Bells!

And ship to ship made signals,
Man answered back to man,
While oft, to cheer and hearten,
The Three Bells nearer ran;

And the captain from her taffrail
Sent down his hopeful cry:
"Take heart! Hold on!" he shouted,
"The Three Bells shall lay by!"

All night across the waters
The tossing lights shone clear;
All night from reeling taffrail
The Three Bells sent her cheer.

And when the dreary watches
Of storm and darkness passed,

Just as the wreck lurched under,
All souls were saved at last.

Sail on, Three Bells, forever,
In grateful memory sail!
Ring on, Three Bells of rescue,
Above the wave and gale!

Type of the Love eternal,
Repeat the Master's cry,
As tossing through our darkness
The lights of God draw nigh!

The Witch of Wenham

The house is still standing in Danvers, Mass., where, it is said, a suspected witch was confined overnight in the attic, which was bolted fast. In the morning, when the constable came to take her to Salem for trial, she was missing, although the door was still bolted. Her escape was doubtless aided by her friends, but at the time it was attributed to Satanic interference.

I

Along Crane River's sunny slopes
Blew warm the winds of May,
And over Naumkeag's ancient oaks
The green outgrew the gray.

The grass was green on Rial-side,
The early birds at will
Waked up the violet in its dell,
The wind-flower on its hill.

"Where go you, in your Sunday coat,
Son Andrew, tell me, pray."
"For stripëd perch in Wenham Lake
I go to fish to-day."

"Unharmed of thee in Wenham Lake
The mottled perch shall be:
A blue-eyed witch sits on the bank
And weaves her net for thee.

"She weaves her golden hair; she sings
Her spell-song low and faint;
The wickedest witch in Salem jail
Is to that girl a saint."

"Nay, mother, hold thy cruel tongue;
God knows," the young man cried,
"He never made a whiter soul
Than hers by Wenham side.

"She tends her mother sick and blind,
And every want supplies;
To her above the blessed Book
She lends her soft blue eyes.

"Her voice is glad with holy songs,
Her lips are sweet with prayer;
Go where you will, in ten miles round
Is none more good and fair."

"Son Andrew, for the love of God
And of thy mother, stay!"
She clasped her hands, she wept aloud,
But Andrew rode away.

"O reverend sir, my Andrew's soul
The Wenham witch has caught;
She holds him with the curlëd gold
Whereof her snare is wrought.

"She charms him with her great blue eyes,
She binds him with her hair;
Oh, break the spell with holy words,
Unbind him with a prayer!"

"Take heart," the painful preacher said,
"This mischief shall not be;
The witch shall perish in her sins
And Andrew shall go free.

"Our poor Ann Putnam testifies
She saw her weave a spell,
Bare-armed, loose-haired, at full of moon,
Around a dried-up well.

" 'Spring up, O well!' she softly sang
The Hebrew's old refrain
(For Satan uses Bible words),
Till water flowed amain.

"And many a goodwife heard her speak
By Wenham water words
That made the buttercups take wings
And turn to yellow birds.

"They say that swarming wild bees seek
The hive at her command;
And fishes swim to take their food
From out her dainty hand.

"Meek as she sits in meeting-time,
The godly minister
Notes well the spell that doth compel
The young men's eyes to her.

"The mole upon her dimpled chin
Is Satan's seal and sign;
Her lips are red with evil bread
And stain of unblest wine.

"For Tituba, my Indian, saith
At Quasycung she took
The Black Man's godless sacrament
And signed his dreadful book.

"Last night my sore-afflicted child
Against the young witch cried.
To take her Marshal Herrick rides
Even now to Wenham side."

The marshal in his saddle sat,
His daughter at his knee;
"I go to fetch that arrant witch,
Thy fair playmate," quoth he.

"Her spectre walks the parsonage,
And haunts both hall and stair;
They know her by the great blue eyes
And floating gold of hair."

"They lie, they lie, my father dear!
No foul old witch is she,
But sweet and good and crystal-pure
As Wenham waters be."

"I tell thee, child, the Lord hath set
Before us good and ill,
And woe to all whose carnal loves
Oppose His righteous will.

"Between Him and the powers of hell
Choose thou, my child, to-day:
No sparing hand, no pitying eye,
When God commands to slay!"

He went his way; the old wives shook
With fear as he drew nigh;
The children in the dooryards held
Their breath as he passed by.

Too well they knew the gaunt gray horse
The grim witch-hunter rode,
The pale Apocalyptic beast
By grisly Death bestrode.

II

Oh, fair the face of Wenham Lake
Upon the young girl's shone,
Her tender mouth, her dreaming eyes,
Her yellow hair outblown.

By happy youth and love attuned
To natural harmonies,
The singing birds, the whispering wind,
She sat beneath the trees.

Sat shaping for her bridal dress
Her mother's wedding gown,
When lo! the marshal, writ in hand,
From Alford hill rode down.

His face was hard with cruel fear,
He grasped the maiden's hands:
"Come with me unto Salem town,
For so the law commands!"

"Oh, let me to my mother say
Farewell before I go!"

He closer tied her little hands
  Unto his saddle bow.

"Unhand me," cried she piteously,
  "For thy sweet daughter's sake."
"I'll keep my daughter safe," he said,
  "From the witch of Wenham Lake."

"Oh, leave me for my mother's sake,
  She needs my eyes to see."
"Those eyes, young witch, the crows shall peck
  From off the gallows-tree."

He bore her to a farm-house old
  And up its stairway long,
And closed on her the garret-door
  With iron bolted strong.

The day died out, the night came down:
  Her evening prayer she said,
While, through the dark, strange faces seemed
  To mock her as she prayed.

The present horror deepened all
  The fears her childhood knew;
The awe wherewith the air was filled
  With every breath she drew.

And could it be, she trembling asked,
  Some secret thought or sin
Had shut good angels from her heart
  And let the bad ones in?

Had she in some forgotten dream
  Let go her hold on Heaven,
And sold herself unwittingly
  To spirits unforgiven?

Oh, weird and still the dark hours passed;
  No human sound she heard,
But up and down the chimney stack
  The swallows moaned and stirred.

And o'er her, with a dread surmise
  Of evil sight and sound,
The blind bats on their leathern wings
  Went wheeling round and round.

Low hanging in the midnight sky
  Looked in a half-faced moon.
Was it a dream, or did she hear
  Her lover's whistled tune?

She forced the oaken scuttle back;
  A whisper reached her ear:
"Slide down the roof to me," it said,
  "So softly none may hear."

She slid along the sloping roof
  Till from its eaves she hung,
And felt the loosened shingles yield
  To which her fingers clung.

Below, her lover stretched his hands
  And touched her feet so small;
"Drop down to me, dear heart," he said,
  "My arms shall break the fall."

He set her on his pillion soft,
  Her arms about him twined;
And, noiseless as if velvet-shod,
  They left the house behind.

But when they reached the open way,
  Full free the rein he cast;
Oh, never through the mirk midnight
  Rode man and maid more fast.

Along the wild wood-paths they sped,
  The bridgeless streams they swam;
At set of moon they passed the Bass,
  At sunrise Agawam.

At high noon on the Merrimac
  The ancient ferryman
Forgot, at times, his idle oars,
  So fair a freight to scan.

And when from off his grounded boat
He saw them mount and ride,
"God keep her from the evil eye,
And harm of witch!" he cried.

The maiden laughed, as youth will laugh
At all its fears gone by;
"He does not know," she whispered low,
"A little witch am I."

All day he urged his weary horse,
And, in the red sundown,
Drew rein before a friendly door
In distant Berwick town.

A fellow-feeling for the wronged
The Quaker people felt;
And safe beside their kindly hearths
The hunted maiden dwelt,

Until from off its breast the land
The haunting horror threw,
And hatred, born of ghastly dreams,
To shame and pity grew.

Sad were the year's spring morns, and sad
Its golden summer day,
But blithe and glad its withered fields,
And skies of ashen gray;

For spell and charm had power no more,
The spectres ceased to roam,
And scattered households knelt again
Around the hearths of home.

And when once more by Beaver Dam
The meadow-lark outsang,
And once again on all the hills
The early violets sprang,

And all the windy pasture slopes
Lay green within the arms
Of creeks that bore the salted sea
To pleasant inland farms,

The smith filed off the chains he forged,
  The jail-bolts backward fell;
And youth and hoary age came forth
  Like souls escaped from hell.

In the "Old South"

On the 8th of July, 1677, Margaret Brewster with four other Friends went into the South Church in time of meeting, "in sackcloth, with ashes upon her head, barefoot, and her face blackened," and delivered "a warning from the great God of Heaven and Earth to the Rulers and Magistrates of Boston." For the offence she was sentenced to be "whipped at a cart's tail up and down the Town, with twenty lashes."

She came and stood in the Old South Church,
  A wonder and a sign,
With a look the old-time sibyls wore,
  Half-crazed and half-divine.

Save the mournful sackcloth about her wound,
  Unclothed as the primal mother,
With limbs that trembled and eyes that blazed
  With a fire she dare not smother.

Loose on her shoulders fell her hair,
  With sprinkled ashes gray;
She stood in the broad aisle strange and weird
  As a soul at the judgment day.

And the minister paused in his sermon's midst,
  And the people held their breath,
For these were the words the maiden spoke
  Through lips as the lips of death:

"Thus saith the Lord, with equal feet
  All men my courts shall tread,
And priest and ruler no more shall eat
  My people up like bread!

"Repent! repent! ere the Lord shall speak
  In thunder and breaking seals!
Let all souls worship Him in the way
  His light within reveals."

She shook the dust from her naked feet,
And her sackcloth closer drew,
And into the porch of the awe-hushed church
She passed like a ghost from view.

They whipped her away at the tail o' the cart
Through half the streets of the town,
But the words she uttered that day nor fire
Could burn nor water drown.

And now the aisles of the ancient church
By equal feet are trod,
And the bell that swings in its belfry rings
Freedom to worship God!

And now whenever a wrong is done
It thrills the conscious walls;
The stone from the basement cries aloud
And the beam from the timber calls.

There are steeple-houses on every hand,
And pulpits that bless and ban,
And the Lord will not grudge the single church
That is set apart for man.

For in two commandments are all the law
And the prophets under the sun,
And the first is last and the last is first,
And the twain are verily one.

So long as Boston shall Boston be,
And her bay-tides rise and fall,
Shall freedom stand in the Old South Church
And plead for the rights of all!

The Henchman

My lady walks her morning round,
My lady's page her fleet greyhound,
My lady's hair the fond winds stir,
And all the birds make songs for her.

Her thrushes sing in Rathburn bowers,
And Rathburn side is gay with flowers;
But ne'er like hers, in flower or bird,
Was beauty seen or music heard.

The distance of the stars is hers;
The least of all her worshippers,
The dust beneath her dainty heel,
She knows not that I see or feel.

Oh, proud and calm! — she cannot know
Where'er she goes with her I go;
Oh, cold and fair! — she cannot guess
I kneel to share her hound's caress!

Gay knights beside her hunt and hawk,
I rob their ears of her sweet talk;
Her suitors come from east and west,
I steal her smiles from every guest.

Unheard of her, in loving words,
I greet her with the song of birds;
I reach her with her green-armed bowers,
I kiss her with the lips of flowers.

The hound and I are on her trail,
The wind and I uplift her veil;
As if the calm, cold moon she were,
And I the tide, I follow her.

As unrebuked as they, I share
The license of the sun and air,
And in a common homage hide
My worship from her scorn and pride.

World-wide apart, and yet so near,
I breathe her charmëd atmosphere,
Wherein to her my service brings
The reverence due to holy things.

Her maiden pride, her haughty name,
My dumb devotion shall not shame;
The love that no return doth crave
To knightly levels lifts the slave.

No lance have I, in joust or fight,
To splinter in my lady's sight;
But, at her feet, how blest were I
For any need of hers to die!

Rabbi Ishmael

The Rabbi Ishmael, with the woe and sin
Of the world heavy upon him, entering in
The Holy of Holies, saw an awful Face
With terrible splendor filling all the place.
"O Ishmael Ben Elisha!" said a voice,
"What seekest thou? What blessing is thy choice?"
And, knowing that he stood before the Lord,
Within the shadow of the cherubim,
Wide-winged between the blinding light and him,
He bowed himself, and uttered not a word,
But in the silence of his soul was prayer:
"O Thou Eternal! I am one of all,
And nothing ask that others may not share.
Thou art almighty; we are weak and small,
And yet Thy children: let Thy mercy spare!"
Trembling, he raised his eyes, and in the place
Of the insufferable glory, lo! a face
Of more than mortal tenderness, that bent
Graciously down in token of assent,
And, smiling, vanished! With strange joy elate,
The wondering Rabbi sought the temple's gate.
Radiant as Moses from the Mount, he stood
And cried aloud unto the multitude:
"O Israel, hear! The Lord our God is good!
Mine eyes have seen His glory and His grace;
Beyond His judgments shall His love endure;
The mercy of the All Merciful is sure!"

How the Robin Came: An Algonquin Legend

Happy young friends, sit by me,
Under May's blown apple-tree,
While these home-birds in and out
Through the blossoms flit about.

Hear a story, strange and old,
By the wild red Indians told,
How the robin came to be:
Once a great chief left his son, —
Well-beloved, his only one, —
When the boy was well-nigh grown,
In the trial-lodge alone.
Left for tortures long and slow
Youths like him must undergo,
Who their pride of manhood test,
Lacking water, food, and rest.
Seven days the fast he kept,
Seven nights he never slept.
Then the young boy, wrung with pain,
Weak from nature's overstrain,
Faltering, moaned a low complaint:
"Spare me, father, for I faint!"
But the chieftain, haughty-eyed,
Hid his pity in his pride.
"You shall be a hunter good,
Knowing never lack of food:
You shall be a warrior great,
Wise as fox and strong as bear;
Many scalps your belt shall wear,
If with patient heart you wait
Bravely till your task is done.
Better you should starving die
Than that boy and squaw should cry
Shame upon your father's son!"

When next morn the sun's first rays
Glistened on the hemlock sprays,
Straight that lodge the old chief sought,
And boiled samp and moose meat brought.
"Rise and eat, my son!" he said.
Lo, he found the poor boy dead!
As with grief his grave they made,
And his bow beside him laid,
Pipe, and knife, and wampum-braid,
On the lodge-top overhead,
Preening smooth its breast of red
And the brown coat that it wore,
Sat a bird unknown before.
And as if with human tongue,

"Mourn me not," it said, or sung;
"I, a bird, am still your son,
Happier than if hunter fleet,
Or a brave, before your feet
Laying scalps in battle won.
Friend of man, my song shall cheer
Lodge and corn-land; hovering near,
To each wigwam I shall bring
Tidings of the coming spring;
Every child my voice shall know
In the moon of melting snow,
When the maple's red bud swells,
And the wind-flower lifts its bells.
As their fond companion
Men shall henceforth own your son,
And my song shall testify
That of human kin am I."

Thus the Indian legend saith
How, at first, the robin came
With a sweeter life than death,
Bird for boy, and still the same.
If my young friends doubt that this
Is the robin's genesis,
Not in vain is still the myth
If a truth be found therewith:
Unto gentleness belong
Gifts unknown to pride and wrong;
Happier far than hate is praise, —
He who sings than he who slays.

Banished from Massachusetts

1660

On a painting by E. A. Abbey. The General Court of Massachusetts enacted Oct. 19, 1658, that "any person or persons of the cursed sect of Quakers" should, on conviction of the same, be banished, on pain of death, from the jurisdiction of the commonwealth.

Over the threshold of his pleasant home
Set in green clearings passed the exiled Friend,
In simple trust, misdoubting not the end.
"Dear heart of mine!" he said, "the time has come
To trust the Lord for shelter." One long gaze

The goodwife turned on each familiar thing, —
The lowing kine, the orchard blossoming,
The open door that showed the hearth-fire's blaze, —
And calmly answered, "Yes, He will provide."
Silent and slow they crossed the homestead's bound,
Lingering the longest by their child's grave-mound.
"Move on, or stay and hang!" the sheriff cried.
They left behind them more than home or land,
And set sad faces to an alien strand.

Safer with winds and waves than human wrath,
With ravening wolves than those whose zeal for God
Was cruelty to man, the exiles trod
Drear leagues of forest without guide or path,
Or launching frail boats on the uncharted sea,
Round storm-vexed capes, whose teeth of granite ground
The waves to foam, their perilous way they wound,
Enduring all things so their souls were free.
Oh, true confessors, shaming them who did
Anew the wrong their Pilgrim Fathers bore!
For you the Mayflower spread her sail once more,
Freighted with souls, to all that duty bid
Faithful as they who sought an unknown land,
O'er wintry seas, from Holland's Hook of Sand!

So from his lost home to the darkening main,
Bodeful of storm, stout Macy held his way,
And, when the green shore blended with the gray,
His poor wife moaned: "Let us turn back again."
"Nay, woman, weak of faith, kneel down," said he,
"And say thy prayers: the Lord himself will steer;
And led by Him, nor man nor devils I fear!"
So the gray Southwicks, from a rainy sea,
Saw, far and faint, the loom of land, and gave
With feeble voices thanks for friendly ground
Whereon to rest their weary feet, and found
A peaceful death-bed and a quiet grave
Where, ocean-walled, and wiser than his age,
The lord of Shelter scorned the bigot's rage.

Aquidneck's isle, Nantucket's lonely shores,
And Indian-haunted Narragansett saw
The way-worn travellers round their camp-fire draw,
Or heard the plashing of their weary oars.

And every place whereon they rested grew
Happier for pure and gracious womanhood,
And men whose names for stainless honor stood,
Founders of States and rulers wise and true.
The Muse of history yet shall make amends
To those who freedom, peace, and justice taught,
Beyond their dark age led the van of thought,
And left unforfeited the name of Friends.
O mother State, how foiled was thy design!
The gain was theirs, the loss alone was thine.

The Brown Dwarf of Rügen

The hint of this ballad is found in Arndt's *Märchen,* Berlin, 1816. The ballad appeared first in *St. Nicholas,* whose young readers were advised, while smiling at the absurd superstition, to remember that bad companionship and evil habits, desires, and passions are more to be dreaded now than the Elves and Trolls who frightened the children of past ages.

The pleasant isle of Rügen looks the Baltic water o'er,
To the silver-sanded beaches of the Pomeranian shore;

And in the town of Rambin a little boy and maid
Plucked the meadow-flowers together and in the sea-surf played.

Alike were they in beauty if not in their degree:
He was the Amptman's first-born, the miller's child was she.

Now of old the isle of Rügen was full of Dwarfs and Trolls,
The brown-faced little Earth-men, the people without souls;

And for every man and woman in Rügen's island found
Walking in air and sunshine, a Troll was underground.

It chanced the little maiden, one morning, strolled away
Among the haunted Nine Hills, where the elves and goblins play.

That day, in barley fields below, the harvesters had known
Of evil voices in the air, and heard the small horns blown.

She came not back; the search for her in field and wood was vain:
They cried her east, they cried her west, but she came not again.

"She's down among the Brown Dwarfs," said the dream-wives wise
and old,
And prayers were made, and masses said, and Rambin's church bell
tolled.

Five years her father mourned her; and then John Deitrich said:
"I will find my little playmate, be she alive or dead."

He watched among the Nine Hills, he heard the Brown Dwarfs sing,
And saw them dance by moonlight merrily in a ring.

And when their gay-robed leader tossed up his cap of red,
Young Deitrich caught it as it fell, and thrust it on his head.

The Troll came crouching at his feet and wept for lack of it.
"Oh, give me back my magic cap, for your great head unfit!"

"Nay," Deitrich said; "the Dwarf who throws his charmëd cap away,
Must serve its finder at his will, and for his folly pay.

"You stole my pretty Lisbeth, and hid her in the earth;
And you shall ope the door of glass and let me lead her forth."

"She will not come; she's one of us; she's mine!" the Brown Dwarf said;
"The day is set, the cake is baked, to-morrow we shall wed."

"The fell fiend fetch thee!" Deitrich cried, "and keep thy foul tongue
still.
Quick! open, to thy evil world, the glass door of the hill!"

The Dwarf obeyed; and youth and Troll down the long stairway
passed,
And saw in dim and sunless light a country strange and vast.

Weird, rich, and wonderful, he saw the elfin under-land, —
Its palaces of precious stones, its streets of golden sand.

He came unto a banquet-hall with tables richly spread,
Where a young maiden served to him the red wine and the bread.

How fair she seemed among the Trolls so ugly and so wild!
Yet pale and very sorrowful, like one who never smiled!

Her low, sweet voice, her gold-brown hair, her tender blue eyes seemed
Like something he had seen elsewhere or something he had dreamed.

He looked; he clasped her in his arms; he knew the long-lost one;
"O Lisbeth! See thy playmate — I am the Amptman's son!"

She leaned her fair head on his breast, and through her sobs she spoke:
"Oh, take me from this evil place, and from the elfin folk!

"And let me tread the grass-green fields and smell the flowers again,
And feel the soft wind on my cheek and hear the dropping rain!

"And oh, to hear the singing bird, the rustling of the tree,
The lowing cows, the bleat of sheep, the voices of the sea;

"And oh, upon my father's knee to sit beside the door,
And hear the bell of vespers ring in Rambin church once more!"

He kissed her cheek, he kissed her lips; the Brown Dwarf groaned
to see,
And tore his tangled hair and ground his long teeth angrily.

But Deitrich said: "For five long years this tender Christian maid
Has served you in your evil world, and well must she be paid!

"Haste! — hither bring me precious gems, the richest in your store;
Then when we pass the gate of glass, you'll take your cap once more."

No choice was left the baffled Troll, and, murmuring, he obeyed,
And filled the pockets of the youth and apron of the maid.

They left the dreadful under-land and passed the gate of glass;
They felt the sunshine's warm caress, they trod the soft, green grass.

And when, beneath, they saw the Dwarf stretch up to them his brown
And crooked claw-like fingers, they tossed his red cap down.

Oh, never shone so bright a sun, was never sky so blue,
As hand in hand they homeward walked the pleasant meadows
through!

And never sang the birds so sweet in Rambin's woods before,
And never washed the waves so soft along the Baltic shore;

And when beneath his door-yard trees the father met his child,
The bells rung out their merriest peal, the folks with joy ran wild.

And soon from Rambin's holy church the twain came forth as one,
The Amptman kissed a daughter, the miller blest a son.

John Deitrich's fame went far and wide, and nurse and maid crooned o'er
Their cradle song: "Sleep on, sleep well, the Trolls shall come no more!"

For in the haunted Nine Hills he set a cross of stone;
And Elf and Brown Dwarf sought in vain a door where door was none.

The tower he built in Rambin, fair Rügen's pride and boast,
Looked o'er the Baltic water to the Pomeranian coast;

And, for his worth ennobled, and rich beyond compare,
Count Deitrich and his lovely bride dwelt long and happy there.

The Poems of John Greenleaf Whittier

II

SNOW-BOUND

The Editor's Commentary

"SNOW-BOUND" is not only Whittier's most famous poem but one of the treasures of American literature. It owes something to Burns, the poet who first influenced Whittier, especially to "The Cotter's Saturday Night." But "Snow-Bound" is no imitation, no transplanting of a foreign growth into native soil; it is, rather, a transmutation, a conversion of common material into something noble.

Whittier's aim was not exaltation but exactness. He made this plain in the graphic opening lines; he emphasized it in his subtitle, "A Winter Idyl" and in his dedication "To the Memory of the Household It Describes." Frankly autobiographical, the poem mixes the thing observed with the thing remembered: the New England of the fifty-eight-year-old poet is also the small boy's intimate world. It is the remembering boy who sees the snowflakes winging their way in a whirlwind dance, changing the clothes-line posts into "tall sheeted ghosts," turning familiar landmarks into "strange domes and towers" until the well-curb has a Chinese roof and the "long sweep, high aloof, . . . seemed to tell of Pisa's leaning miracle."

But "the chill embargo of the snow" — a phrase Emily Dickinson might have envied — brings the homestead into high relief. The members of the family are naturally contrasted with the visitors: the schoolmaster, "brisk wielder of the birch and rule," who delighted to sing, play games, and transform dread Olympus into huckleberry hill; the "not unfeared, half-welcome" eccentric Harriet Livermore, an incongruously exotic personality, "rebuking with her cultured phrase" the Whittiers' "homeliness of words and ways"; the guileless uncle, "innocent of books"; the spinster aunt; the sore-tried elder sister — a richly realized gallery of ever-living portraits.

The descriptive paragraphs introducing "Snow-Bound," as well as the notes preceding other poems in this volume, were written for his *Collected Poems* by Whittier himself.

Snow-Bound: A Winter Idyl

TO THE MEMORY OF THE HOUSEHOLD IT DESCRIBES
THIS POEM IS DEDICATED BY THE AUTHOR

The inmates of the family at the Whittier homestead who are referred to in the poem were my father, mother, my brother and two sisters, and my uncle and aunt, both unmarried. In addition, there was the district school master, who boarded with us. The "not unfeared, half-welcome guest" was Harriet Livermore, daughter of Judge Livermore, of New Hampshire, a young woman of fine natural ability, enthusiastic, eccentric, with slight control over her violent temper, which sometimes made her religious profession doubtful. She was equally ready to exhort in school-house prayer-meetings and dance in a Washington ball-room, while her father was a member of congress. She early embraced the doctrine of the Second Advent, and felt it her duty to proclaim the Lord's speedy coming. With this message she crossed the Atlantic and spent the greater part of a long life in travelling over Europe and Asia. She lived some time with Lady Hester Stanhope, a woman as fantastic and mentally strained as herself, on the slope of Mt. Lebanon, but finally quarrelled with her in regard to two white horses with red marks on their backs which suggested the idea of saddles, on which her titled hostess expected to ride into Jerusalem with the Lord. A friend of mine found her, when quite an old woman, wandering in Syria with a tribe of Arabs, who with the Oriental notion that madness is inspiration, accepted her as their prophetess and leader. At the time referred to in *Snow-Bound* she was boarding at the Rocks Village, about two miles from us.

In my boyhood, in our lonely farm-house, we had scanty sources of information; few books and only a small weekly newspaper. Our only annual was the Almanac. Under such circumstances story-telling was a necessary resource in the long winter evenings. My father when a young man had traversed the wilderness to Canada, and could tell us of his adventures with Indians and wild beasts, and of his sojourn in the French villages. My uncle was ready with his record of hunting and fishing and, it must be confessed, with stories which he at least half believed, of witchcraft and apparitions. My mother, who was born in the Indian-haunted region of Somersworth, New Hampshire, between Dover and Portsmouth, told us of the inroads of the savages, and the narrow escape of her ancestors. She described strange people who lived on the Piscataqua and Cocheco, among whom was Bantam the sorcerer. I have in my possession the wizard's "conjuring book," which he solemnly opened when consulted. It is a copy of Cornelius Agrippa's *Magic,* printed in 1651, dedicated to Dr. Robert Child, who, like Michael Scott, had learned

"the art of glammorie
In Padua beyond the sea,"

and who is famous in the annals of Massachusetts, where he was at one time a resident, as the first man who dared petition the General Court for liberty of conscience. The full title of the book is *Three Books of Occult Philosophy, by Henry Cornelius Agrippa, Knight, Doctor of both Laws, Counsellor to Cæsar's Sacred Majesty and Judge of the Prerogative Court.*

The sun that brief December day
Rose cheerless over hills of gray,
And, darkly circled, gave at noon
A sadder light than waning moon.
Slow tracing down the thickening sky
Its mute and ominous prophecy,

A portent seeming less than threat,
It sank from sight before it set.
A chill no coat, however stout,
Of homespun stuff could quite shut out,
A hard, dull bitterness of cold,
That checked, mid-vein, the circling race
Of life-blood in the sharpened face,
The coming of the snow-storm told.
The wind blew east; we heard the roar
Of Ocean on his wintry shore,
And felt the strong pulse throbbing there
Beat with low rhythm our inland air.

Meanwhile we did our nightly chores,—
Brought in the wood from out of doors,
Littered the stalls, and from the mows
Raked down the herd's-grass for the cows:
Heard the horse whinnying for his corn;
And, sharply clashing horn on horn,
Impatient down the stanchion rows
The cattle shake their walnut bows;
While, peering from his early perch
Upon the scaffold's pole of birch,
The cock his crested helmet bent
And down his querulous challenge sent.

Unwarmed by any sunset light
The gray day darkened into night,
A night made hoary with the swarm
And whirl-dance of the blinding storm,
As zigzag, wavering to and fro,
Crossed and recrossed the wingëd snow:
And ere the early bedtime came
The white drift piled the window-frame,
And through the glass the clothes-line posts
Looked in like tall and sheeted ghosts.

So all night long the storm roared on:
The morning broke without a sun;
In tiny spherule traced with lines
Of Nature's geometric signs,
In starry flake, and pellicle,
All day the hoary meteor fell;
And, when the second morning shone,

SNOW-BOUND

And, darkly circled, gave at noon
A sadder light than waning moon

We looked upon a world unknown,
On nothing we could call our own.
Around the glistening wonder bent
The blue walls of the firmament,
No cloud above, no earth below, —
A universe of sky and snow!
The old familiar sights of ours
Took marvellous shapes; strange domes and towers
Rose up where sty or corn-crib stood,
Or garden-wall, or belt of wood;
A smooth white mound the brush-pile showed,
A fenceless drift what once was road;
The bridle-post an old man sat
With loose-flung coat and high cocked hat;
The well-curb had a Chinese roof;
And even the long sweep, high aloof,
In its slant splendor, seemed to tell
Of Pisa's leaning miracle.

A prompt, decisive man, no breath
Our father wasted: "Boys, a path!"
Well pleased, (for when did farmer boy
Count such a summons less than joy?)
Our buskins on our feet we drew;
With mittened hands, and caps drawn low,
To guard our necks and ears from snow,
We cut the solid whiteness through.
And, where the drift was deepest, made
A tunnel walled and overlaid
With dazzling crystal: we had read
Of rare Aladdin's wondrous cave,
And to our own his name we gave,
With many a wish the luck were ours
To test his lamp's supernal powers.
We reached the barn with merry din,
And roused the prisoned brutes within.
The old horse thrust his long head out,
And grave with wonder gazed about;
The cock his lusty greeting said,
And forth his speckled harem led;
The oxen lashed their tails, and hooked,
And mild reproach of hunger looked;
The hornëd patriarch of the sheep,
Like Egypt's Amun roused from sleep,

Shook his sage head with gesture mute,
And emphasized with stamp of foot.

All day the gusty north-wind bore
The loosening drift its breath before;
Low circling round its southern zone,
The sun through dazzling snow-mist shone.
No church-bell lent its Christian tone
To the savage air, no social smoke
Curled over woods of snow-hung oak.
A solitude made more intense
By dreary-voicëd elements,
The shrieking of the mindless wind,
The moaning tree-boughs swaying blind,
And on the glass the unmeaning beat
Of ghostly finger-tips of sleet.
Beyond the circle of our hearth
No welcome sound of toil or mirth
Unbound the spell, and testified
Of human life and thought outside.
We minded that the sharpest ear
The buried brooklet could not hear,
The music of whose liquid lip
Had been to us companionship,
And, in our lonely life, had grown
To have an almost human tone.

As night drew on, and, from the crest
Of wooded knolls that ridged the west,
The sun, a snow-blown traveller, sank
From sight beneath the smothering bank,
We piled, with care, our nightly stack
Of wood against the chimney-back, —
The oaken log, green, huge, and thick,
And on its top the stout back-stick;
The knotty forestick laid apart,
And filled between with curious art
The ragged brush; then, hovering near,
We watched the first red blaze appear,
Heard the sharp crackle, caught the gleam
On whitewashed wall and sagging beam,
Until the old, rude-furnished room
Burst, flower-like, into rosy bloom;
While radiant with a mimic flame

Outside the sparkling drift became,
And through the bare-boughed lilac-tree
Our own warm hearth seemed blazing free.
The crane and pendent trammels showed,
The Turks' heads on the andirons glowed;
While childish fancy, prompt to tell
The meaning of the miracle,
Whispered the old rhyme: "*Under the tree,*
When fire outdoors burns merrily,
There the witches are making tea."

The moon above the eastern wood
Shone at its full; the hill-range stood
Transfigured in the silver flood,
Its blown snows flashing cold and keen,
Dead white, save where some sharp ravine
Took shadow, or the sombre green
Of hemlocks turned to pitchy black
Against the whiteness at their back.
For such a world and such a night
Most fitting that unwarming light,
Which only seemed where'er it fell
To make the coldness visible.

Shut in from all the world without,
We sat the clean-winged hearth about,
Content to let the north-wind roar
In baffled rage at pane and door,
While the red logs before us beat
The frost-line back with tropic heat;
And ever, when a louder blast
Shook beam and rafter as it passed,
The merrier up its roaring draught
The great throat of the chimney laughed;
The house-dog on his paws outspread
Laid to the fire his drowsy head,
The cat's dark silhouette on the wall
A couchant tiger's seemed to fall;
And, for the winter fireside meet,
Between the andirons' straddling feet,
The mug of cider simmered slow,
The apples sputtered in a row,
And, close at hand, the basket stood
With nuts from brown October's wood.

What matter how the night behaved?
What matter how the north-wind raved?
Blow high, blow low, not all its snow
Could quench our hearth-fire's ruddy glow.
O Time and Change! — with hair as gray
As was my sire's that winter day,
How strange it seems, with so much gone
Of life and love, to still live on!
Ah, brother! only I and thou
Are left of all that circle now, —
The dear home faces whereupon
That fitful firelight paled and shone.
Henceforward, listen as we will,
The voices of that hearth are still;
Look where we may, the wide earth o'er,
Those lighted faces smile no more.
We tread the paths their feet have worn,
  We sit beneath their orchard trees,
  We hear, like them, the hum of bees
And rustle of the bladed corn;
We turn the pages that they read,
  Their written words we linger o'er,
But in the sun they cast no shade,
No voice is heard, no sign is made,
  No step is on the conscious floor!
Yet Love will dream, and Faith will trust,
(Since He who knows our need is just,)
That somehow, somewhere, meet we must.
Alas for him who never sees
The stars shine through his cypress-trees!
Who, hopeless, lays his dead away,
Nor looks to see the breaking day
Across the mournful marbles play!
Who hath not learned, in hours of faith,
  The truth to flesh and sense unknown,
That Life is ever lord of Death,
  And Love can never lose its own!

We sped the time with stories old,
Wrought puzzles out, and riddles told,
Or stammered from our school-book lore
"The Chief of Gambia's golden shore."
How often since, when all the land
Was clay in Slavery's shaping hand,

As if a far-blown trumpet stirred
The languorous sin-sick air, I heard:
"Does not the voice of reason cry,
  Claim the first right which Nature gave,
From the red scourge of bondage fly,
  Nor deign to live a burdened slave!"
Our father rode again his ride
On Memphremagog's wooded side;
Sat down again to moose and samp
In trapper's hut and Indian camp;
Lived o'er the old idyllic ease
Beneath St. François' hemlock-trees;
Again for him the moonlight shone
On Norman cap and bodiced zone;
Again he heard the violin play
Which led the village dance away.
And mingled in its merry whirl
The grandam and the laughing girl.
Or, nearer home, our steps he led
Where Salisbury's level marshes spread
  Mile-wide as flies the laden bee;
Where merry mowers, hale and strong,
Swept, scythe on scythe, their swaths along
  The low green prairies of the sea.
We shared the fishing off Boar's Head,
  And round the rocky Isles of Shoals
  The hake-broil on the drift-wood coals;
The chowder on the sand-beach made,
Dipped by the hungry, steaming hot,
With spoons of clam-shell from the pot.
We heard the tales of witchcraft old,
And dream and sign and marvel told
To sleepy listeners as they lay
Stretched idly on the salted hay,
Adrift along the winding shores,
When favoring breezes deigned to blow
The square sail of the gundelow
And idle lay the useless oars.

Our mother, while she turned her wheel
Or run the new-knit stocking-heel,
Told how the Indian hordes came down
At midnight on Cocheco town,
And how her own great-uncle bore

His cruel scalp-mark to fourscore.
Recalling, in her fitting phrase,
  So rich and picturesque and free,
  (The common unrhymed poetry
Of simple life and country ways,)
The story of her early days, —
She made us welcome to her home;
Old hearths grew wide to give us room;
We stole with her a frightened look
At the gray wizard's conjuring-book,
The fame whereof went far and wide
Through all the simple country side;
We heard the hawks at twilight play,
The boat-horn on Piscataqua,
The loon's weird laughter far away;
We fished her little trout-brook, knew
What flowers in wood and meadow grew,
What sunny hillsides autumn-brown
She climbed to shake the ripe nuts down,
Saw where in sheltered cove and bay
The ducks' black squadron anchored lay,
And heard the wild-geese calling loud
Beneath the gray November cloud.

Then, haply, with a look more grave,
And soberer tone, some tale she gave
From painful Sewel's ancient tome,
Beloved in every Quaker home,
Of faith fire-winged by martyrdom,
Or Chalkley's Journal, old and quaint, —
Gentlest of skippers, rare sea-saint! —
Who, when the dreary calms prevailed,
And water-butt and bread-cask failed,
And cruel, hungry eyes pursued
His portly presence mad for food,
With dark hints muttered under breath
Of casting lots for life or death,
Offered, if Heaven withheld supplies,
To be himself the sacrifice.
Then, suddenly, as if to save
The good man from his living grave,
A ripple on the water grew,
A school of porpoise flashed in view.
"Take, eat," he said, "and be content;

These fishes in my stead are sent
By Him who gave the tangled ram
To spare the child of Abraham."

Our uncle, innocent of books,
Was rich in lore of fields and brooks,
The ancient teachers never dumb
Of Nature's unhoused lyceum.
In moons and tides and weather wise,
He read the clouds as prophecies,
And foul or fair could well divine,
By many an occult hint and sign,
Holding the cunning-warded keys
To all the woodcraft mysteries;
Himself to Nature's heart so near
That all her voices in his ear
Of beast or bird had meanings clear,
Like Apollonius of old,
Who knew the tales the sparrows told,
Or Hermes, who interpreted
What the sage cranes of Nilus said;
A simple, guileless, childlike man,
Content to live where life began;
Strong only on his native grounds,
The little world of sights and sounds
Whose girdle was the parish bounds,
Whereof his fondly partial pride
The common features magnified,
As Surrey hills to mountains grew
In White of Selborne's loving view, —
He told how teal and loon he shot,
And how the eagle's eggs he got,
The feats on pond and river done,
The prodigies of rod and gun;
Till, warming with the tales he told,
Forgotten was the outside cold,
The bitter wind unheeded blew,
From ripening corn the pigeons flew,
The partridge drummed i' the wood, the mink
Went fishing down the river-brink.
In fields with bean or clover gay,
The woodchuck, like a hermit gray,
  Peered from the doorway of his cell;
The muskrat plied the mason's trade,

And tier by tier his mud-walls laid;
And from the shagbark overhead
The grizzled squirrel dropped his shell.

Next, the dear aunt, whose smile of cheer
And voice in dreams I see and hear, —
The sweetest woman ever Fate
Perverse denied a household mate,
Who, lonely, homeless, not the less
Found peace in love's unselfishness,
And welcome whereso'er she went,
A calm and gracious element,
Whose presence seemed the sweet income
And womanly atmosphere of home, —
Called up her girlhood memories,
The huskings and the apple-bees,
The sleigh-rides and the summer sails,
Weaving through all the poor details
And homespun warp of circumstance
A golden woof-thread of romance.
For well she kept her genial mood
And simple faith of maidenhood;
Before her still a cloud-land lay,
The mirage loomed across her way;
The morning dew, that dries so soon
With others, glistened at her noon;
Through years of toil and soil and care,
From glossy tress to thin gray hair,
All unprofaned she held apart
The virgin fancies of the heart.
Be shame to him of woman born
Who hath for such but thought of scorn.

There, too, our elder sister plied
Her evening task the stand beside;
A full, rich nature, free to trust,
Truthful and almost sternly just,
Impulsive, earnest, prompt to act,
And make her generous thought a fact,
Keeping with many a light disguise
The secret of self-sacrifice.
O heart sore-tried! thou hast the best
That Heaven itself could give thee, — rest,
Rest from all bitter thoughts and things!

SNOW-BOUND

Before our door the straggling train
Drew up, an added team to gain

How many a poor one's blessing went
With thee beneath the low green tent
Whose curtain never outward swings!

As one who held herself a part
Of all she saw, and let her heart
Against the household bosom lean,
Upon the motley-braided mat
Our youngest and our dearest sat,
Lifting her large, sweet, asking eyes,
Now bathed in the unfading green
And holy peace of Paradise.
Oh, looking from some heavenly hill,
Or from the shade of saintly palms,
Or silver reach of river calms,
Do those large eyes behold me still?
With me one little year ago: —
The chill weight of the winter snow
For months upon her grave has lain;
And now, when summer south-winds blow
And brier and harebell bloom again,
I tread the pleasant paths we trod,
I see the violet-sprinkled sod
Whereon she leaned, too frail and weak
The hillside flowers she loved to seek,
Yet following me where'er I went
With dark eyes full of love's content.
The birds are glad; the brier-rose fills
The air with sweetness; all the hills
Stretch green to June's unclouded sky;
But still I wait with ear and eye
For something gone which should be nigh,
A loss in all familiar things,
In flower that blooms, and bird that sings.
And yet, dear heart! remembering thee,
Am I not richer than of old?
Safe in thy immortality,
What change can reach the wealth I hold?
What chance can mar the pearl and gold
Thy love hath left in trust with me?
And while in life's late afternoon,
Where cool and long the shadows grow,
I walk to meet the night that soon
Shall shape and shadow overflow,

I cannot feel that thou art far,
Since near at need the angels are;
And when the sunset gates unbar,
  Shall I not see thee waiting stand,
And, white against the evening star,
  The welcome of thy beckoning hand?

Brisk wielder of the birch and rule,
The master of the district school
Held at the fire his favored place,
Its warm glow lit a laughing face
Fresh-hued and fair, where scarce appeared
The uncertain prophecy of beard.
He teased the mitten-blinded cat,
Played cross-pins on my uncle's hat,
Sang songs, and told us what befalls
In classic Dartmouth's college halls.
Born the wild Northern hills among,
From whence his yeoman father wrung
By patient toil subsistence scant,
Not competence and yet not want,
He early gained the power to pay
His cheerful, self-reliant way;
Could doff at ease his scholar's gown
To peddle wares from town to town;
Or through the long vacation's reach
In lonely lowland districts teach,
Where all the droll experience found
At stranger hearths in boarding round,
The moonlit skater's keen delight,
The sleigh-drive through the frosty night,
The rustic party, with its rough
Accompaniment of blind-man's-buff,
And whirling-plate, and forfeits paid,
His winter task a pastime made.
Happy the snow-locked homes wherein
He tuned his merry violin,
Or played the athlete in the barn,
Or held the good dame's winding-yarn,
Or mirth-provoking versions told
Of classic legends rare and old,
Wherein the scenes of Greece and Rome
Had all the commonplace of home,
And little seemed at best the odds

'Twixt Yankee pedlers and old gods;
Where Pindus-born Arachthus took
The guise of any grist-mill brook,
And dread Olympus at his will
Became a huckleberry hill.

A careless boy that night he seemed;
 But at his desk he had the look
And air of one who wisely schemed,
 And hostage from the future took
 In trainëd thought and lore of book.
Large-brained, clear-eyed, of such as he
Shall Freedom's young apostles be,
Who, following in War's bloody trail,
Shall every lingering wrong assail;
All chains from limb and spirit strike,
Uplift the black and white alike;
Scatter before their swift advance
The darkness and the ignorance,
The pride, the lust, the squalid sloth,
Which nurtured Treason's monstrous growth,
Made murder pastime, and the hell
Of prison-torture possible;
The cruel lie of caste refute,
Old forms remould, and substitute
For Slavery's lash the freeman's will,
For blind routine, wise-handed skill;
A school-house plant on every hill,
Stretching in radiate nerve-lines thence
The quick wires of intelligence;
Till North and South together brought
Shall own the same electric thought,
In peace a common flag salute,
And, side by side in labor's free
And unresentful rivalry,
Harvest the fields wherein they fought.

Another guest that winter night
Flashed back from lustrous eyes the light.
Unmarked by time, and yet not young,
The honeyed music of her tongue
And words of meekness scarcely told
A nature passionate and bold,
Strong, self-concentred, spurning guide,

Its milder features dwarfed beside
Her unbent will's majestic pride.
She sat among us, at the best,
A not unfeared, half-welcome guest,
Rebuking with her cultured phrase
Our homeliness of words and ways.
A certain pard-like, treacherous grace
Swayed the lithe limbs and drooped the lash,
Lent the white teeth their dazzling flash;
And under low brows, black with night,
Rayed out at times a dangerous light;
The sharp heat-lightnings of her face
Presaging ill to him whom Fate
Condemned to share her love or hate.
A woman tropical, intense
In thought and act, in soul and sense,
She blended in a like degree
The vixen and the devotee,
Revealing with each freak or feint
  The temper of Petruchio's Kate,
The raptures of Siena's saint.
Her tapering hand and rounded wrist
Had facile power to form a fist;
The warm, dark languish of her eyes
Was never safe from wrath's surprise.
Brows saintly calm and lips devout
Knew every change of scowl and pout;
And the sweet voice had notes more high
And shrill for social battle-cry.

Since then what old cathedral town
Has missed her pilgrim staff and gown,
What convent-gate has held its lock
Against the challenge of her knock!
Through Smyrna's plague-hushed thoroughfares,
Up sea-set Malta's rocky stairs,
Gray olive slopes of hills that hem
Thy tombs and shrines, Jerusalem,
Or startling on her desert throne
The crazy Queen of Lebanon
With claims fantastic as her own,
Her tireless feet have held their way;
And still, unrestful, bowed, and gray,
She watches under Eastern skies,

With hope each day renewed and fresh,
The Lord's quick coming in the flesh,
Whereof she dreams and prophesies!

Where'er her troubled path may be,
The Lord's sweet pity with her go!
The outward wayward life we see,
The hidden springs we may not know.
Nor is it given us to discern
What threads the fatal sisters spun,
Through what ancestral years has run
The sorrow with the woman born,
What forged her cruel chain of moods,
What set her feet in solitudes,
And held the love within her mute,
What mingled madness in the blood,
A life-long discord and annoy,
Water of tears with oil of joy,
And hid within the folded bud
Perversities of flower and fruit.
It is not ours to separate
The tangled skein of will and fate,
To show what metes and bounds should stand
Upon the soul's debatable land,
And between choice and Providence
Divide the circle of events;
But He who knows our frame is just,
Merciful and compassionate,
And full of sweet assurances
And hope for all the language is,
That He remembereth we are dust!

At last the great logs, crumbling low,
Sent out a dull and duller glow,
The bull's-eye watch that hung in view,
Ticking its weary circuit through,
Pointed with mutely warning sign
Its black hand to the hour of nine.
That sign the pleasant circle broke:
My uncle ceased his pipe to smoke,
Knocked from its bowl the refuse gray,
And laid it tenderly away;
Then roused himself to safely cover
The dull red brands with ashes over.

And while, with care, our mother laid
The work aside, her steps she stayed
One moment, seeking to express
Her grateful sense of happiness
For food and shelter, warmth and health,
And love's contentment more than wealth,
With simple wishes (not the weak,
Vain prayers which no fulfilment seek,
But such as warm the generous heart,
O'er-prompt to do with Heaven its part)
That none might lack, that bitter night,
For bread and clothing, warmth and light.

Within our beds awhile we heard
The wind that round the gables roared,
With now and then a ruder shock,
Which made our very bedsteads rock.
We heard the loosened clapboards tost,
The board-nails snapping in the frost;
And on us, through the unplastered wall,
Felt the light sifted snow-flakes fall.
But sleep stole on, as sleep will do
When hearts are light and life is new;
Faint and more faint the murmurs grew,
Till in the summer-land of dreams
They softened to the sound of streams,
Low stir of leaves, and dip of oars,
And lapsing waves on quiet shores.

Next morn we wakened with the shout
Of merry voices high and clear;
And saw the teamsters drawing near
To break the drifted highways out.
Down the long hillside treading slow
We saw the half-buried oxen go,
Shaking the snow from heads uptost,
Their straining nostrils white with frost.
Before our door the straggling train
Drew up, an added team to gain.
The elders threshed their hands a-cold,
  Passed, with the cider-mug, their jokes
  From lip to lip; the younger folks
Down the loose snow-banks, wrestling, rolled,
Then toiled again the cavalcade

O'er windy hill, through clogged ravine,
And woodland paths that wound between
Low drooping pine-boughs winter-weighed.
From every barn a team afoot,
At every house a new recruit,
Where, drawn by Nature's subtlest law,
Haply the watchful young men saw
Sweet doorway pictures of the curls
And curious eyes of merry girls,
Lifting their hands in mock defence
Against the snow-ball's compliments,
And reading in each missive tost
The charm with Eden never lost.

We heard once more the sleigh-bells' sound;
And, following where the teamsters led,
The wise old Doctor went his round,
Just pausing at our door to say,
In the brief autocratic way
Of one who, prompt at Duty's call,
Was free to urge her claim on all,
That some poor neighbor sick abed
At night our mother's aid would need.
For, one in generous thought and deed,
What mattered in the sufferer's sight
The Quaker matron's inward light,
The Doctor's mail of Calvin's creed?
All hearts confess the saints elect
Who, twain in faith, in love agree,
And melt not in an acid sect
The Christian pearl of charity!

So days went on: a week had passed
Since the great world was heard from last.
The Almanac we studied o'er,
Read and reread our little store
Of books and pamphlets, scarce a score;
One harmless novel, mostly hid
From younger eyes, a book forbid,
And poetry, (or good or bad,
A single book was all we had,)
Where Ellwood's meek, drab-skirted Muse,
A stranger to the heathen Nine,
Sang, with a somewhat nasal whine,

The wars of David and the Jews.
At last the floundering carrier bore
The village paper to our door.
Lo! broadening outward as we read,
To warmer zones the horizon spread
In panoramic length unrolled
We saw the marvels that it told.
Before us passed the painted Creeks,
And daft McGregor on his raids
In Costa Rica's everglades.
And up Taygetos winding slow
Rode Ypsilanti's Mainote Greeks,
A Turk's head at each saddle-bow!
Welcome to us its week-old news,
Its corner for the rustic Muse,
Its monthly gauge of snow and rain,
Its record, mingling in a breath
The wedding bell and dirge of death:
Jest, anecdote, and love-lorn tale,
The latest culprit sent to jail;
Its hue and cry of stolen and lost,
Its vendue sales and goods at cost,
And traffic calling loud for gain.
We felt the stir of hall and street,
The pulse of life that round us beat;
The chill embargo of the snow
Was melted in the genial glow;
Wide swung again our ice-locked door,
And all the world was ours once more!

Clasp, Angel of the backward look
And folded wings of ashen gray
And voice of echoes far away,
The brazen covers of thy book;
The weird palimpsest old and vast,
Wherein thou hid'st the spectral past;
Where, closely mingling, pale and glow
The characters of joy and woe;
The monographs of outlived years,
Or smile-illumed or dim with tears,
Green hills of life that slope to death,
And haunts of home, whose vistaed trees
Shade off to mournful cypresses
With the white amaranths underneath.

Even while I look, I can but heed
  The restless sands' incessant fall,
Importunate hours that hours succeed,
Each clamorous with its own sharp need,
  And duty keeping pace with all.
Shut down and clasp the heavy lids;
I hear again the voice that bids
The dreamer leave his dream midway
For larger hopes and graver fears:
Life greatens in these later years,
The century's aloe flowers to-day!

Yet, haply, in some lull of life,
Some Truce of God which breaks its strife,
The worldling's eyes shall gather dew,
  Dreaming in throngful city ways
Of winter joys his boyhood knew;
And dear and early friends — the few
Who yet remain — shall pause to view
  These Flemish pictures of old days;
Sit with me by the homestead hearth,
And stretch the hands of memory forth
  To warm them at the wood-fire's blaze!
And thanks untraced to lips unknown
Shall greet me like the odors blown
From unseen meadows newly mown,
Or lilies floating in some pond,
Wood-fringed, the wayside gaze beyond;
The traveller owns the grateful sense
Of sweetness near, he knows not whence,
And, pausing, takes with forehead bare
The benediction of the air.

The Poems of John Greenleaf Whittier

III

OF PLACES AND PEOPLE

The Editor's Commentary

"Of Places and People" contains poems selected from three separate groups: "Poems of Nature," "Personal Poems," and "Occasional Poems." Some of the verses have become part of our education; some are still sung as hymns; a few rise above time and circumstance into the timelessness of pure poetry.

Such a poem is "Ichabod," a denunciation which might easily have been vituperative but is all the more bitter because of its quiet scorn. It was occasioned by Daniel Webster's support of the Fugitive Slave Law and his speech urging the North to appease the South. No personal enmity prompted it; on the contrary, Whittier penned the protest in one of the saddest moments of his life. "I saw, as I wrote, with painful clearness, its sure results: the Slave Power arrogant and defiant, strengthened and encouraged to carry out its scheme for the extension of its baleful system, or the dissolution of the Union, the guaranties of personal liberty . . . and the whole country made the hunting-ground of slave-catchers."

Two years later Webster died, and the resentment was softened. "The consciousness of a common inheritance of frailty and weakness modifies the severity of judgment," wrote Whittier, and years later composed a sequel to "Ichabod." In "The Lost Occasion" the poet gave utterance "to an almost universal regret that the great statesman did not live to see the flag which he loved trampled under the feet of Slavery, and, in view of this desecration, make his last days glorious in defense of 'Liberty and Union, one and inseparable.' "

The moral principle sustains and illumines the personal no less than the important poems. But the religious poems, even the hymns, while sometimes sententious, are never sanctimonious. The Quaker conscience is colored by a pagan consciousness. Toil is sweetened with esthetic rewards no less than with homestead produce; God is not only the Lord of hosts but the Painter of fruits and flowers. "Beauty," said Emerson, "is its own excuse for being." But Whittier assures us even more confidently:

> The good is always beautiful,
> The beautiful is good.

Ichabod

So fallen! so lost! the light withdrawn
Which once he wore!
The glory from his gray hairs gone
Forevermore!

Revile him not, the Tempter hath
A snare for all;
And pitying tears, not scorn and wrath,
Befit his fall!

Oh, dumb be passion's stormy rage,
When he who might
Have lighted up and led his age,
Falls back in night.

Scorn! would the angels laugh, to mark
A bright soul driven,
Fiend-goaded, down the endless dark,
From hope and heaven!

Let not the land once proud of him
Insult him now,
Nor brand with deeper shame his dim,
Dishonored brow.

But let its humbled sons, instead,
From sea to lake,
A long lament, as for the dead,
In sadness make.

Of all we loved and honored, naught
Save power remains;
A fallen angel's pride of thought,
Still strong in chains.

All else is gone; from those great eyes
The soul has fled:
When faith is lost, when honor dies,
The man is dead!

Then, pay the reverence of old days
To his dead fame;
Walk backward, with averted gaze,
And hide the shame!

The Lost Occasion

Some die too late and some too soon,
At early morning, heat of noon,
Or the chill evening twilight. Thou,
Whom the rich heavens did so endow
With eyes of power and Jove's own brow,
With all the massive strength that fills
Thy home-horizon's granite hills,
With rarest gifts of heart and head
From manliest stock inherited,
New England's stateliest type of man,
In port and speech Olympian;
Whom no one met, at first, but took
A second awed and wondering look
(As turned, perchance, the eyes of Greece
On Phidias' unveiled masterpiece);
Whose words in simplest homespun clad,
The Saxon strength of Cædmon's had,
With power reserved at need to reach
The Roman forum's loftiest speech,
Sweet with persuasion, eloquent
In passion, cool in argument,
Or, ponderous, falling on thy foes
As fell the Norse god's hammer blows,
Crushing as if with Talus' flail
Through Error's logic-woven mail,
And failing only when they tried
The adamant of the righteous side, —
Thou, foiled in aim and hope, bereaved
Of old friends, by the new deceived,
Too soon for us, too soon for thee,
Beside thy lonely Northern sea,
Where long and low the marsh-lands spread,
Laid wearily down thy august head.

Thou shouldst have lived to feel below
Thy feet Disunion's fierce upthrow;
The late-sprung mine that underlaid
Thy sad concessions vainly made.
Thou shouldst have seen from Sumter's wall
The star-flag of the Union fall,
And armed rebellion pressing on
The broken lines of Washington!
No stronger voice than thine had then
Called out the utmost might of men,

To make the Union's charter free
And strengthen law by liberty.
How had that stern arbitrament
To thy gray age youth's vigor lent,
Shaming ambition's paltry prize
Before thy disillusioned eyes;
Breaking the spell about thee wound
Like the green withes that Samson bound;
Redeeming in one effort grand,
Thyself and thy imperilled land!
Ah, cruel fate, that closed to thee,
O sleeper by the Northern sea,
The gates of opportunity!
God fills the gaps of human need,
Each crisis brings its word and deed.
Wise men and strong we did not lack;
But still, with memory turning back,
In the dark hours we thought of thee,
And thy lone grave beside the sea.

Above that grave the east winds blow,
And from the marsh-lands drifting slow
The sea-fog comes, with evermore
The wave-wash of a lonely shore,
And sea-bird's melancholy cry,
As Nature fain would typify
The sadness of a closing scene,
The loss of that which should have been.
But, where thy native mountains bare
Their foreheads to diviner air,
Fit emblem of enduring fame,
One lofty summit keeps thy name.
For thee the cosmic forces did
The rearing of that pyramid,
The prescient ages shaping with
Fire, flood, and frost thy monolith.
Sunrise and sunset lay thereon
With hands of light their benison,
The stars of midnight pause to set
Their jewels in its coronet.
And evermore that mountain mass
Seems climbing from the shadowy pass
To light, as if to manifest
Thy nobler self, thy life at best!

Autumn Thoughts

Gone hath the Spring, with all its flowers,
 And gone the Summer's pomp and show,
And Autumn, in his leafless bowers,
 Is waiting for the Winter's snow.

I said to Earth, so cold and gray,
 "An emblem of myself thou art."
"Not so," the Earth did seem to say,
 "For Spring shall warm my frozen heart."

I soothe my wintry sleep with dreams
 Of warmer sun and softer rain,
And wait to hear the sound of streams
 And songs of merry birds again.

But thou, from whom the Spring hath gone,
 For whom the flowers no longer blow,
Who standest blighted and forlorn,
 Like Autumn waiting for the snow;

No hope is thine of sunnier hours,
 Thy Winter shall no more depart;
No Spring revive thy wasted flowers,
 Nor Summer warm thy frozen heart.

The Frost Spirit

He comes, — he comes, — the Frost Spirit comes! You may trace his footsteps now
On the naked woods and the blasted fields and the brown hill's withered brow.
He has smitten the leaves of the gray old trees where their pleasant green came forth,
And the winds, which follow wherever he goes, have shaken them down to earth.

He comes, — he comes, — the Frost Spirit comes! from the frozen Labrador,
From the icy bridge of the Northern seas, which the white bear wanders o'er,
Where the fisherman's sail is stiff with ice, and the luckless forms below
In the sunless cold of the lingering night into marble statues grow!

He comes, — he comes, — the Frost Spirit comes! on the rushing Northern blast,

THE FROST SPIRIT

He has smitten the leaves of the gray
old trees where their pleasant green came forth

And the dark Norwegian pines have bowed as his fearful breath went
past.
With an unscorched wing he has hurried on, where the fires of Hecla
glow
On the darkly beautiful sky above and the ancient ice below.

He comes, — he comes, — the Frost Spirit comes! and the quiet lake
shall feel
The torpid touch of his glazing breath, and ring to the skater's heel;
And the streams which danced on the broken rocks, or sang to the lean-
ing grass,
Shall bow again to their winter chain, and in mournful silence pass.

He comes, — he comes, — the Frost Spirit comes! Let us meet him as
we may,
And turn with the light of the parlor-fire his evil power away;
And gather closer the circle round, when that firelight dances high,
And laugh at the shriek of the baffled Fiend as his sounding wing
goes by!

The Merrimac

Stream of my fathers! sweetly still
The sunset rays thy valley fill;
Poured slantwise down the long defile,
Wave, wood, and spire beneath them smile.
I see the winding Powow fold
The green hill in its belt of gold,
And following down its wavy line,
Its sparkling waters blend with thine.
There's not a tree upon thy side,
Nor rock, which thy returning tide
As yet hath left abrupt and stark
Above thy evening water-mark;
No calm cove with its rocky hem,
No isle whose emerald swells begem
Thy broad, smooth current; not a sail
Bowed to the freshening ocean gale;
No small boat with its busy oars,
Nor gray wall sloping to thy shores;
Nor farm-house with its maple shade,
Or rigid poplar colonnade,
But lies distinct and full in sight,
Beneath this gush of sunset light.

Centuries ago, that harbor-bar,
Stretching its length of foam afar,
And Salisbury's beach of shining sand,
And yonder island's wave-smoothed strand,
Saw the adventurer's tiny sail,
Flit, stooping from the eastern gale;
And o'er these woods and waters broke
The cheer from Britain's hearts of oak,
As brightly on the voyager's eye,
Weary of forest, sea, and sky,
Breaking the dull continuous wood,
The Merrimac rolled down his flood;
Mingling that clear pellucid brook,
Which channels vast Agioochook
When spring-time's sun and shower unlock
The frozen fountains of the rock,
And more abundant waters given
From that pure lake, "The Smile of Heaven,"
Tributes from vale and mountain-side, —
With ocean's dark, eternal tide!

On yonder rocky cape, which braves
The stormy challenge of the waves,
Midst tangled vine and dwarfish wood,
The hardy Anglo-Saxon stood,
Planting upon the topmost crag
The staff of England's battle-flag;
And, while from out its heavy fold
Saint George's crimson cross unrolled,
Midst roll of drum and trumpet blare,
And weapons brandishing in air,
He gave to that lone promontory
The sweetest name in all his story;
Of her, the flower of Islam's daughters,
Whose harems look on Stamboul's waters, —
Who, when the chance of war had bound
The Moslem chain his limbs around,
Wreathed o'er with silk that iron chain,
Soothed with her smiles his hours of pain,
And fondly to her youthful slave
A dearer gift than freedom gave.

But look! the yellow light no more
Streams down on wave and verdant shore;

And clearly on the calm air swells
The twilight voice of distant bells.
From Ocean's bosom, white and thin,
The mists come slowly rolling in;
Hills, woods, the river's rocky rim,
Amidst the sea-like vapor swim,
While yonder lonely coast-light, set
Within its wave-washed minaret,
Half quenched, a beamless star and pale,
Shines dimly through its cloudy veil!

Home of my fathers! — I have stood
Where Hudson rolled his lordly flood:
Seen sunrise rest and sunset fade
Along his frowning Palisade;
Looked down the Appalachian peak
On Juniata's silver streak;
Have seen along his valley gleam
The Mohawk's softly winding stream;
The level light of sunset shine
Through broad Potomac's hem of pine;
And autumn's rainbow-tinted banner
Hang lightly o'er the Susquehanna;
Yet wheresoe'er his step might be,
Thy wandering child looked back to thee!
Heard in his dreams thy river's sound
Of murmuring on its pebbly bound,
The unforgotten swell and roar
Of waves on thy familiar shore;
And saw, amidst the curtained gloom
And quiet of his lonely room,
Thy sunset scenes before him pass;
As, in Agrippa's magic glass,
The loved and lost arose to view,
Remembered groves in greenness grew,
Bathed still in childhood's morning dew,
Along whose bowers of beauty swept
Whatever Memory's mourners wept,
Sweet faces, which the charnel kept,
Young, gentle eyes, which long had slept;
And while the gazer leaned to trace,
More near, some dear familiar face,
He wept to find the vision flown, —
A phantom and a dream alone!

Hampton Beach

The sunlight glitters keen and bright,
Where, miles away,
Lies stretching to my dazzled sight
A luminous belt, a misty light,
Beyond the dark pine bluffs and wastes of sandy gray.

The tremulous shadow of the Sea!
Against its ground
Of silvery light, rock, hill, and tree,
Still as a picture, clear and free,
With varying outline mark the coast for miles around.

On — on — we tread with loose-flung rein
Our seaward way,
Through dark-green fields and blossoming grain,
Where the wild brier-rose skirts the lane,
And bends above our heads the flowering locust spray.

Ha! like a kind hand on my brow
Comes this fresh breeze,
Cooling its dull and feverish glow,
While through my being seems to flow
The breath of a new life, the healing of the seas!

Now rest we, where this grassy mound
His feet hath set
In the great waters, which have bound
His granite ankles greenly round
With long and tangled moss, and weeds with cool spray wet.

Good-by to Pain and Care! I take
Mine ease to-day:
Here where these sunny waters break,
And ripples this keen breeze, I shake
All burdens from the heart, all weary thoughts away.

I draw a freer breath, I seem
Like all I see —
Waves in the sun, the white-winged gleam
Of sea-birds in the slanting beam,
And far-off sails which flit before the southwind free.

So when Time's veil shall fall asunder,
The soul may know

No fearful change, nor sudden wonder,
Nor sink the weight of mystery under,
But with the upward rise, and with the vastness grow.

And all we shrink from now may seem
No new revealing;
Familiar as our childhood's stream,
Or pleasant memory of a dream
The loved and cherished Past upon the new life stealing.

Serene and mild the untried light
May have its dawning;
And, as in summer's northern night
The evening and the dawn unite,
The sunset hues of Time blend with the soul's new morning.

I sit alone; in foam and spray
Wave after wave
Breaks on the rocks which, stern and gray,
Shoulder the broken tide away,
Or murmurs hoarse and strong through mossy cleft and cave.

What heed I of the dusty land
And noisy town?
I see the mighty deep expand
From its white line of glimmering sand
To where the blue of heaven on bluer waves shuts down!

In listless quietude of mind,
I yield to all
The change of cloud and wave and wind;
And passive on the flood reclined,
I wander with the waves, and with them rise and fall.

But look, thou dreamer! wave and shore
In shadow lie;
The night-wind warns me back once more
To where, my native hill-tops o'er,
Bends like an arch of fire the glowing sunset sky.

So then, beach, bluff, and wave, farewell!
I bear with me
No token stone nor glittering shell,
But long and oft shall Memory tell
Of this brief thoughtful hour of musing by the Sea.

April

"The spring comes slowly up this way."
Christabel.

'Tis the noon of the spring-time, yet never a bird
In the wind-shaken elm or the maple is heard;
For green meadow-grasses wide levels of snow,
And blowing of drifts where the crocus should blow;
Where wind-flower and violet, amber and white,
On south-sloping brooksides should smile in the light,
O'er the cold winter-beds of their late-waking roots
The frosty flake eddies, the ice-crystal shoots;
And, longing for light, under wind-driven heaps,
Round the boles of the pine-wood the ground-laurel creeps,
Unkissed of the sunshine, unbaptized of showers,
With buds scarcely swelled, which should burst into flowers!
We wait for thy coming, sweet wind of the south!
For the touch of thy light wings, the kiss of thy mouth;
For the yearly evangel thou bearest from God,
Resurrection and life to the graves of the sod!
Up our long river-valley, for days, have not ceased
The wail and the shriek of the bitter northeast,
Raw and chill, as if winnowed through ices and snow,
All the way from the land of the wild Esquimau,
Until all our dreams of the land of the blest,
Like that red hunter's, turn to the sunny southwest.
O soul of the spring-time, its light and its breath,
Bring warmth to this coldness, bring life to this death;
Renew the great miracle; let us behold
The stone from the mouth of the sepulchre rolled,
And Nature, like Lazarus, rise, as of old!
Let our faith, which in darkness and coldness has lain,
Revive with the warmth and the brightness again,
And in blooming of flower and budding of tree
The symbols and types of our destiny see;
The life of the spring-time, the life of the whole,
And, as sun to the sleeping earth, love to the soul!

A Dream of Summer

Bland as the morning breath of June
The southwest breezes play;
And, through its haze, the winter noon
Seems warm as summer's day.
The snow-plumed Angel of the North

Has dropped his icy spear;
Again the mossy earth looks forth,
Again the streams gush clear.

The fox his hillside cell forsakes,
The muskrat leaves his nook,
The bluebird in the meadow brakes
Is singing with the brook.
"Bear up, O Mother Nature!" cry
Bird, breeze, and streamlet free;
"Our winter voices prophesy
Of summer days to thee!"

So, in those winters of the soul,
By bitter blasts and drear
O'erswept from Memory's frozen pole,
Will sunny days appear.
Reviving Hope and Faith, they show
The soul its living powers,
And how beneath the winter's snow
Lie germs of summer flowers!

The Night is mother of the Day,
The Winter of the Spring,
And ever upon old Decay
The greenest mosses cling.
Behind the cloud the starlight lurks,
Through showers the sunbeams fall;
For God, who loveth all His works,
Has left His hope with all!

Summer by the Lakeside

LAKE WINNIPESAUKEE

I. NOON

White clouds, whose shadows haunt the deep,
Light mists, whose soft embraces keep
The sunshine on the hills asleep!

O isles of calm! O dark, still wood!
And stiller skies that overbrood
Your rest with deeper quietude!

O shapes and hues, dim beckoning, through
Yon mountain gaps, my longing view
Beyond the purple and the blue,

To stiller sea and greener land,
And softer lights and airs more bland,
And skies, — the hollow of God's hand!

Transfused through you, O mountain friends!
With mine your solemn spirit blends,
And life no more hath separate ends.

I read each misty mountain sign,
I know the voice of wave and pine,
And I am yours, and ye are mine.

Life's burdens fall, its discords cease,
I lapse into the glad release
Of Nature's own exceeding peace.

O welcome calm of heart and mind!
As falls yon fir-tree's loosened rind
To leave a tenderer growth behind,

So fall the weary years away;
A child again, my head I lay
Upon the lap of this sweet day.

This western wind hath Lethean powers,
Yon noonday cloud nepenthe showers,
The lake is white with lotus-flowers!

Even Duty's voice is faint and low,
And slumberous Conscience, waking slow,
Forgets her blotted scroll to show.

The Shadow which pursues us all,
Whose ever-nearing steps appall,
Whose voice we hear behind us call, —

That Shadow blends with mountain gray,
It speaks but what the light waves say, —
Death walks apart from Fear to-day!

A DREAM OF SUMMER

Again the mossy earth looks forth,
Again the streams gush clear

Rocked on her breast, these pines and I
Alike on Nature's love rely;
And equal seems to live or die.

Assured that He whose presence fills
With light the spaces of these hills
No evil to His creatures wills,

The simple faith remains, that He
Will do, whatever that may be,
The best alike for man and tree.

What mosses over one shall grow,
What light and life the other know,
Unanxious, leaving Him to show.

II. EVENING

Yon mountain's side is black with night,
While, broad-orbed, o'er its gleaming crown
The moon, slow-rounding into sight,
On the hushed inland sea looks down.

How start to light the clustering isles,
Each silver-hemmed! How sharply show
The shadows of their rocky piles,
And tree-tops in the wave below!

How far and strange the mountains seem,
Dim-looming through the pale, still light!
The vague, vast grouping of a dream,
They stretch into the solemn night.

Beneath, lake, wood, and peopled vale,
Hushed by that presence grand and grave,
Are silent, save the cricket's wail,
And low response of leaf and wave.

Fair scenes! whereto the Day and Night
Make rival love, I leave ye soon,
What time before the eastern light
The pale ghost of the setting moon

Shall hide behind yon rocky spines,
  And the young archer, Morn, shall break
His arrows on the mountain pines,
  And, golden-sandalled, walk the lake!

Farewell! around this smiling bay
  Gay-hearted Health, and Life in bloom,
With lighter steps than mine, may stray
  In radiant summers yet to come.

But none shall more regretful leave
  These waters and these hills than I:
Or, distant, fonder dream how eve
  Or dawn is painting wave and sky;

How rising moons shine sad and mild
  On wooded isle and silvering bay;
Or setting suns beyond the piled
  And purple mountains lead the day;

Nor laughing girl, nor bearding boy,
  Nor full-pulsed manhood, lingering here,
Shall add, to life's abounding joy,
  The charmed repose to suffering dear.

Still waits kind Nature to impart
  Her choicest gifts to such as gain
An entrance to her loving heart
  Through the sharp discipline of pain.

Forever from the Hand that takes
  One blessing from us others fall;
And, soon or late, our Father makes
  His perfect recompense to all!

Oh, watched by Silence and the Night,
  And folded in the strong embrace
Of the great mountains, with the light
  Of the sweet heavens upon thy face,

Lake of the Northland! keep thy dower
  Of beauty still, and while above
Thy solemn mountains speak of power,
  Be thou the mirror of God's love.

The Mayflowers

Sad Mayflower! watched by winter stars,
And nursed by winter gales,
With petals of the sleeted spars,
And leaves of frozen sails!

What had she in those dreary hours,
Within her ice-rimmed bay,
In common with the wild-wood flowers,
The first sweet smiles of May?

Yet, "God be praised!" the Pilgrim said,
Who saw the blossoms peer
Above the brown leaves, dry and dead,
"Behold our Mayflower here!"

"God wills it: here our rest shall be,
Our years of wandering o'er;
For us the Mayflower of the sea
Shall spread her sails no more."

O sacred flowers of faith and hope,
As sweetly now as then
Ye bloom on many a birchen slope,
In many a pine-dark glen.

Behind the sea-wall's rugged length,
Unchanged, your leaves unfold,
Like love behind the manly strength
Of the brave hearts of old.

So live the fathers in their sons,
Their sturdy faith be ours,
And ours the love that overruns
Its rocky strength with flowers.

The Pilgrim's wild and wintry day
Its shadow round us draws;
The Mayflower of his stormy bay,
Our Freedom's struggling cause.

But warmer suns erelong shall bring
To life the frozen sod;
And through dead leaves of hope shall spring
Afresh the flowers of God!

The First Flowers

For ages, on our river borders,
These tassels in their tawny bloom,
And willowy studs of downy silver,
Have prophesied of Spring to come.

For ages have the unbound waters
Smiled on them from their pebbly hem,
And the clear carol of the robin
And song of bluebird welcomed them.

But never yet from smiling river,
Or song of early bird, have they
Been greeted with a gladder welcome
Than whispers from my heart to-day.

They break the spell of cold and darkness,
The weary watch of sleepless pain;
And from my heart, as from the river,
The ice of winter melts again.

Thanks, Mary! for this wild-wood token
Of Freya's footsteps drawing near;
Almost, as in the rune of Asgard,
The growing of the grass I hear.

It is as if the pine-trees called me
From ceilëd room and silent books,
To see the dance of woodland shadows,
And hear the song of April brooks!

As in the old Teutonic ballad
Of Odenwald live bird and tree,
Together live in bloom and music,
I blend in song thy flowers and thee.

Earth's rocky tablets bear forever
The dint of rain and small bird's track:
Who knows but that my idle verses
May leave some trace by Merrimac!

The bird that trod the mellow layers
Of the young earth is sought in vain;
The cloud is gone that wove the sandstone,
From God's design, with threads of rain!

So, when this fluid age we live in
Shall stiffen round my careless rhyme,
Who made the vagrant tracks may puzzle
The savants of the coming time;

And, following out their dim suggestions,
Some idly-curious hand may draw
My doubtful portraiture, as Cuvier
Drew fish and bird from fin and claw.

And maidens in the far-off twilights,
Singing my words to breeze and stream,
Shall wonder if the old-time Mary
Were real, or the rhymer's dream!

The Old Burying-Ground

Our vales are sweet with fern and rose,
Our hills are maple-crowned;
But not from them our fathers chose
The village burying-ground.

The dreariest spot in all the land
To Death they set apart;
With scanty grace from Nature's hand,
And none from that of art.

A winding wall of mossy stone,
Frost-flung and broken, lines
A lonesome acre thinly grown
With grass and wandering vines.

Without the wall a birch-tree shows
Its drooped and tasselled head;
Within, a stag-horn sumach grows,
Fern-leafed, with spikes of red.

There, sheep that graze the neighboring plain
Like white ghosts come and go,
The farm-horse drags his fetlock chain,
The cow-bell tinkles slow.

Low moans the river from its bed,
The distant pines reply;
Like mourners shrinking from the dead,
They stand apart and sigh.

Unshaded smites the summer sun,
Unchecked the winter blast;
The school-girl learns the place to shun,
With glances backward cast.

For thus our fathers testified,
That he might read who ran,
The emptiness of human pride,
The nothingness of man.

They dared not plant the grave with flowers,
Nor dress the funeral sod,
Where, with a love as deep as ours,
They left their dead with God.

The hard and thorny path they kept
From beauty turned aside;
Nor missed they over those who slept
The grace to life denied.

Yet still the wilding flowers would blow,
The golden leaves would fall,
The seasons come, the seasons go,
And God be good to all.

Above the graves the blackberry hung
In bloom and green its wreath,
And harebells swung as if they rung
The chimes of peace beneath.

The beauty Nature loves to share,
The gifts she hath for all,
The common light, the common air,
O'ercrept the graveyard's wall.

It knew the glow of eventide,
The sunrise and the noon,
And glorified and sanctified
It slept beneath the moon.

With flowers or snow-flakes for its sod,
Around the seasons ran,
And evermore the love of God
Rebuked the fear of man.

We dwell with fears on either hand
Within a daily strife,
And spectral problems waiting stand
Before the gates of life.

The doubts we vainly seek to solve,
The truths we know, are one;
The known and nameless stars revolve
Around the Central Sun.

And if we reap as we have sown,
And take the dole we deal,
The law of pain is love alone,
The wounding is to heal.

Unharmed from change to change we glide,
We fall as in our dreams;
The far-off terror at our side
A smiling angel seems.

Secure on God's all-tender heart
Alike rest great and small;
Why fear to lose our little part,
When He is pledged for all?

O fearful heart and troubled brain!
Take hope and strength from this, —
That Nature never hints in vain,
Nor prophesies amiss.

Her wild birds sing the same sweet stave,
Her lights and airs are given
Alike to playground and the grave;
And over both is Heaven.

The Pressed Gentian

The time of gifts has come again,
And, on my northern window-pane,
Outlined against the day's brief light,
A Christmas token hangs in sight.
The wayside travellers, as they pass,
Mark the gray disk of clouded glass;
And the dull blankness seems, perchance,
Folly to their wise ignorance.

They cannot from their outlook see
The perfect grace it hath for me;
For there the flower, whose fringes through
The frosty breath of autumn blew,
Turns from without its face of bloom
To the warm tropic of my room,
As fair as when beside its brook
The hue of bending skies it took.

So from the trodden ways of earth,
Seem some sweet souls who veil their worth,
And offer to the careless glance
The clouding gray of circumstance.
They blossom best where hearth-fires burn,
To loving eyes alone they turn
The flowers of inward grace, that hide
Their beauty from the world outside.

But deeper meanings come to me,
My half-immortal flower, from thee!
Man judges from a partial view,
None ever yet his brother knew;
The Eternal Eye that sees the whole
May better read the darkened soul,
And find, to outward sense denied,
The flower upon its inmost side!

Sweet Fern

The subtle power in perfume found
  Nor priest nor sibyl vainly learned;
On Grecian shrine or Aztec mound
  No censer idly burned.

SWEET FERN

A sudden waft of west wind blew
The breath of the sweet fern

That power the old-time worships knew,
The Corybantes' frenzied dance,
The Pythian priestess swooning through
The wonderland of trance.

And Nature holds, in wood and field,
Her thousand sunlit censers still;
To spells of flower and shrub we yield
Against or with our will.

I climbed a hill path strange and new
With slow feet, pausing at each turn;
A sudden waft of west wind blew
The breath of the sweet fern.

That fragrance from my vision swept
The alien landscape; in its stead,
Up fairer hills of youth I stepped,
As light of heart as tread.

I saw my boyhood's lakelet shine
Once more through rifts of woodland shade;
I knew my river's winding line
By morning mist betrayed.

With me June's freshness, lapsing brook,
Murmurs of leaf and bee, the call
Of birds, and one in voice and look
In keeping with them all.

A fern beside the way we went
She plucked, and, smiling, held it up,
While from her hand the wild, sweet scent
I drank as from a cup.

O potent witchery of smell!
The dust-dry leaves to life return,
And she who plucked them owns the spell
And lifts her ghostly fern.

Or sense or spirit? Who shall say
What touch the chord of memory thrills?
It passed, and left the August day
Ablaze on lonely hills.

A Mystery

The river hemmed with leaning trees
Wound through its meadows green;
A low, blue line of mountains showed
The open pines between.

One sharp, tall peak above them all
Clear into sunlight sprang:
I saw the river of my dreams,
The mountains that I sang!

No clue of memory led me on,
But well the ways I knew;
A feeling of familiar things
With every footstep grew.

Not otherwise above its crag
Could lean the blasted pine;
Not otherwise the maple hold
Aloft its red ensign.

So up the long and shorn foot-hills
The mountain road should creep;
So, green and low, the meadow fold
Its red-haired kine asleep.

The river wound as it should wind;
Their place the mountains took;
The white torn fringes of their clouds
Wore no unwonted look.

Yet ne'er before that river's rim
Was pressed by feet of mine,
Never before mine eyes had crossed
That broken mountain line.

A presence, strange at once and known,
Walked with me as my guide;
The skirts of some forgotten life
Trailed noiseless at my side.

Was it a dim-remembered dream?
Or glimpse through æons old?
The secret which the mountains kept
The river never told.

But from the vision ere it passed
A tender hope I drew,
And, pleasant as a dawn of spring,
The thought within me grew,

That love would temper every change,
And soften all surprise,
And, misty with the dreams of earth,
The hills of Heaven arise.

The Trailing Arbutus

I wandered lonely where the pine-trees made
Against the bitter East their barricade,
And, guided by its sweet
Perfume, I found, within a narrow dell,
The trailing spring flower tinted like a shell
Amid dry leaves and mosses at my feet.

From under dead boughs, for whose loss the pines
Moaned ceaseless overhead, the blossoming vines
Lifted their glad surprise,
While yet the bluebird smoothed in leafless trees
His feathers ruffled by the chill sea-breeze,
And snow-drifts lingered under April skies.

As, pausing, o'er the lonely flower I bent,
I thought of lives thus lowly, clogged and pent,
Which yet find room,
Through care and cumber, coldness and decay,
To lend a sweetness to the ungenial day,
And make the sad earth happier for their bloom.

Bryant on His Seventieth Birthday

We praise not now the poet's art,
The rounded beauty of his song;
Who weighs him from his life apart
Must do his nobler nature wrong.

Not for the eye, familiar grown
With charms to common sight denied, —

The marvellous gift he shares alone
With him who walked on Rydal-side;

Not for rapt hymn nor woodland lay,
Too grave for smiles, too sweet for tears;
We speak his praise who wears to-day
The glory of his seventy years.

When Peace brings Freedom in her train,
Let happy lips his songs rehearse;
His life is now his noblest strain,
His manhood better than his verse!

Thank God! his hand on Nature's keys
Its cunning keeps at life's full span;
But, dimmed and dwarfed, in times like these,
The poet seems beside the man!

So be it! let the garlands die,
The singer's wreath, the painter's meed,
Let our names perish, if thereby
Our country may be saved and freed!

Wordsworth

WRITTEN ON A BLANK LEAF OF HIS MEMOIRS

Dear friends, who read the world aright,
And in its common forms discern
A beauty and a harmony
The many never learn!

Kindred in soul of him who found
In simple flower and leaf and stone
The impulse of the sweetest lays
Our Saxon tongue has known, —

Accept this record of a life
As sweet and pure, as calm and good,
As a long day of blandest June
In green field and in wood.

How welcome to our ears, long pained
By strife of sect and party noise,

THE LAST WALK IN AUTUMN

With mingled sound of horns and bells,
A far-heard clang, the mild geese fly

The brook-like murmur of his song
  Of nature's simple joys!

The violet by its mossy stone,
  The primrose by the river's brim,
And chance-sown daffodil, have found
  Immortal life through him.

The sunrise on his breezy lake,
  The rosy tints his sunset brought,
World-seen, are gladdening all the vales
  And mountain-peaks of thought.

Art builds on sand; the works of pride
  And human passion change and fall;
But that which shares the life of God
  With Him surviveth all.

The Last Walk in Autumn

I

O'er the bare woods, whose outstretched hands
  Plead with the leaden heavens in vain,
I see, beyond the valley lands,
  The sea's long level dim with rain.
Around me all things, stark and dumb,
Seem praying for the snows to come,
And, for the summer bloom and greenness gone,
With winter's sunset lights and dazzling morn atone.

II

Along the river's summer walk,
  The withered tufts of asters nod;
And trembles on its arid stalk
  The hoar plume of the golden-rod.
And on a ground of sombre fir,
And azure-studded juniper,
The silver birch its buds of purple shows,
And scarlet berries tell where bloomed the sweet wild-rose!

III

With mingled sound of horns and bells,
  A far-heard clang, the wild geese fly,
Storm-sent, from Arctic moors and fells
  Like a great arrow through the sky,
Two dusky lines converged in one,
Chasing the southward-flying sun;
While the brave snow-bird and the hardy jay
Call to them from the pines, as if to bid them stay.

IV

I passed this way a year ago:
  The wind blew south; the noon of day
Was warm as June's; and save that snow
  Flecked the low mountains far away,
And that the vernal-seeming breeze
Mocked faded grass and leafless trees,
I might have dreamed of summer as I lay,
Watching the fallen leaves with the soft wind at play.

V

Since then, the winter blasts have piled
  The white pagodas of the snow
On these rough slopes, and, strong and wild,
  Yon river, in its overflow
Of spring-time rain and sun, set free,
Crashed with its ices to the sea;
And over these gray fields, then green and gold,
The summer corn has waved, the thunder's organ rolled.

VI

Rich gift of God! A year of time!
  What pomp of rise and shut of day,
What hues wherewith our Northern clime
  Makes autumn's dropping woodlands gay,
What airs outblown from ferny dells,
And clover-bloom and sweetbrier smells,
What songs of brooks and birds, what fruits and flowers,
Green woods and moonlit snows, have in its round been ours!

VII

I know not how, in other lands,
The changing seasons come and go;
What splendors fall on Syrian sands,
What purple lights on Alpine snow!
Nor how the pomp of sunrise waits
On Venice at her watery gates;
A dream alone to me is Arno's vale,
And the Alhambra's halls are but a traveller's tale.

VIII

Yet, on life's current, he who drifts
Is one with him who rows or sails;
And he who wanders widest lifts
No more of beauty's jealous veils
Than he who from his doorway sees
The miracle of flowers and trees,
Feels the warm Orient in the noonday air,
And from cloud minarets hears the sunset call to prayer!

IX

The eye may well be glad that looks
Where Pharpar's fountains rise and fall;
But he who sees his native brooks
Laugh in the sun, has seen them all.
The marble palaces of Ind
Rise round him in the snow and wind;
From his lone sweetbrier Persian Hafiz smiles,
And Rome's cathedral awe is in his woodland aisles.

X

And thus it is my fancy blends
The near at hand and far and rare;
And while the same horizon bends
Above the silver-sprinkled hair
Which flashed the light of morning skies
On childhood's wonder-lifted eyes,
Within its round of sea and sky and field,
Earth wheels with all her zones, the Kosmos stands revealed.

XI

And thus the sick man on his bed,
The toiler to his task-work bound,
Behold their prison-walls outspread,
Their clipped horizon widen round!
While freedom-giving fancy waits,
Like Peter's angel at the gates,
The power is theirs to baffle care and pain,
To bring the lost world back, and make it theirs again!

XII

What lack of goodly company,
When masters of the ancient lyre
Obey my call, and trace for me
Their words of mingled tears and fire!
I talk with Bacon, grave and wise,
I read the world with Pascal's eyes;
And priest and sage, with solemn brows austere,
And poets, garland-bound, the Lords of Thought, draw near.

XIII

Methinks, O friend, I hear thee say,
"In vain the human heart we mock;
Bring living guests who love the day,
Not ghosts who fly at crow of cock!
The herbs we share with flesh and blood
Are better than ambrosial food
With laurelled shades." I grant it, nothing loath,
But doubly blest is he who can partake of both.

XIV

He who might Plato's banquet grace,
Have I not seen before me sit,
And watched his puritanic face,
With more than Eastern wisdom lit?
Shrewd mystic! who, upon the back
Of his Poor Richard's Almanac
Writing the Sufi's song, the Gentoo's dream,
Links Manu's age of thought to Fulton's age of steam!

XV

Here too, of answering love secure,
Have I not welcomed to my hearth
The gentle pilgrim troubadour,
Whose songs have girdled half the earth;
Whose pages, like the magic mat
Whereon the Eastern lover sat,
Have borne me over Rhine-land's purple vines,
And Nubia's tawny sands, and Phrygia's mountain pines!

XVI

And he, who to the lettered wealth
Of ages adds the lore unpriced,
The wisdom and the moral health,
The ethics of the school of Christ;
The statesman to his holy trust,
As the Athenian archon, just,
Struck down, exiled like him for truth alone,
Has he not graced my home with beauty all his own?

XVII

What greetings smile, what farewells wave,
What loved ones enter and depart!
The good, the beautiful, the brave,
The Heaven-lent treasures of the heart!
How conscious seems the frozen sod
And beechen slope whereon they trod!
The oak-leaves rustle, and the dry grass bends
Beneath the shadowy feet of lost or absent friends.

XVIII

Then ask not why to these bleak hills
I cling, as clings the tufted moss,
To bear the winter's lingering chills,
The mocking spring's perpetual loss.
I dream of lands where summer smiles,
And soft winds blow from spicy isles,
But scarce would Ceylon's breath of flowers be sweet,
Could I not feel thy soil, New England, at my feet!

XIX

At times I long for gentler skies,
And bathe in dreams of softer air,
But homesick tears would fill the eyes
That saw the Cross without the Bear.
The pine must whisper to the palm,
The north-wind break the tropic calm;
And with the dreamy languor of the Line,
The North's keen virtue blend, and strength to beauty join.

XX

Better to stem with heart and hand
The roaring tide of life, than lie,
Unmindful, on its flowery strand,
Of God's occasions drifting by!
Better with naked nerve to bear
The needles of this goading air,
Than, in the lap of sensual ease, forego
The godlike power to do, the godlike aim to know.

XXI

Home of my heart! to me more fair
Than gay Versailles or Windsor's halls,
The painted, shingly town-house where
The freeman's vote for Freedom falls!
The simple roof where prayer is made,
Than Gothic groin and colonnade;
The living temple of the heart of man,
Than Rome's sky-mocking vault, or many-spired Milan!

XXII

More dear thy equal village schools,
Where rich and poor the Bible read,
Than classic halls where Priestcraft rules,
And Learning wears the chains of Creed;
Thy glad Thanksgiving, gathering in
The scattered sheaves of home and kin,
Than the mad license ushering Lenten pains,
Or holidays of slaves who laugh and dance in chains.

XXIII

And sweet homes nestle in these dales,
And perch along these wooded swells;
And, blest beyond Arcadian vales,
They hear the sound of Sabbath bells!
Here dwells no perfect man sublime,
Nor woman winged before her time,
But with the faults and follies of the race,
Old home-bred virtues hold their not unhonored place.

XXIV

Here manhood struggles for the sake
Of mother, sister, daughter, wife,
The graces and the loves which make
The music of the march of life;
And woman, in her daily round
Of duty, walks on holy ground.
No unpaid menial tills the soil, nor here
Is the bad lesson learned at human rights to sneer.

XXV

Then let the icy north-wind blow
The trumpets of the coming storm,
To arrowy sleat and blinding snow
Yon slanting lines of rain transform.
Young hearts shall hail the drifted cold,
As gayly as I did of old;
And I, who watch them through the frosty pane,
Unenvious, live in them my boyhood o'er again.

XXVI

And I will trust that He who heeds
The life that hides in mead and wold,
Who hangs yon alder's crimson beads,
And stains these mosses green and gold,
Will still, as He hath done, incline
His gracious care to me and mine;
Grant what we ask aright, from wrong debar,
And, as the earth grows dark, make brighter every star!

XXVII

I have not seen, I may not see,
My hopes for man take form in fact,
But God will give the victory
In due time; in that faith I act.
And he who sees the future sure,
The baffling present may endure,
And bless, meanwhile, the unseen Hand that leads
The heart's desires beyond the halting step of deeds.

XXVIII

And thou, my song, I send thee forth,
Where harsher songs of mine have flown;
Go, find a place at home and hearth
Where'er thy singer's name is known;
Revive for him the kindly thought
Of friends; and they who love him not,
Touched by some strain of thine, perchance may take
The hand he proffers all, and thank him for thy sake.

Channing

Not vainly did old poets tell,
Nor vainly did old genius paint
God's great and crowning miracle,
The hero and the saint!

For even in a faithless day
Can we our sainted ones discern;
And feel, while with them on the way,
Our hearts within us burn.

And thus the common tongue and pen
Which, world-wide, echo Channing's fame,
As one of Heaven's anointed men,
Have sanctified his name.

In vain shall Rome her portals bar,
And shut from him her saintly prize,
Whom, in the world's great calendar,
All men shall canonize.

THE LAST WALK IN AUTUMN

No unpaid menial tills the soil, nor here
Is the bad lesson learned at human rights to sneer

By Narragansett's sunny bay,
Beneath his green embowering wood,
To me it seems but yesterday
Since at his side I stood.

The slopes lay green with summer rains,
The western wind blew fresh and free,
And glimmered down the orchard lanes
The white surf of the sea.

With us was one, who, calm and true,
Life's highest purpose understood,
And, like his blessed Master, knew
The joy of doing good.

Unlearned, unknown to lettered fame,
Yet on the lips of England's poor
And toiling millions dwelt his name,
With blessings evermore.

Unknown to power or place, yet where
The sun looks o'er the Carib sea,
It blended with the freeman's prayer
And song of jubilee.

He told of England's sin and wrong,
The ills her suffering children know,
The squalor of the city's throng,
The green field's want and woe.

O'er Channing's face the tenderness
Of sympathetic sorrow stole,
Like a still shadow, passionless,
The sorrow of the soul.

But when the generous Briton told
How hearts were answering to his own,
And Freedom's rising murmur rolled
Up to the dull-eared throne,

I saw, methought, a glad surprise
Thrill through that frail and pain-worn frame,
And, kindling in those deep, calm eyes,
A still and earnest flame.

His few, brief words were such as move
The human heart, — the Faith-sown seeds
Which ripen in the soil of love
To high heroic deeds.

No bars of sect or clime were felt,
The Babel strife of tongues had ceased,
And at one common altar knelt
The Quaker and the priest.

And not in vain: with strength renewed,
And zeal refreshed, and hope less dim,
For that brief meeting, each pursued
The path allotted him.

How echoes yet each Western hill
And vale with Channing's dying word!
How are the hearts of freemen still
By that great warning stirred!

The stranger treads his native soil,
And pleads, with zeal unfelt before,
The honest right of British toil,
The claim of England's poor.

Before him time-wrought barriers fall,
Old fears subside, old hatreds melt,
And, stretching o'er the sea's blue wall,
The Saxon greets the Celt.

The yeoman on the Scottish lines,
The Sheffield grinder, worn and grim,
The delver in the Cornwall mines,
Look up with hope to him.

Swart smiters of the glowing steel,
Dark feeders of the forge's flame,
Pale watchers at the loom and wheel,
Repeat his honored name.

And thus the influence of that hour
Of converse on Rhode Island's strand
Lives in the calm, resistless power
Which moves our fatherland.

God blesses still the generous thought,
And still the fitting word He speeds,
And Truth, at His requiring taught,
He quickens into deeds.

Where is the victory of the grave?
What dust upon the spirit lies?
God keeps the sacred life he gave, —
The prophet never dies!

Brown of Ossawatomie

John Brown of Ossawatomie spake on his dying day:
"I will not have to shrive my soul a priest in Slavery's pay.
But let some poor slave-mother whom I have striven to free,
With her children, from the gallows-stair put up a prayer for me!"

John Brown of Ossawatomie, they led him out to die;
And lo! a poor slave-mother with her little child pressed nigh.
Then the bold, blue eye grew tender, and the old harsh face grew mild,
As he stooped between the jeering ranks and kissed the negro's child!

The shadows of his stormy life that moment fell apart;
And they who blamed the bloody hand forgave the loving heart.
That kiss from all its guilty means redeemed the good intent,
And round the grisly fighter's hair the martyr's aureole bent!

Perish with him the folly that seeks through evil good!
Long live the generous purpose unstained with human blood!
Not the raid of midnight terror, but the thought which underlies;
Not the borderer's pride of daring, but the Christian's sacrifice.

Nevermore may yon Blue Ridges the Northern rifle hear,
Nor see the light of blazing homes flash on the negro's spear.
But let the free-winged angel Truth their guarded passes scale,
To teach that right is more than might, and justice more than mail!

So vainly shall Virginia set her battle in array;
In vain her trampling squadrons knead the winter snow with clay.
She may strike the pouncing eagle, but she dares not harm the dove;
And every gate she bars to Hate shall open wide to Love!

A Song of Harvest

This day, two hundred years ago,
The wild grape by the river's side,
And tasteless groundnut trailing low,
The table of the woods supplied.

Unknown the apple's red and gold,
The blushing tint of peach and pear;
The mirror of the Powow told
No tale of orchards ripe and rare.

Wild as the fruits he scorned to till,
These vales the idle Indian trod;
Nor knew the glad, creative skill,
The joy of him who toils with God.

O Painter of the fruits and flowers!
We thank Thee for thy wise design
Whereby these human hands of ours
In Nature's garden work with Thine.

And thanks that from our daily need
The joy of simple faith is born;
That he who smites the summer weed,
May trust Thee for the autumn corn.

Give fools their gold, and knaves their power;
Let fortune's bubbles rise and fall;
Who sows a field, or trains a flower,
Or plants a tree, is more than all.

For he who blesses most is blest;
And God and man shall own his worth
Who toils to leave as his bequest
An added beauty to the earth.

And, soon or late, to all that sow,
The time of harvest shall be given;
The flower shall bloom, the fruit shall grow,
If not on earth, at last in heaven.

A SONG OF HARVEST

And, soon or late, to all that sow,
The time of harvest shall be given

Garibaldi

In trance and dream of old, God's prophet saw
The casting down of thrones. Thou, watching lone
The hot Sardinian coast-line, hazy-hilled,
Where, fringing round Caprera's rocky zone
With foam, the slow waves gather and withdraw,
Behold'st the vision of the seer fulfilled,
And hear'st the sea-winds burdened with a sound
Of falling chains, as, one by one, unbound,
The nations lift their right hands up and swear
Their oath of freedom. From the chalk-white wall
Of England, from the black Carpathian range,
Along the Danube and the Theiss, through all
The passes of the Spanish Pyrenees,
And from the Seine's thronged banks, a murmur strange
And glad floats to thee o'er thy summer seas
On the salt wind that stirs thy whitening hair, —
The song of freedom's bloodless victories!
Rejoice, O Garibaldi! Though thy sword
Failed at Rome's gates, and blood seemed vainly poured
Where, in Christ's name, the crownëd infidel
Of France wrought murder with the arms of hell
On that sad mountain slope whose ghostly dead,
Unmindful of the gray exorcist's ban,
Walk, unappeased, the chambered Vatican,
And draw the curtains of Napoleon's bed!
God's providence is not blind, but, full of eyes,
It searches all the refuges of lies;
And in His time and way, the accursed things
Before whose evil feet thy battle-gage
Has clashed defiance from hot youth to age
Shall perish. All men shall be priests and kings,
One royal brotherhood, one church made free
By love, which is the law of liberty!

The Poet and the Children: LONGFELLOW

With a glory of winter sunshine
Over his locks of gray,
In the old historic mansion
He sat on his last birthday;

[THE POET AND THE CHILDREN]

With his books and his pleasant pictures,
And his household and his kin,
While a sound as of myriads singing
From far and near stole in.

It came from his own fair city,
From the prairie's boundless plain,
From the Golden Gate of sunset,
And the cedarn woods of Maine.

And his heart grew warm within him,
And his moistening eyes grew dim,
For he knew that his country's children
Were singing the songs of him:

The lays of his life's glad morning,
The psalms of his evening time,
Whose echoes shall float forever
On the winds of every clime.

All their beautiful consolations,
Sent forth like birds of cheer,
Came flocking back to his windows,
And sang in the Poet's ear.

Grateful, but solemn and tender,
The music rose and fell
With a joy akin to sadness
And a greeting like farewell.

With a sense of awe he listened
To the voices sweet and young;
The last of earth and the first of heaven
Seemed in the songs they sung.

And waiting a little longer
For the wonderful change to come,
He heard the Summoning Angel,
Who calls God's children home!

And to him in a holier welcome
Was the mystical meaning given
Of the words of the blessed Master:
"Of such is the kingdom of heaven!"

Eva

Suggested by Mrs. Stowe's tale of *Uncle Tom's Cabin,* and written when the characters in the tale were realities by the fireside of countless American homes.

Dry the tears for holy Eva,
With the blessed angels leave her;
Of the form so soft and fair
Give to earth the tender care.

For the golden locks of Eva
Let the sunny south-land give her
Flowery pillow of repose,
Orange-bloom and budding rose.

In the better home of Eva
Let the shining ones receive her,
With the welcome-voicëd psalm,
Harp of gold and waving palm!

All is light and peace with Eva;
There the darkness cometh never;
Tears are wiped, and fetters fall,
And the Lord is all in all.

Weep no more for happy Eva,
Wrong and sin no more shall grieve her;
Care and pain and weariness
Lost in love so measureless.

Gentle Eva, loving Eva,
Child confessor, true believer,
Listener at the Master's knee,
"Suffer such to come to me."

Or, for faith like thine, sweet Eva,
Lighting all the solemn river,
And the blessings of the poor
Wafting to the heavenly shore!

Chicago

The great fire at Chicago was on 8–10 October, 1871.

Men said at vespers: "All is well!"
In one wild night the city fell;
Fell shrines of prayer and marts of gain
Before the fiery hurricane.

[CHICAGO]

On threescore spires had sunset shone,
Where ghastly sunrise looked on none.
Men clasped each other's hands, and said:
"The City of the West is dead!"

Brave hearts who fought, in slow retreat,
The fiends of fire from street to street,
Turned, powerless, to the blinding glare,
The dumb defiance of despair.

A sudden impulse thrilled each wire
That signalled round that sea of fire;
Swift words of cheer, warm heart-throbs came;
In tears of pity died the flame!

From East, from West, from South and North,
The messages of hope shot forth,
And, underneath the severing wave,
The world, full-handed, reached to save.

Fair seemed the old; but fairer still
The new, the dreary void shall fill
With dearer homes than those o'erthrown,
For love shall lay each corner-stone.

Rise, stricken city! from thee throw
The ashen sackcloth of thy woe;
And build, as to Amphion's strain,
To songs of cheer thy walls again!

How shrivelled in thy hot distress
The primal sin of selfishness!
How instant rose, to take thy part,
The angel in the human heart!

Ah! not in vain the flames that tossed
Above thy dreadful holocaust;
The Christ again has preached through thee
The Gospel of Humanity!

Then lift once more thy towers on high,
And fret with spires the western sky,
To tell that God is yet with us,
And love is still miraculous!

LEXINGTON

Swift as their summons came they left
The plough mid-furrow standing still

Hymn

FOR THE OPENING OF PLYMOUTH CHURCH, ST. PAUL, MINNESOTA

All things are Thine: no gift have we,
Lord of all gifts, to offer Thee;
And hence with grateful hearts to-day,
Thy own before Thy feet we lay.

Thy will was in the builders' thought;
Thy hand unseen amidst us wrought;
Through mortal motive, scheme and plan,
Thy wise eternal purpose ran.

No lack Thy perfect fulness knew;
For human needs and longings grew
This house of prayer, this home of rest,
In the fair garden of the West.

In weakness and in want we call
On Thee for whom the heavens are small;
Thy glory is Thy children's good,
Thy joy Thy tender Fatherhood.

O Father! deign these walls to bless,
Fill with Thy love their emptiness,
And let their door a gateway be
To lead us from ourselves to Thee!

Lexington

1775

No Berserk thirst of blood had they,
No battle-joy was theirs, who set
Against the alien bayonet
Their homespun breasts in that old day.

Their feet had trodden peaceful ways;
They loved not strife, they dreaded pain;
They saw not, what to us is plain,
That God would make man's wrath His praise.

No seers were they, but simple men;
Its vast results the future hid;
The meaning of the work they did
Was strange and dark and doubtful then.

Swift as their summons came they left
  The plough mid-furrow standing still,
  The half-ground corn grist in the mill,
The spade in earth, the axe in cleft.

They went where duty seemed to call,
  They scarcely asked the reason why;
  They only knew they could but die,
And death was not the worst of all!

Of man for man the sacrifice,
  All that was theirs to give, they gave.
  The flowers that blossomed from their grave
Have sown themselves beneath all skies.

Their death-shot shook the feudal tower,
  And shattered slavery's chain as well;
  On the sky's dome, as on a bell,
Its echo struck the world's great hour.

That fateful echo is not dumb:
  The nations listening to its sound
  Wait, from a century's vantage-ground,
The holier triumphs yet to come, —

The bridal time of Law and Love,
  The gladness of the world's release,
  When, war-sick, at the feet of Peace
The hawk shall nestle with the dove! —

The golden age of brotherhood
  Unknown to other rivalries
  Than of the mild humanities,
And gracious interchange of good,

When closer strand shall lean to strand,
  Till meet, beneath saluting flags,
  The eagle of our mountain-crags,
The lion of our Motherland!

Centennial Hymn

Written for the opening of the International Exhibition, Philadelphia, 1876

I

Our fathers' God! from out whose hand
The centuries fall like grains of sand,
We meet to-day, united, free,
And loyal to our land and Thee,
To thank Thee for the era done,
And trust Thee for the opening one.

II

Here, where of old, by Thy design,
The fathers spake that word of Thine
Whose echo is the glad refrain
Of rended bolt and falling chain,
To grace our festal time, from all
The zones of earth our guests we call.

III

Be with us while the New World greets
The Old World thronging all its streets,
Unveiling all the triumphs won
By art or toil beneath the sun;
And unto common good ordain
This rivalship of hand and brain.

IV

Thou, who hast here in concord furled
The war flags of a gathered world,
Beneath our Western skies fulfil
The Orient's mission of good-will,
And, freighted with love's Golden Fleece,
Send back its Argonauts of peace.

V

For art and labor met in truce,
For beauty made the bride of use,
We thank Thee; but, withal, we crave
The austere virtues strong to save,

The honor proof to place or gold,
The manhood never bought nor sold!

VI

Oh make Thou us, through centuries long,
In peace secure, in justice strong;
Around our gift of freedom draw
The safeguards of thy righteous law:
And, cast in some diviner mould,
Let the new cycle shame the old!

Hymn of the Children

Thine are all the gifts, O God!
  Thine the broken bread;
Let the naked feet be shod,
  And the starving fed.

Let Thy children, by Thy grace,
  Give as they abound,
Till the poor have breathing-space,
  And the lost are found.

Wiser than the miser's hoards
  Is the giver's choice;
Sweeter than the song of birds
  Is the thankful voice.

Welcome smiles on faces sad
  As the flowers of spring;
Let the tender hearts be glad
  With the joy they bring.

Happier for their pity's sake
  Make their sports and plays,
And from lips of childhood take
  Thy perfected praise!

Garden

O Painter of the fruits and flowers,
We own Thy wise design,
Whereby these human hands of ours
May share the work of Thine!

Apart from Thee we plant in vain
The root and sow the seed;
Thy early and Thy later rain,
Thy sun and dew we need.

Our toil is sweet with thankfulness,
Our burden is our boon;
The curse of Earth's gray morning is
The blessing of its noon.

Why search the wide world everywhere
For Eden's unknown ground?
That garden of the primal pair
May nevermore be found.

But, blest by Thee, our patient toil
May right the ancient wrong,
And give to every clime and soil
The beauty lost so long.

Our homestead flowers and fruited trees
May Eden's orchard shame;
We taste the tempting sweets of these
Like Eve, without her blame.

And, North and South and East and West,
The pride of every zone,
The fairest, rarest, and the best
May all be made our own.

Its earliest shrines the young world sought
In hill-groves and in bowers,
The fittest offerings thither brought
Were Thy own fruits and flowers.

And still with reverent hands we cull
Thy gifts each year renewed;
The good is always beautiful,
The beautiful is good.

The Bartholdi Statue

1886

The land, that, from the rule of kings,
In freeing us, itself made free,
Our Old World Sister, to us brings
Her sculptured Dream of Liberty:

Unlike the shapes on Egypt's sands
Uplifted by the toil-worn slave,
On Freedom's soil with freemen's hands
We rear the symbol free hands gave.

O France, the beautiful! to thee
Once more a debt of love we owe:
In peace beneath thy Colors Three,
We hail a later Rochambeau!

Rise, stately Symbol! holding forth
Thy light and hope to all who sit
In chains and darkness! Belt the earth
With watch-fires from thy torch uplit!

Reveal the primal mandate still
Which Chaos heard and ceased to be,
Trace on mid-air th' Eternal Will
In signs of fire: "Let man be free!"

Shine far, shine free, a guiding light
To Reason's ways and Virtue's aim,
A lightning-flash the wretch to smite
Who shields his license with thy name!

The Poems of John Greenleaf Whittier

IV

THE TENT ON THE BEACH

The Editor's Commentary

To a large extent "The Tent on the Beach" is autobiographical. Whittier describes himself in the lines beginning "And one there was, a dreamer born" — and if the portrait is not completely rounded, it is at least a sad and nostalgic picture of a young poet who had "a mission to fulfil" painted by one who no longer had to fight "the ban of Church and State, the fierce mob's hounding down."

Whittier was sixty when he published "The Tent on the Beach." Originally he planned to follow the scheme of the Decameron, interweaving characters and stories, the method followed, among others, by Chaucer in *The Canterbury Tales* and by Longfellow in *Tales of a Wayside Inn.* But he abandoned this, possibly because it was hackneyed, and connected the poems with the merest thread of narrative. The three characters were scarcely disguised real people: the poet himself and his two friends, the publisher James T. Fields, "the lettered magnate," and the poet Bayard Taylor, "the free cosmopolite."

Even the setting was real. The scene was "the long line of sandy beach which defines almost the whole of the New Hampshire sea-coast, especially marked near its southern extremity by the salt meadows of Hampton. The Hampton River winds its way through these meadows and the reader may, if he choose, imagine my tent pitched near its mouth."

It is not surprising that seven of the ten narratives — and the seven best — are native in substance as well as theme. This is especially emphasized by "Abraham Davenport," one of Whittier's most dramatic poems and his one employment of resonant blank verse instead of the reliable — and sometimes too-ready — rhyme.

THE TENT ON THE BEACH

Sometimes along the wheel-deep sand
A one-horse wagon slowly crawled

The Tent on the Beach

I would not sin, in this half-playful strain, —
  Too light perhaps for serious years, though born
Of the enforced leisure of slow pain, —
  Against the pure ideal which has drawn
My feet to follow its far-shining gleam.
A simple plot is mine: legends and runes
Of credulous days, old fancies that have lain
Silent from boyhood taking voice again,
Warmed into life once more, even as the tunes
That, frozen in the fabled hunting-horn,
Thawed into sound: — a winter fireside dream
Of dawns and sunsets by the summer sea,
Whose sands are traversed by a silent throng
Of voyagers from that vaster mystery
Of which it is an emblem; — and the dear
Memory of one who might have tuned my song
To sweeter music by her delicate ear.

When heats as of a tropic clime
  Burned all our inland valleys through,
Three friends, the guests of summer time,
  Pitched their white tent where sea-winds blew.
Behind them, marshes, seamed and crossed
With narrow creeks, and flower-embossed,
Stretched to the dark oak wood, whose leafy arms
Screened from the stormy East the pleasant inland farms.

At full of tide their bolder shore
  Of sun-bleached sand the waters beat;
At ebb, a smooth and glistening floor
  They touched with light, receding feet.
Northward a green bluff broke the chain
Of sand-hills; southward stretched a plain
Of salt grass, with a river winding down,
Sail-whitened, and beyond the steeples of the town, —

Whence sometimes, when the wind was light
  And dull the thunder of the beach,
They heard the bells of morn and night
  Swing, miles away, their silver speech.
Above low scarp and turf-grown wall
They saw the fort-flag rise and fall;
And, the first star to signal twilight's hour,
The lamp-fire glimmer down from the tall light-house tower.

They rested there, escaped awhile
From cares that wear the life away,
To eat the lotus of the Nile
And drink the poppies of Cathay, —
To fling their loads of custom down,
Like drift-weed, on the sand-slopes brown,
And in the sea-waves drown the restless pack
Of duties, claims, and needs that barked upon their track.

One, with his beard scarce silvered, bore
A ready credence in his looks,
A lettered magnate, lording o'er
An ever-widening realm of books.
In him brain-currents, near and far,
Converged as in a Leyden jar;
The old, dead authors thronged him round about,
And Elzevir's gray ghosts from leathern graves looked out.

He knew each living pundit well,
Could weigh the gifts of him or her,
And well the market value tell
Of poet and philosopher.
But if he lost, the scenes behind,
Somewhat of reverence vague and blind,
Finding the actors human at the best,
No readier lips than his the good he saw confessed.

His boyhood fancies not outgrown,
He loved himself the singer's art;
Tenderly, gently, by his own
He knew and judged an author's heart.
No Rhadamanthine brow of doom
Bowed the dazed pedant from his room;
And bards, whose name is legion, if denied,
Bore off alike intact their verses and their pride.

Pleasant it was to roam about
The lettered world as he had done,
And see the lords of song without
Their singing robes and garlands on.
With Wordsworth paddle Rydal mere,
Taste rugged Elliott's home-brewed beer,
And with the ears of Rogers, at fourscore,
Hear Garrick's buskined tread and Walpole's wit once more.

And one there was, a dreamer born,
Who, with a mission to fulfil,
Had left the Muses' haunts to turn
The crank of an opinion-mill,
Making his rustic reed of song
A weapon in the war with wrong,
Yoking his fancy to the breaking-plough
That beam-deep turned the soil for truth to spring and grow.

Too quiet seemed the man to ride
The wingëd Hippogriff Reform;
Was his a voice from side to side
To pierce the tumult of the storm?
A silent, shy, peace-loving man,
He seemed no fiery partisan
To hold his way against the public frown,
The ban of Church and State, the fierce mob's hounding down.

For while he wrought with strenuous will
The work his hands had found to do,
He heard the fitful music still
Of winds that out of dream-land blew.
The din about him could not drown
What the strange voices whispered down;
Along his task-field weird processions swept,
The visionary pomp of stately phantoms stepped.

The common air was thick with dreams, —
He told them to the toiling crowd;
Such music as the woods and streams
Sang in his ear he sang aloud;
In still, shut bays, on windy capes,
He heard the call of beckoning shapes,
And, as the gray old shadows prompted him,
To homely moulds of rhyme he shaped their legends grim.

He rested now his weary hands,
And lightly moralized and laughed,
As, tracing on the shifting sands
A burlesque of his paper-craft,
He saw the careless waves o'errun
His words, as time before had done,
Each day's tide-water washing clean away,
Like letters from the sand, the work of yesterday.

And one, whose Arab face was tanned
By tropic sun and boreal frost,
So travelled there was scarce a land
Or people left him to exhaust,
In idling mood had from him hurled
The poor squeezed orange of the world,
And in the tent-shade, sat beneath a palm,
Smoked, cross-legged like a Turk, in Oriental calm.

The very waves that washed the sand
Below him, he had seen before
Whitening the Scandinavian strand
And sultry Mauritanian shore.
From ice-rimmed isles, from summer seas
Palm-fringed, they bore him messages;
He heard the plaintive Nubian songs again,
And mule-bells tinkling down the mountain-paths of Spain.

His memory round the ransacked earth
On Puck's long girdle slid at ease;
And, instant, to the valley's girth
Of mountains, spice isles of the seas,
Faith flowered in minster stones, Art's guess
At truth and beauty, found access;
Yet loved the while, that free cosmopolite,
Old friends, old ways, and kept his boyhood's dreams in sight.

Untouched as yet by wealth and pride,
That virgin innocence of beach:
No shingly monster, hundred-eyed,
Stared its gray sand-birds out of reach;
Unhoused, save where, at intervals,
The white tents showed their canvas walls,
Where brief sojourners, in the cool, soft air,
Forgot their inland heats, hard toil, and year-long care.

Sometimes along the wheel-deep sand
A one-horse wagon slowly crawled,
Deep laden with a youthful band,
Whose look some homestead old recalled;
Brother perchance, and sisters twain,
And one whose blue eyes told, more plain
Than the free language of her rosy lip,
Of the still dearer claim of love's relationship.

With cheeks of russet-orchard tint,
The light laugh of their native rills,
The perfume of their garden's mint,
The breezy freedom of the hills,
They bore, in unrestrained delight,
The motto of the Garter's knight,
Careless as if from every gazing thing
Hid by their innocence, as Gyges by his ring.

The clanging sea-fowl came and went,
The hunter's gun in the marshes rang;
At nightfall from a neighboring tent
A flute-voiced woman sweetly sang.
Loose-haired, barefooted, hand-in-hand,
Young girls went tripping down the sand;
And youths and maidens, sitting in the moon,
Dreamed o'er the old fond dream from which we wake too soon.

At times their fishing-lines they plied,
With an old Triton at the oar,
Salt as the sea-wind, tough and dried
As a lean cusk from Labrador.
Strange tales he told of wreck and storm, —
Had seen the sea-snake's awful form,
And heard the ghosts on Haley's Isle complain,
Speak him off shore, and beg a passage to old Spain!

And there, on breezy morns, they saw
The fishing-schooners outward run,
Their low-bent sails in tack and flaw
Turned white or dark to shade and sun.
Sometimes, in calms of closing day,
They watched the spectral mirage play,
Saw low, far islands looming tall and nigh,
And ships, with upturned keels, sail like a sea the sky.

Sometimes a cloud, with thunder black,
Stooped low upon the darkening main,
Piercing the waves along its track
With the slant javelins of rain.
And when west-wind and sunshine warm
Chased out to sea its wrecks of storm,
They saw the prismy hues in thin spray showers
Where the green buds of waves burst into white froth flowers.

And when along the line of shore
The mists crept upward chill and damp,
Stretched, careless, on their sandy floor
Beneath the flaring lantern lamp,
They talked of all things old and new,
Read, slept, and dreamed as idlers do;
And in the unquestioned freedom of the tent,
Body and o'er-taxed mind to healthful ease unbent.

Once, when the sunset splendors died,
And, trampling up the sloping sand,
In lines outreaching far and wide,
The white-maned billows swept to land,
Dim seen across the gathering shade,
A vast and ghostly cavalcade,
They sat around their lighted kerosene,
Hearing the deep bass roar their every pause between.

Then, urged thereto, the Editor
Within his full portfolio dipped,
Feigning excuse while searching for
(With secret pride) his manuscript.
His pale face flushed from eye to beard,
With nervous cough his throat he cleared,
And, in a voice so tremulous it betrayed
The anxious fondness of an author's heart, he read:

The Grave by the Lake

Where the Great Lake's sunny smiles
Dimple round its hundred isles,
And the mountain's granite ledge
Cleaves the water like a wedge,
Ringed about with smooth, gray stones,
Rest the giant's mighty bones.

Close beside, in shade and gleam,
Laughs and ripples Melvin stream;
Melvin water, mountain-born,
All fair flowers its banks adorn;
All the woodland voices meet,
Mingling with its murmurs sweet.

Over lowlands forest-grown,
Over waters island-strown,
Over silver-sanded beach,
Leaf-locked bay and misty reach,
Melvin stream and burial-heap,
Watch and ward the mountains keep.

Who that Titan cromlech fills?
Forest-kaiser, lord o' the hills?
Knight who on the birchen tree
Carved his savage heraldry?
Priest o' the pine-wood temples dim,
Prophet, sage, or wizard grim?

Rugged type of primal man,
Grim utilitarian,
Loving woods for hunt and prowl,
Lake and hill for fish and fowl,
As the brown bear blind and dull
To the grand and beautiful:

Not for him the lesson drawn
From the mountains smit with dawn.
Star-rise, moon-rise, flowers of May,
Sunset's purple bloom of day, —
Took his life no hue from thence,
Poor amid such affluence?

Haply unto hill and tree
All too near akin was he:
Unto him who stands afar
Nature's marvels greatest are;
Who the mountain purple seeks
Must not climb the higher peaks.

Yet who knows, in winter tramp,
Or the midnight of the camp,
What revealings faint and far,
Stealing down from moon and star,
Kindled in that human clod
Thought of destiny and God?

Stateliest forest patriarch,
Grand in robes of skin and bark,

What sepulchral mysteries,
What weird funeral-rites, were his?
What sharp wail, what drear lament,
Back scared wolf and eagle sent?

Now, whate'er he may have been,
Low he lies as other men;
On his mound the partridge drums,
There the noisy blue-jay comes;
Rank nor name nor pomp has he
In the grave's democracy.

Part thy blue lips, Northern lake!
Moss-grown rocks, your silence break!
Tell the tale, thou ancient tree!
Thou, too, slide-worn Ossipee!
Speak, and tell us how and when
Lived and died this king of men!

Wordless moans the ancient pine;
Lake and mountain give no sign;
Vain to trace this ring of stones;
Vain the search of crumbling bones:
Deepest of all mysteries,
And the saddest, silence is.

Nameless, noteless, clay with clay
Mingles slowly day by day;
But somewhere, for good or ill,
That dark soul is living still;
Somewhere yet that atom's force
Moves the light-poised universe.

Strange that on his burial-sod
Harebells bloom, and golden-rod,
While the soul's dark horoscope
Holds no starry sign of hope!
Is the Unseen with sight at odds?
Nature's pity more than God's?

Thus I mused by Melvin's side,
While the summer eventide
Made the woods and inland sea
And the mountains mystery;

And the hush of earth and air
Seemed the pause before a prayer, —

Prayer for him, for all who rest,
Mother Earth, upon thy breast, —
Lapped on Christian turf, or hid
In rock-cave or pyramid:
All who sleep, as all who live,
Well may need the prayer, "Forgive!"

Desert-smothered caravan,
Knee-deep dust that once was man,
Battle-trenches ghastly piled,
Ocean-floors with white bones tiled,
Crowded tomb and mounded sod,
Dumbly crave that prayer to God.

Oh, the generations old
Over whom no church-bells tolled,
Christless, lifting up blind eyes
To the silence of the skies!
For the innumerable dead
Is my soul disquieted.

Where be now these silent hosts?
Where the camping-ground of ghosts?
Where the spectral conscripts led
To the white tents of the dead?
What strange shore or chartless sea
Holds the awful mystery?

Then the warm sky stooped to make
Double sunset in the lake;
While above I saw with it,
Range on range, the mountains lit;
And the calm and splendor stole
Like an answer to my soul.

Hear'st thou, O of little faith,
What to thee the mountain saith,
What is whispered by the trees? —
"Cast on God thy care for these;
Trust Him, if thy sight be dim:
Doubt for them is doubt of Him.

"Blind must be their close-shut eyes
Where like night the sunshine lies,
Fiery-linked the self-forged chain
Binding ever sin to pain,
Strong their prison-house of will,
But without He waiteth still.

"Not with hatred's undertow
Doth the Love Eternal flow;
Every chain that spirits wear
Crumbles in the breath of prayer;
And the penitent's desire
Opens every gate of fire.

"Still Thy love, O Christ arisen,
Yearns to reach these souls in Prison!
Through all depths of sin and loss
Drops the plummet of Thy cross!
Never yet abyss was found
Deeper than that cross could sound!"

Therefore well may Nature keep
Equal faith with all who sleep,
Set her watch of hills around
Christian grave and heathen mound,
And to cairn and kirkyard send
Summer's flowery dividend.

Keep, O pleasant Melvin stream,
Thy sweet laugh in shade and gleam!
On the Indian's grassy tomb
Swing, O flowers, your bells of bloom!
Deep below, as high above,
Sweeps the circle of God's love.

He paused and questioned with his eye
 The hearers' verdict on his song.
A low voice asked: "Is't well to pry
 Into the secrets which belong
Only to God? — The life to be
Is still the unguessed mystery:
Unscaled, unpierced the cloudy walls remain,
We beat with dream and wish the soundless doors in vain.

"But faith beyond our sight may go."
He said: "The gracious Fatherhood
Can only know above, below,
Eternal purposes of good.
From our free heritage of will,
The bitter springs of pain and ill
Flow only in all worlds. The perfect day
Of God is shadowless, and love is love alway."

"I know," she said, "the letter kills;
That on our arid fields of strife
And heat of clashing texts distils
The dew of spirit and of life.
But, searching still the written Word,
I fain would find, Thus saith the Lord,
A voucher for the hope I also feel
That sin can give no wound beyond love's power to heal."

"Pray," said the Man of Books, "give o'er
A theme too vast for time and place.
Go on, Sir Poet, ride once more
Your hobby at his old free pace.
But let him keep, with step discreet,
The solid earth beneath his feet.
In the great mystery which around us lies,
The wisest is a fool, the fool Heaven-helped is wise."

The Traveller said: "If songs have creeds,
Their choice of them let singers make;
But Art no other sanction needs
Than beauty for its own fair sake.
It grinds not in the mill of use,
Nor asks for leave, nor begs excuse;
It makes the flexile laws it deigns to own,
And gives its atmosphere its color and its tone.

"Confess, old friend, your austere school
Has left your fancy little chance;
You square to reason's rigid rule
The flowing outlines of romance.
With conscience keen from exercise,
And chronic fear of compromise,
You check the free play of your rhymes, to clap
A moral underneath, and spring it like a trap."

The sweet voice answered: "Better so
  Than bolder flights that know no check;
Better to use the bit, than throw
  The reins all loose on fancy's neck.
The liberal range of Art should be
The breadth of Christian liberty,
Restrained alone by challenge and alarm
Where its charmed footsteps tread the border land of harm.

"Beyond the poet's sweet dream lives
  The eternal epic of the man.
He wisest is who only gives,
  True to himself, the best he can;
Who, drifting in the winds of praise,
The inward monitor obeys;
And, with the boldness that confesses fear,
Takes in the crowded sail, and lets his conscience steer.

"Thanks for the fitting word he speaks,
  Nor less for doubtful work unspoken,
For the false model that he breaks,
  As for the moulded grace unbroken;
For what is missed and what remains,
For losses which are truest gains,
For reverence conscious of the Eternal eye,
And truth too fair to need the garnish of a lie."

Laughing, the Critic bowed. "I yield
  The point without another word;
Who ever yet a case appealed
  Where beauty's judgment had been heard?
And you, my good friend, owe to me
Your warmest thanks for such a plea,
As true withal as sweet. For my offence
Of cavil, let her words be ample recompense."

Across the sea one lighthouse star,
  With crimson ray that came and went,
Revolving on its tower afar,
  Looked through the doorway of the tent.
While outward, over sand-slopes wet,
The lamp flashed down its yellow jet
On the long wash of waves, with red and green
Tangles of weltering weed through the white foam-wreaths
  seen.

" 'Sing while we may, — another day
May bring enough of sorrow'; — thus
Our Traveller in his own sweet lay,
His Crimean camp-song, hints to us,"
The lady said. "So let it be;
Sing us a song," exclaimed all three.
She smiled: "I can but marvel at your choice
To hear our poet's words through my poor borrowed voice."

Her window opens to the bay,
On glistening light or misty gray,
And there at dawn and set of day
In prayer she kneels.
"Dear Lord!" she saith, "to many a home
From wind and wave the wanderers come;
I only see the tossing foam
Of stranger keels.

"Blown out and in by summer gales,
The stately ships, with crowded sails,
And sailors leaning o'er their rails,
Before me glide;
They come, they go, but nevermore,
Spice-laden from the Indian shore,
I see his swift-winged Isidore
The waves divide.

"O Thou! with whom the night is day
And one the near and far away,
Look out on yon gray waste, and say
Where lingers he.
Alive, perchance, on some lone beach
Or thirsty isle beyond the reach
Of man, he hears the mocking speech
Of wind and sea.

"O dread and cruel deep, reveal
The secret which thy waves conceal,
And, ye wild sea-birds, hither wheel
And tell your tale.
Let winds that tossed his raven hair
A message from my lost one bear, —
Some thought of me, a last fond prayer
Or dying wail!

"Come, with your dreariest truth shut out
The fears that haunt me round about;
O God! I cannot bear this doubt
That stifles breath.
The worst is better than the dread;
Give me but leave to mourn my dead
Asleep in trust and hope, instead
Of life in death!"

It might have been the evening breeze
That whispered in the garden trees,
It might have been the sound of seas
That rose and fell;
But, with her heart, if not her ear,
The old loved voice she seemed to hear:
"I wait to meet thee: be of cheer,
For all is well!"

The sweet voice into silence went,
A silence which was almost pain
As through it rolled the long lament,
The cadence of the mournful main.
Glancing his written pages o'er,
The Reader tried his part once more;
Leaving the land of hackmatack and pine
For Tuscan valleys glad with olive and with vine.

The Brother of Mercy

Piero Luca, known of all the town
As the gray porter by the Pitti wall
Where the noon shadows of the gardens fall,
Sick and in dolor, waited to lay down
His last sad burden, and beside his mat
The barefoot monk of La Certosa sat.

Unseen, in square and blossoming garden drifted,
Soft sunset lights through green Val d' Arno sifted;
Unheard, below the living shuttles shifted
Backward and forth, and wove, in love or strife,
In mirth or pain, the mottled web of life:
But when at last came upward from the street

Tinkle of bell and tread of measured feet,
The sick man started, strove to rise in vain,
Sinking back heavily with a moan of pain.
And the monk said, " 'Tis but the Brotherhood
Of Mercy going on some errand good:
Their black masks by the palace-wall I see."
Piero answered faintly, "Woe is me!
This day for the first time in forty years
In vain the bell hath sounded in my ears,
Calling me with my brethren of the mask,
Beggar and prince alike, to some new task
Of love or pity, — haply from the street
To bear a wretch plague-stricken, or, with feet
Hushed to the quickened ear and feverish brain,
To tread the crowded lazaretto's floors,
Down the long twilight of the corridors,
Midst tossing arms and faces full of pain.
I loved the work: it was its own reward.
I never counted on it to offset
My sins, which are many, or make less my debt
To the free grace and mercy of our Lord;
But somehow, father, it has come to be
In these long years so much a part of me,
I should not know myself, if lacking it,
But with the work the worker too would die,
And in my place some other self would sit
Joyful or sad, — what matters, if not I?
And now all's over. Woe is me!" — "My son,"
The monk said soothingly, "thy work is done;
And no more as a servant, but the guest
Of God thou enterest thy eternal rest.
No toil, no tears, no sorrow for the lost,
Shall mar thy perfect bliss. Thou shalt sit down
Clad in white robes, and wear a golden crown
Forever and forever." — Piero tossed
On his sick-pillow: "Miserable me!
I am too poor for such grand company;
The crown would be too heavy for this gray
Old head; and God forgive me if I say
It would be hard to sit there night and day,
Like an image in the Tribune, doing naught
With these hard hands, that all my life have wrought,
Not for bread only, but for pity's sake.
I'm dull at prayers: I could not keep awake,

Counting my beads. Mine's but a crazy head,
Scarce worth the saving, if all else be dead.
And if one goes to heaven without a heart,
God knows he leaves behind his better part.
I love my fellow-men: the worst I know
I would do good to. Will death change me so
That I shall sit among the lazy saints,
Turning a deaf ear to the sore complaints
Of souls that suffer? Why, I never yet
Left a poor dog in the *strada* hard beset,
Or ass o'erladen! Must I rate man less
Than dog or ass, in holy selfishness?
Methinks (Lord, pardon, if the thought be sin!)
The world of pain were better, if therein
One's heart might still be human, and desires
Of natural pity drop upon its fires
Some cooling tears."
Thereat the pale monk crossed
His brow, and muttering, "Madman! thou art lost!"
Took up his pyx and fled; and, left alone,
The sick man closed his eyes with a great groan
That sank into a prayer, "Thy will be done!"

Then was he made aware, by soul or ear,
Of somewhat pure and holy bending o'er him,
And of a voice like that of her who bore him,
Tender and most compassionate: "Never fear!
For heaven is love, as God himself is love;
Thy work below shall be thy work above."
And when he looked, lo! in the stern monk's place
He saw the shining of an angel's face!

The Traveller broke the pause. "I've seen
The Brothers down the long street steal,
Black, silent, masked, the crowd between,
And felt to doff my hat and kneel
With heart, if not with knee, in prayer,
For blessings on their pious care."
The Reader wiped his glasses: "Friends of mine,
We'll try our home-brewed next, instead of foreign wine."

The Wreck of Rivermouth

The Goody Cole who figures in this poem and *The Changeling* was Eunice Cole, who for a quarter of a century or more was feared, persecuted, and hated as the witch of Hampton. She lived alone in a hovel a little distant from the spot where the Hampton Academy now stands, and there she died, unattended. When her death was discovered, she was hastily covered up in the earth near by, and a stake driven through her body, to exorcise the evil spirit. Rev. Stephen Bachiler or Batchelder was one of the ablest of the early New England preachers. His marriage late in life to a woman regarded by his church as disreputable induced him to return to England, where he enjoyed the esteem and favor of Oliver Cromwell during the Protectorate.

Rivermouth Rocks are fair to see,
By dawn or sunset shone across,
When the ebb of the sea has left them free
To dry their fringes of gold-green moss:
For there the river comes winding down,
From salt sea-meadows and uplands brown,
And waves on the outer rocks afoam
Shout to its waters, "Welcome home!"

And fair are the sunny isles in view
East of the grisly Head of the Boar,
And Agamenticus lifts its blue
Disk of a cloud the woodlands o'er;
And southerly, when the tide is down,
'Twixt white sea-waves and sand-hills brown,
The beach-birds dance and the gray gulls wheel
Over a floor of burnished steel.

Once, in the old Colonial days,
Two hundred years ago and more,
A boat sailed down through the winding ways
Of Hampton River to that low shore,
Full of a goodly company
Sailing out on the summer sea,
Veering to catch the land-breeze light,
With the Boar to left and the Rocks to right.

In Hampton meadows, where mowers laid
Their scythes to the swaths of salted grass,
"Ah, well-a-day! our hay must be made!"
A young man sighed, who saw them pass.
Loud laughed his fellows to see him stand
Whetting his scythe with a listless hand,
Hearing a voice in a far-off song,
Watching a white hand beckoning long.

"Fie on the witch!" cried a merry girl,
As they rounded the point where Goody Cole
Sat by her door with her wheel atwirl,
A bent and blear-eyed poor old soul.
"Oho!" she muttered, "ye're brave to-day!
But I hear the little waves laugh and say,
'The broth will be cold that waits at home;
For it's one to go, but another to come!' "

"She's cursed," said the skipper; "speak her fair:
I'm scary always to see her shake
Her wicked head, with its wild gray hair,
And nose like a hawk, and eyes like a snake."
But merrily still, with laugh and shout,
From Hampton River the boat sailed out,
Till the huts and the flakes on Star seemed nigh,
And they lost the scent of the pines of Rye.

They dropped their lines in the lazy tide,
Drawing up haddock and mottled cod;
They saw not the Shadow that walked beside,
They heard not the feet with silence shod.
But thicker and thicker a hot mist grew,
Shot by the lightnings through and through;
And muffled growls, like the growl of a beast,
Ran along the sky from west to east.

Then the skipper looked from the darkening sea
Up to the dimmed and wading sun;
But he spake like a brave man cheerily,
"Yet there is time for our homeward run."
Veering and tacking, they backward wore;
And just as a breath from the woods ashore
Blew out to whisper of danger past,
The wrath of the storm came down at last!

The skipper hauled at the heavy sail:
"God be our help!" he only cried,
As the roaring gale, like the stroke of a flail,
Smote the boat on its starboard side.
The Shoalsmen looked, but saw alone
Dark films of rain-cloud slantwise blown,
Wild rocks lit up by the lightning's glare,
The strife and torment of sea and air.

Goody Cole looked out from her door:
  The Isles of Shoals were drowned and gone,
Scarcely she saw the Head of the Boar
  Toss the foam from tusks of stone.
She clasped her hands with a grip of pain,
The tear on her cheek was not of rain:
"They are lost," she muttered, "boat and crew!
Lord, forgive me! my words were true!"

Suddenly seaward swept the squall;
  The low sun smote through cloudy rack;
The Shoals stood clear in the light, and all
  The trend of the coast lay hard and black.
But far and wide as eye could reach,
No life was seen upon wave or beach;
The boat that went out at morning never
Sailed back again into Hampton River.

O mower, lean on thy bended snath,
  Look from the meadows green and low:
The wind of the sea is a waft of death,
  The waves are singing a song of woe!
By silent river, by moaning sea,
Long and vain shall thy watching be:
Never again shall the sweet voice call,
Never the white hand rise and fall!

O Rivermouth Rocks, how sad a sight
  Ye saw in the light of breaking day!
Dead faces looking up cold and white
  From sand and seaweed where they lay.
The mad old witch-wife wailed and wept,
And cursed the tide as it backward crept:
"Crawl back, crawl back, blue water-snake!
Leave your dead for the hearts that break!"

Solemn it was in that old day
  In Hampton town and its log-built church,
Where side by side the coffins lay
  And the mourners stood in aisle and porch.
In the singing-seats young eyes were dim,
The voices faltered that raised the hymn,
And Father Dalton, grave and stern,
Sobbed through his prayer and wept in turn.

But his ancient colleague did not pray;
　Under the weight of his fourscore years
He stood apart with the iron-gray
　Of his strong brows knitted to hide his tears;
And a fair-faced woman of doubtful fame,
Linking her own with his honored name,
Subtle as sin, at his side withstood
The felt reproach of her neighborhood.

Apart with them, like them forbid,
　Old Goody Cole looked drearily round,
As, two by two, with their faces hid,
　The mourners walked to the burying-ground.
She let the staff from her clasped hands fall:
"Lord, forgive us! we're sinners all!"
And the voice of the old man answered her:
"Amen!" said Father Bachiler.

So, as I sat upon Appledore
　In the calm of a closing summer day,
And the broken lines of Hampton shore
　In purple [illegible]land lay,
The Riverm[illegible]eir story told;
And waves ag[illegible] sunset gold,
Rising and break[illegible]g in steady chime,
Beat the rhythm and kept the time.

And the sunset paled, and warmed once more
　With a softer, tenderer after-glow;
In the east was moon-rise, with boats off-shore
　And sails in the distance drifting slow.
The beacon glimmered from Portsmouth bar,
The White Isle kindled its great red star;
And life and death in my old-time lay
Mingled in peace like the night and day!

　"Well!" said the Man of Books, "your story
　　Is really not ill told in verse.
　As the Celt said of purgatory,
　　One might go farther and fare worse."
　The Reader smiled; and once again
　With steadier voice took up his strain,
While the fair singer from the neighboring tent
Drew near, and at his side a graceful listener bent.

THE WRECK OF RIVERMOUTH

In Hampton meadows, where mowers laid
Their scythes to the swaths of salted grass

For the fairest maid in Hampton
They needed not to search,
Who saw young Anna Favor
Come walking into church, —

Or bringing from the meadows,
At set of harvest-day,
The frolic of the blackbirds,
The sweetness of the hay.

Now the weariest of all mothers,
The saddest two years' bride,
She scowls in the face of her husband,
And spurns her child aside.

"Rake out the red coals, goodman, —
For there the child shall lie,
Till the black witch comes to fetch her
And both [illegible] fly.

"It [illegible] r,
It [illegible] d into [illegible]
"The [illegible] ,
And le [illegible] e wh [illegible]

"Oh, fair [illegible] ,
Blue eyes, [illegible] ,
But this is ugly and wrinkled,
Cross, and cunning, and old.

"I hate the touch of her fingers,
I hate the feel of her skin;
It's not the milk from my bosom,
But my blood, that she sucks in.

"My face grows sharp with the torment;
Look! my arms are skin and bone!
Rake open the red coals, goodman,
And the witch shall have her own.

"She'll come when she hears it crying,
In the shape of an owl or bat,
And she'll bring us our darling Anna
In place of her screeching brat."

Then the goodman, Ezra Dalton,
Laid his hand upon her head:
"Thy sorrow is great, O woman!
I sorrow with thee," he said.

"The paths to trouble are many,
And never but one sure way
Leads out to the light beyond it:
My poor wife, let us pray."

Then he said to the great All-Father,
"Thy daughter is weak and blind;
Let her sight come back, and clothe her
Once more in her right mind.

"Lead her out of this evil shadow,
Out of these fancies wild;
Let the holy love of the mother
Turn again to her child.

"Make her lips like the [illegible]
Kissing her bl[illegible]
Let her hands, lik[illegible]
Rest on her lit[illegible]

"Comfort the soul of [illegible],
Open her prison-door,
And thine shall be all the glory
And praise forevermore."

Then into the face of its mother
The baby looked up and smiled;
And the cloud of her soul was lifted,
And she knew her little child.

A beam of the slant west sunshine
Made the wan face almost fair,
Lit the blue eyes' patient wonder
And the rings of pale gold hair.

She kissed it on lip and forehead,
She kissed it on cheek and chin,
And she bared her snow-white bosom
To the lips so pale and thin.

Oh, fair on her bridal morning
  Was the maid who blushed and smiled,
But fairer to Ezra Dalton
  Looked the mother of his child.

With more than a lover's fondness
  He stooped to her worn young face,
And the nursing child and the mother
  He folded in one embrace.

"Blessed be God!" he murmured.
  "Blessed be God!" she said;
"For I see, who once was blinded, —
  I live, who once was dead.

"Now mount and ride, my goodman,
  As thou lovest thy own soul!
Woe's me, if my wicked fancies
  Be the death of Goody Cole!"

His horse he saddled and bridled,
  And into the night rode he,
Now through the great black woodland,
  Now by the white-beached sea.

He rode through the silent clearings,
  He came to the ferry wide,
And thrice he called to the boatman
  Asleep on the other side.

He set his horse to the river,
  He swam to Newbury town,
And he called up Justice Sewall
  In his nightcap and his gown.

And the grave and worshipful justice
  (Upon whose soul be peace!)
Set his name to the jailer's warrant
  For Goodwife Cole's release.

Then through the night the hoof-beats
  Went sounding like a flail;
And Goody Cole at cockcrow
  Came forth from Ipswich jail.

"Here is a rhyme: I hardly dare
To venture on its theme worn out;
What seems so sweet by Doon and Ayr
Sounds simply silly hereabout;
And pipes by lips Arcadian blown
Are only tin horns at our own.
Yet still the muse of pastoral walks with us,
While Hosea Biglow sings, our new Theocritus."

The Maids of Attitash

In sky and wave the white clouds swam,
And the blue hills of Nottingham
Through gaps of leafy green
Across the lake were seen,

When, in the shadow of the ash
That dreams its dream in Attitash,
In the warm summer weather,
Two maidens sat together.

They sat and watched in idle mood
The gleam and shade of lake and wood;
The beach the keen light smote,
The white sail of a boat;

Swan flocks of lilies shoreward lying,
In sweetness, not in music, dying;
Hardhack, and virgin's-bower,
And white-spiked clethra-flower.

With careless ears they heard the plash
And breezy wash of Attitash,
The wood-bird's plaintive cry,
The locust's sharp reply.

And teased the while, with playful hand,
The shaggy dog of Newfoundland,
Whose uncouth frolic spilled
Their baskets berry-filled.

Then one, the beauty of whose eyes
Was evermore a great surprise,

Tossed back her queenly head,
And lightly laughing, said:

"No bridegroom's hand be mine to hold
That is not lined with yellow gold;
I tread no cottage-floor;
I own no lover poor.

"My love must come on silken wings,
With bridal lights of diamond rings,
Not foul with kitchen smirch,
With tallow-dip for torch."

The other, on whose modest head
Was lesser dower of beauty shed,
With look for home-hearths meet,
And voice exceeding sweet,

Answered, "We will not rivals be;
Take thou the gold, leave love to me;
Mine be the cottage small,
And thine the rich man's hall.

"I know, indeed, that wealth is good;
But lowly roof and simple food,
With love that hath no doubt,
Are more than gold without."

Hard by a farmer hale and young
His cradle in the rye-field swung,
Tracking the yellow plain
With windrows of ripe grain.

And still, whene'er he paused to whet
His scythe, the sidelong glance he met
Of large dark eyes, where strove
False pride and secret love.

Be strong, young mower of the grain;
That love shall overmatch disdain,
Its instincts soon or late
The heart shall vindicate.

In blouse of gray, with fishing-rod,
Half screened by leaves, a stranger trod

The margin of the pond,
Watching the group beyond.

The supreme hours unnoted come;
Unfelt the turning tides of doom;
And so the maids laughed on,
Nor dreamed what Fate had done, —

Nor knew the step was Destiny's
That rustled in the birchen trees,
As, with their lives forecast,
Fisher and mower passed.

Erelong by lake and rivulet side
The summer roses paled and died,
And Autumn's fingers shed
The maple's leaves of red.

Through the long gold-hazed afternoon,
Alone, but for the diving loon,
The partridge in the brake,
The black duck on the lake,

Beneath the shadow of the ash
Sat man and maid by Attitash;
And earth and air made room
For human hearts to bloom.

Soft spread the carpets of the sod,
And scarlet-oak and golden-rod
With blushes and with smiles
Lit up the forest aisles.

The mellow light the lake aslant,
The pebbled margin's ripple-chant
Attempered and low-toned,
The tender mystery owned.

And through the dream the lovers dreamed
Sweet sounds stole in and soft lights streamed;
The sunshine seemed to bless,
The air was a caress.

Not she who lightly laughed is there,
With scornful toss of midnight hair,

Her dark, disdainful eyes,
And proud lip worldly-wise.

Her haughty vow is still unsaid,
But all she dreamed and coveted
Wears, half to her surprise,
The youthful farmer's guise!

With more than all her old-time pride
She walks the rye-field at his side,
Careless of cot or hall,
Since love transfigures all.

Rich beyond dreams, the vantage-ground
Of life is gained; her hands have found
The talisman of old
That changes all to gold.

While she who could for love dispense
With all its glittering accidents,
And trust her heart alone,
Finds love and gold her own.

What wealth can buy or art can build
Awaits her; but her cup is filled
Even now unto the brim;
Her world is love and him!

The while he heard, the Book-man drew
A length of make-believing face,
With smothered mischief laughing through:
"Why, you shall sit in Ramsay's place,
And, with his Gentle Shepherd, keep
On Yankee hills immortal sheep,
While love-lorn swains and maids the seas beyond
Hold dreamy tryst around your huckleberry-pond."

The Traveller laughed: "Sir Galahad
Singing of love the Trouvere's lay!
How should he know the blindfold lad
From one of Vulcan's forge-boys?" — "Nay,
He better sees who stands outside
Than they who in procession ride,"

The Reader answered: "Selectmen and squire
Miss, while they make, the show that wayside folks
admire.

"Here is a wild tale of the North,
Our travelled friend will own as one
Fit for a Norland Christmas hearth
And lips of Christian Andersen.
They tell it in the valleys green
Of the fair island he has seen,
Low lying off the pleasant Swedish shore,
Washed by the Baltic Sea, and watched by Elsinore."

Kallundborg Church

"Build at Kallundborg by the sea
A church as stately as church may be,
And there shalt thou wed my daughter fair,"
Said the Lord of Nesvek to Esbern Snare.

And the Baron laughed. But Esbern said,
"Though I lose my soul, I will Helva wed!"
And off he strode, in his pride of will,
To the Troll who dwelt in Ulshoi hill.

"Build, O Troll, a church for me
At Kallundborg by the mighty sea;
Build it stately, and build it fair,
Build it quickly," said Esbern Snare.

But the sly Dwarf said, "No work is wrought
By Trolls of the Hills, O man, for naught.
What wilt thou give for thy church so fair?"
"Set thy own price," quoth Esbern Snare.

"When Kallundborg church is builded well,
Thou must the name of its builder tell,
Or thy heart and thy eyes must be my boon."
"Build," said Esbern, "and build it soon."

By night and by day the Troll wrought on;
He hewed the timbers, he piled the stone;
But day by day, as the walls rose fair,
Darker and sadder grew Esbern Snare.

He listened by night, he watched by day,
He sought and thought, but he dared not pray;
In vain he called on the Elle-maids shy,
And the Neck and the Nis gave no reply.

Of his evil bargain far and wide
A rumor ran through the country-side;
And Helva of Nesvek, young and fair,
Prayed for the soul of Esbern Snare.

And now the church was wellnigh done;
One pillar it lacked, and one alone;
And the grim Troll muttered, "Fool thou art!
To-morrow gives me thy eyes and heart!"

By Kallundborg in black despair,
Through wood and meadow, walked Esbern Snare,
Till, worn and weary, the strong man sank
Under the birches on Ulshoi bank.

At his last day's work he heard the Troll
Hammer and delve in the quarry's hole;
Before him the church stood large and fair:
"I have builded my tomb," said Esbern Snare.

And he closed his eyes the sight to hide,
When he heard a light step at his side:
"O Esbern Snare!" a sweet voice said,
"Would I might die now in thy stead!"

With a grasp by love and by fear made strong,
He held her fast, and he held her long;
With the beating heart of a bird afeard,
She hid her face in his flame-red beard.

"O love!" he cried, "let me look to-day
In thine eyes ere mine are plucked away;
Let me hold thee close, let me feel thy heart
Ere mine by the Troll is torn apart!

"I sinned, O Helva, for love of thee!
Pray that the Lord Christ pardon me!"
But fast as she prayed, and faster still,
Hammered the Troll in Ulshoi hill.

He knew, as he wrought, that a loving heart
Was somehow baffling his evil art;
For more than spell of Elf or Troll
Is a maiden's prayer for her lover's soul.

And Esbern listened, and caught the sound
Of a Troll-wife singing underground:
"To-morrow comes Fine, father thine:
Lie still and hush thee, baby mine!

"Lie still, my darling! next sunrise
Thou'lt play with Esbern Snare's heart and eyes!"
"Ho! ho!" quoth Esbern, "is that your game?
Thanks to the Troll-wife, I know his name!"

The Troll he heard him, and hurried on
To Kallundborg church with the lacking stone.
"Too late, Gaffer Fine!" cried Esbern Snare;
And Troll and pillar vanished in air!

That night the harvesters heard the sound
Of a woman sobbing underground,
And the voice of the Hill-Troll loud with blame
Of the careless singer who told his name.

Of the Troll of the Church they sing the rune
By the Northern Sea in the harvest moon;
And the fishers of Zealand hear him still
Scolding his wife in Ulshoi hill.

And seaward over its groves of birch
Still looks the tower of Kallundborg church,
Where, first at its altar, a wedded pair,
Stood Helva of Nesvek and Esbern Snare!

"What," asked the Traveller, "would our sires,
The old Norse story-tellers, say
Of sun-graved pictures, ocean wires,
And smoking steamboats of to-day?
And this, O lady, by your leave,
Recalls your song of yester eve:
Pray, let us have that Cable-hymn once more."
"Hear, hear!" the Book-man cried, "the lady has the floor.

"These noisy waves below perhaps
To such a strain will lend their ear,
With softer voice and lighter lapse
Come stealing up the sands to hear,
And what they once refused to do
For old King Knut accord to you.
Nay, even the fishes shall your listeners be,
As once, the legend runs, they heard St. Anthony."

The Cable Hymn

O lonely bay of Trinity,
O dreary shores, give ear!
Lean down unto the white-lipped sea
The voice of God to hear!

From world to world His couriers fly,
Thought-winged and shod with fire;
The angel of His stormy sky
Rides down the sunken wire.

What saith the herald of the Lord?
"The world's long strife is done;
Close wedded by that mystic cord,
Its continents are one.

"And one in heart, as one in blood,
Shall all her peoples be;
The hands of human brotherhood
Are clasped beneath the sea.

"Through Orient seas, o'er Afric's plain
And Asian mountains borne,
The vigor of the Northern brain
Shall nerve the world outworn.

"From clime to clime, from shore to shore,
Shall thrill the magic thread;
The new Prometheus steals once more
The fire that wakes the dead."

Throb on, strong pulse of thunder! beat
From answering beach to beach;

Fuse nations in thy kindly heat,
  And melt the chains of each!

Wild terror of the sky above,
  Glide tamed and dumb below!
Bear gently, Ocean's carrier-dove,
  Thy errands to and fro.

Weave on, swift shuttle of the Lord,
  Beneath the deep so far,
The bridal robe of earth's accord,
  The funeral shroud of war!

For lo! the fall of Ocean's wall
  Space mocked and time outrun;
And round the world the thought of all
  Is as the thought of one!

The poles unite, the zones agree,
  The tongues of striving cease;
As on the Sea of Galilee
  The Christ is whispering, Peace!

"Glad prophecy! to this at last,"
  The Reader said, "shall all things come.
Forgotten be the bugle's blast,
  And battle-music of the drum.
A little while the world may run
Its old mad way, with needle-gun
And ironclad, but truth, at last, shall reign:
The cradle-song of Christ was never sung in vain!"

Shifting his scattered papers, "Here,"
  He said, as died the faint applause,
"Is something that I found last year
  Down on the island known as Orr's.
I had it from a fair-haired girl
Who, oddly, bore the name of Pearl,
(As if by some droll freak of circumstance,)
Classic, or wellnigh so, in Harriet Stowe's romance."

The Dead Ship of Harpswell

What flecks the outer gray beyond
  The sundown's golden trail?
The white flash of a sea-bird's wing,
  Or gleam of slanting sail?
Let young eyes watch from Neck and Point,
  And sea-worn elders pray, —
The ghost of what was once a ship
  Is sailing up the bay!

From gray sea-fog, from icy drift,
  From peril and from pain,
The home-bound fisher greets thy lights,
  O hundred-harbored Maine!
But many a keel shall seaward turn,
  And many a sail outstand,
When, tall and white, the Dead Ship looms
  Against the dusk of land.

She rounds the headland's bristling pines;
  She threads the isle-set bay;
No spur of breeze can speed her on,
  Nor ebb of tide delay.
Old men still walk the Isle of Orr
  Who tell her date and name,
Old shipwrights sit in Freeport yards
  Who hewed her oaken frame.

What weary doom of baffled quest,
  Thou sad sea-ghost, is thine?
What makes thee in the haunts of home
  A wonder and a sign?
No foot is on thy silent deck,
  Upon thy helm no hand;
No ripple hath the soundless wind
  That smites thee from the land!

For never comes the ship to port,
  Howe'er the breeze may be;
Just when she nears the waiting shore
  She drifts again to sea.
No tack of sail, nor turn of helm,
  Nor sheer of veering side;
Stern-fore she drives to sea and night,
  Against the wind and tide.

In vain o'er Harpswell Neck the star
  Of evening guides her in;
In vain for her the lamps are lit
  Within thy tower, Seguin!
In vain the harbor-boat shall hail,
  In vain the pilot call;
No hand shall reef her spectral sail,
  Or let her anchor fall.

Shake, brown old wives, with dreary joy,
  Your gray-head hints of ill;
And, over sick-beds whispering low,
  Your prophecies fulfil.
Some home amid yon birchen trees
  Shall drape its door with woe;
And slowly where the Dead Ship sails,
  The burial boat shall row!

From Wolf Neck and from Flying Point,
  From island and from main,
From sheltered cove and tided creek,
  Shall glide the funeral train.
The dead-boat with the bearers four,
  The mourners at her stern, —
And one shall go the silent way
  Who shall no more return!

And men shall sigh, and women weep,
  Whose dear ones pale and pine,
And sadly over sunset seas
  Await the ghostly sign.
They know not that its sails are filled
  By pity's tender breath,
Nor see the Angel at the helm
  Who steers the Ship of Death!

"Chill as a down-east breeze should be,"
  The Book-man said. "A ghostly touch
The legend has. I'm glad to see
  Your flying Yankee beat the Dutch."
"Well, here is something of the sort
Which one midsummer day I caught
In Narragansett Bay, for lack of fish."
"We wait," the Traveller said; "serve hot or cold
  your dish."

The Palatine

Leagues north, as fly the gull and auk,
Point Judith watches with eye of hawk;
Leagues south, thy beacon flames, Montauk!

Lonely and wind-shorn, wood-forsaken,
With never a tree for Spring to waken,
For tryst of lovers or farewells taken,

Circled by waters that never freeze,
Beaten by billow and swept by breeze,
Lieth the island of Manisees,

Set at the mouth of the Sound to hold
The coast lights up on its turret old,
Yellow with moss and sea-fog mould.

Dreary the land when gust and sleet
At its doors and windows howl and beat,
And Winter laughs at its fires of peat!

But in summer time, when pool and pond,
Held in the laps of valleys fond,
Are blue as the glimpses of sea beyond;

When the hills are sweet with the brier-rose,
And, hid in the warm, soft dells, unclose
Flowers the mainland rarely knows;

When boats to their morning fishing go,
And, held to the wind and slanting low,
Whitening and darkening the small sails show, —

Then is that lonely island fair;
And the pale health-seeker findeth there
The wine of life in its pleasant air.

No greener valleys the sun invite,
On smoother beaches no sea-birds light,
No blue waves shatter to foam more white!

There, circling ever their narrow range,
Quaint tradition and legend strange
Live on unchallenged, and know no change.

Old wives spinning their webs of tow,
Or rocking weirdly to and fro
In and out of the peat's dull glow,

And old men mending their nets of twine,
Talk together of dream and sign,
Talk of the lost ship Palatine, —

The ship that, a hundred years before,
Freighted deep with its goodly store,
In the gales of the equinox went ashore.

The eager islanders one by one
Counted the shots of her signal gun,
And heard the crash when she drove right on!

Into the teeth of death she sped:
(May God forgive the hands that fed
The false lights over the rocky Head!)

O men and brothers! what sights were there!
White upturned faces, hands stretched in prayer!
Where waves had pity, could ye not spare?

Down swooped the wreckers, like birds of prey
Tearing the heart of the ship away,
And the dead had never a word to say.

And then, with ghastly shimmer and shine
Over the rocks and the seething brine,
They burned the wreck of the Palatine.

In their cruel hearts, as they homeward sped,
"The sea and the rocks are dumb," they said:
"There'll be no reckoning with the dead."

But the year went round, and when once more
Along their foam-white curves of shore
They heard the line-storm rave and roar,

Behold! again, with shimmer and shine,
Over the rocks and the seething brine,
The flaming wreck of the Palatine!

THE PALATINE

And then with ghastly shimmer and shine...
They burned the wreck of the Palatine

So, haply in fitter words than these,
Mending their nets on their patient knees,
They tell the legend of Manisees.

Nor looks nor tones a doubt betray;
"It is known to us all," they quietly say;
"We too have seen it in our day."

Is there, then, no death for a word once spoken?
Was never a deed but left its token
Written on tables never broken?

Do the elements subtle reflections give?
Do pictures of all the ages live
On Nature's infinite negative,

Which, half in sport, in malice half,
She shows at times, with shudder or laugh,
Phantom and shadow in photograph?

For still, on many a moonless night,
From Kingston Head and from Montauk light
The spectre kindles and burns in sight.

Now low and dim, now clear and higher,
Leaps up the terrible Ghost of Fire,
Then, slowly sinking, the flames expire.

And the wise Sound skippers, though skies be fine,
Reef their sails when they see the sign
Of the blazing wreck of the Palatine!

"A fitter tale to scream than sing,"
The Book-man said. "Well, fancy, then,"
The Reader answered, "on the wing
The sea-birds shriek it, not for men,
But in the ear of wave and breeze!"
The Traveller mused: "Your Manisees
Is fairy-land: off Narragansett shore
Who ever saw the isle or heard its name before?

" 'Tis some strange land of Flyaway,
Whose dreamy shore the ship beguiles,
St. Brandan's in its sea-mist gray,
Or sunset loom of Fortunate Isles!"

"No ghost, but solid turf and rock
Is the good island known as Block,"
The Reader said. "For beauty and for ease
I chose its Indian name, soft-flowing Manisees!

"But let it pass; here is a bit
Of unrhymed story, with a hint
Of the old preaching mood in it,
The sort of sidelong moral squint
Our friend objects to, which has grown,
I fear, a habit of my own.
'Twas written when the Asian plague drew near,
And the land held its breath and paled with sudden fear."

Abraham Davenport

The famous Dark Day of New England, May 19, 1780, was a physical puzzle for many years to our ancestors, but its occurrence brought something more than philosophical speculation into the minds of those who passed through it. The incident of Colonel Abraham Davenport's sturdy protest is a matter of history.

In the old days (a custom laid aside
With breeches and cocked hats) the people sent
Their wisest men to make the public laws.
And so, from a brown homestead, where the Sound
Drinks the small tribute of the Mianas,
Waved over by the woods of Rippowams,
And hallowed by pure lives and tranquil deaths,
Stamford sent up to the councils of the State
Wisdom and grace in Abraham Davenport.

'Twas on a May-day of the far old year
Seventeen hundred eighty, that there fell
Over the bloom and sweet life of the Spring,
Over the fresh earth and the heaven of noon,
A horror of great darkness, like the night
In day of which the Norland sagas tell, —
The Twilight of the Gods. The low-hung sky
Was black with ominous clouds, save where its rim
Was fringed with a dull glow, like that which climbs
The crater's sides from the red hell below.
Birds ceased to sing, and all the barn-yard fowls
Roosted; the cattle at the pasture bars
Lowed, and looked homeward; bats on leathern wings

Flitted abroad; the sounds of labor died;
Men prayed, and women wept; all ears grew sharp
To hear the doom-blast of the trumpet shatter
The black sky, that the dreadful face of Christ
Might look from the rent clouds, not as he looked
A loving guest at Bethany, but stern
As Justice and inexorable Law.

Meanwhile in the old State House, dim as ghosts,
Sat the lawgivers of Connecticut,
Trembling beneath their legislative robes.
"It is the Lord's Great Day! Let us adjourn,"
Some said; and then, as if with one accord,
All eyes were turned to Abraham Davenport.
He rose, slow cleaving with his steady voice
The intolerable hush. "This well may be
The Day of Judgment which the world awaits;
But be it so or not, I only know
My present duty, and my Lord's command
To occupy till He come. So at the post
Where He hath set me in His providence,
I choose, for one, to meet Him face to face, —
No faithless servant frightened from my task,
But ready when the Lord of the harvest calls;
And therefore, with all reverence, I would say,
Let God do His work, we will see to ours.
Bring in the candles." And they brought them in.

Then by the flaring lights the Speaker read,
Albeit with husky voice and shaking hands,
An act to amend an act to regulate
The shad and alewive fisheries. Whereupon
Wisely and well spake Abraham Davenport,
Straight to the question, with no figures of speech
Save the ten Arab signs, yet not without
The shrewd dry humor natural to the man:
His awe-struck colleagues listening all the while,
Between the pauses of his argument,
To hear the thunder of the wrath of God
Break from the hollow trumpet of the cloud.

And there he stands in memory to this day,
Erect, self-poised, a rugged face, half seen
Against the background of unnatural dark,

A witness to the ages as they pass,
That simple duty hath no place for fear.

He ceased: just then the ocean seemed
To lift a half-faced moon in sight;
And, shore-ward, o'er the waters gleamed,
From crest to crest, a line of light,
Such as of old, with solemn awe,
The fishers by Gennesaret saw,
When dry-shod o'er it walked the Son of God,
Tracking the waves with light where'er his sandals trod.

Silently for a space each eye
Upon that sudden glory turned:
Cool from the land the breeze blew by,
The tent-ropes flapped, the long beach churned
Its waves to foam; on either hand
Stretched, far as sight, the hills of sand;
With bays of marsh, and capes of bush and tree,
The wood's black shore-line loomed beyond the meadowy sea.

The lady rose to leave. "One song,
Or hymn," they urged, "before we part."
And she, with lips to which belong
Sweet intuitions of all art,
Gave to the winds of night a strain
Which they who heard would hear again;
And to her voice the solemn ocean lent,
Touching its harp of sand, a deep accompaniment.

The Worship of Nature

The harp at Nature's advent strung
Has never ceased to play;
The song the stars of morning sung
Has never died away.

And prayer is made, and praise is given,
By all things near and far;
The ocean looketh up to heaven,
And mirrors every star.

Its waves are kneeling on the strand,
As kneels the human knee,
Their white locks bowing to the sand,
The priesthood of the sea!

They pour their glittering treasures forth,
Their gifts of pearl they bring,
And all the listening hills of earth
Take up the song they sing.

The green earth sends her incense up
From many a mountain shrine;
From folded leaf and dewy cup
She pours her sacred wine.

The mists above the morning rills
Rise white as wings of prayer;
The altar-curtains of the hills
Are sunset's purple air.

The winds with hymns of praise are loud,
Or low with sobs of pain, —
The thunder-organ of the cloud,
The dropping tears of rain.

With drooping head and branches crossed
The twilight forest grieves,
Or speaks with tongues of Pentecost
From all its sunlit leaves.

The blue sky is the temple's arch,
Its transept earth and air,
The music of its starry march
The chorus of a prayer.

So Nature keeps the reverent frame
With which her years began,
And all her signs and voices shame
The prayerless heart of man.

The singer ceased. The moon's white rays
Fell on the rapt, still face of her.
"*Allah il Allah!* He hath praise

From all things," said the Traveller.
"Oft from the desert's silent nights,
And mountain hymns of sunset lights,
My heart has felt rebuke, as in his tent
The Moslem's prayer has shamed my Christian knee
unbent."

He paused, and lo! far, faint, and slow
The bells in Newbury's steeples tolled
The twelve dead hours; the lamp burned low;
The singer sought her canvas fold.
One sadly said, "At break of day
We strike our tent and go our way."
But one made answer cheerily, "Never fear,
We'll pitch this tent of ours in type another year."

The Poems of John Greenleaf Whittier

V

WAR AND ANTI-SLAVERY

The Editor's Commentary

WHITTIER'S *Complete Collected Poetical Works* lists almost a hundred poems devoted to the battle against slavery, the oncoming crisis, and the Civil War. Most of these are anti-slavery verses, and most of them are severely dated. They were written in heat and often in haste, to chastise a statesman who advocated the suppression of free speech, to celebrate a Negro liberator, to expostulate against oppression and champion emancipation. Yet, in spite of the topical references, the excessive rhetoric, and the too prolonged hortatory tone, they survive not only as pronouncements but as personal documents. "The Rendition" turns an incredible scene into nightmare reality. "Le Marais du Cygne" describes (or rather, transcribes) a massacre in lines that are both terse and powerful. "The Kansas Emigrants" was sent to the first company of Free State men as a marching song, and was sung to the tune of "Auld Lang Syne" as they rode toward their new home. "It was one of those prophecies," wrote Edward Everett Hale, "for which poets are born, uttered before the event and not after."

"Barbara Frietchie" is the idealization of an event; to be precise, it is the telescoping of two events. Whittier had heard the story of a "worthy and highly esteemed gentlewoman, intensely loyal . . . holding her Union flag sacred and keeping it with her Bible." When the Confederate troops halted before her house, she fearlessly shook her cane in their faces and drove them out. But, although Barbara Frietchie was no myth, it was a Mrs. Quantrell who flew her flag in the faces of the Confederates — and, as Whittier naïvely added in a note, "it is possible that there has been a blending of the two incidents."

BARBARA FRIETCHIE

"Shoot, if you must, this old gray head,
But spare your country's flag," she said

Barbara Frietchie

Up from the meadows rich with corn,
Clear in the cool September morn,

The clustered spires of Frederick stand
Green-walled by the hills of Maryland.

Round about them orchards sweep,
Apple and peach tree fruited deep,

Fair as the garden of the Lord
To the eyes of the famished rebel horde,

On that pleasant morn of the early fall
When Lee marched over the mountain-wall;

Over the mountains winding down,
Horse and foot, into Frederick town.

Forty flags with their silver stars,
Forty flags with their crimson bars,

Flapped in the morning wind: the sun
Of noon looked down, and saw not one.

Up rose old Barbara Frietchie then,
Bowed with her fourscore years and ten;

Bravest of all in Frederick town,
She took up the flag the men hauled down,

In her attic window the staff she set,
To show that one heart was loyal yet.

Up the street came the rebel tread,
Stonewall Jackson riding ahead.

Under his slouched hat left and right
He glanced; the old flag met his sight.

"Halt!" — the dust-brown ranks stood fast.
"Fire!" — out blazed the rifle-blast.

It shivered the window, pane and sash;
It rent the banner with seam and gash.

Quick, as it fell, from the broken staff
Dame Barbara snatched the silken scarf.

She leaned far out on the window-sill,
And shook it forth with a royal will.

"Shoot, if you must, this old gray head,
But spare your country's flag," she said.

A shade of sadness, a blush of shame,
Over the face of the leader came;

The nobler nature within him stirred
To life at that woman's deed and word;

"Who touches a hair of yon gray head
Dies like a dog! March on!" he said.

All day long through Frederick street
Sounded the tread of marching feet:

All day long that free flag tost
Over the heads of the rebel host.

Ever its torn folds rose and fell
On the loyal winds that loved it well;

And through the hill-gaps sunset light
Shone over it with a warm good-night.

Barbara Frietchie's work is o'er,
And the Rebel rides on his raids no more.

Peace and order and beauty draw
Round thy symbol of light and law;

And ever the stars above look down
On thy stars below in Frederick town!

Honor to her! and let a tear
Fall, for her sake, on Stonewall's bier.

Over Barbara Frietchie's grave,
Flag of Freedom and Union, wave!

Toussaint L'Ouverture

Toussaint L'Ouverture, the black chieftain of Hayti, was a slave on the plantation "de Libertas," belonging to M. Bayou. When the rising of the Negroes took place, in 1791, Toussaint refused to join them until he had aided M. Bayou and his family to escape to Baltimore. The white man had discovered in Toussaint many noble qualities, and had instructed him in some of the first branches of education; and the preservation of his life was owing to the Negro's gratitude for this kindness.

In 1797, Toussaint L'Ouverture was appointed, by the French government, General-in-Chief of the armies of St. Domingo, and, as such, signed the Convention with General Maitland for the evacuation of the island by the British. From this period until 1801 the island, under the government of Toussaint, was happy, tranquil, and prosperous. The miserable attempt of Napoleon to reëstablish slavery in St. Domingo, although it failed of its intended object, proved fatal to the Negro chieftain. Treacherously seized by Leclerc, he was hurried on board a vessel by night, and conveyed to France, where he was confined in a cold subterranean dungeon, at Besançon, where, in April, 1803, he died.

'Twas night. The tranquil moonlight smile
  With which Heaven dreams of Earth, shed down
Its beauty on the Indian isle, —
  On broad green field and white-walled town;
And inland waste of rock and wood,
In searching sunshine, wild and rude,
Rose, mellowed through the silver gleam,
Soft as the landscape of a dream.
All motionless and dewy wet,
Tree, vine, and flower in shadow met:
The myrtle with its snowy bloom,
Crossing the nightshade's solemn gloom, —
The white cecropia's silver rind
Relieved by deeper green behind,
The orange with its fruit of gold,
The lithe paullinia's verdant fold,
The passion-flower with symbol holy,
Twining its tendrils long and lowly,
The rhexias dark, and cassia tall,
And proudly rising over all,
The kingly palm's imperial stem,
Crowned with its leafy diadem,
Star-like, beneath whose sombre shade,
The fiery-winged cucullo played!

How lovely was thine aspect, then,
  Fair island of the Western Sea!
Lavish of beauty, even when
Thy brutes were happier than thy men,
  For they, at least, were free!
Regardless of thy glorious clime,
  Unmindful of thy soil of flowers,

The toiling Negro sighed, that Time
　No faster sped his hours.
For, by the dewy moonlight still,
He fed the weary-turning mill,
Or bent him in the chill morass,
To pluck the long and tangled grass,
And hear above his scar-worn back
The heavy slave-whip's frequent crack:
While in his heart one evil thought
In solitary madness wrought,
One baleful fire surviving still
　The quenching of the immortal mind,
　One sterner passion of his kind,
Which even fetters could not kill,
The savage hope, to deal, erelong,
A vengeance bitterer than his wrong!

Hark to that cry! long, loud, and shrill,
From field and forest, rock and hill,
Thrilling and horrible it rang,
　Around, beneath, above;
The wild beast from his cavern sprang,
　The wild bird from her grove!
Nor fear, nor joy, nor agony
Were mingled in that midnight cry;
But like the lion's growl of wrath,
When falls that hunter in his path
Whose barbëd arrow, deeply set,
Is rankling in his bosom yet,
It told of hate, full, deep, and strong,
Of vengeance kindling out of wrong;
It was as if the crimes of years —
The unrequited toil, the tears,
The shame and hate, which liken well
Earth's garden to the nether hell —
Had found in nature's self a tongue,
On which the gathered horror hung;
As if from cliff, and stream, and glen
Burst on the startled ears of men
That voice which rises unto God,
Solemn and stern, — the cry of blood!
It ceased, and all was still once more,
Save ocean chafing on his shore,
The sighing of the wind between

The broad banana's leaves of green,
Or bough by restless plumage shook,
Or murmuring voice of mountain brook.

Brief was the silence. Once again
  Pealed to the skies that frantic yell,
Glowed on the heavens a fiery stain,
  And flashes rose and fell;
And painted on the blood-red sky,
Dark, naked arms were tossed on high;
And, round the white man's lordly hall,
  Trod, fierce and free, the brute he made;
And those who crept along the wall,
And answered to his lightest call
  With more than spaniel dread,
The creatures of his lawless beck,
Were trampling on his very neck!
And on the night-air, wild and clear,
Rose woman's shriek of more than fear;
For bloodied arms were round her thrown,
And dark cheeks pressed against her own.

Then, injured Afric! for the shame
Of thy own daughters, vengeance came
Full on the scornful hearts of those,
Who mocked thee in thy nameless woes,
And to thy hapless children gave
One choice, — pollution or the grave!
Where then was he whose fiery zeal
Had taught the trampled heart to feel,
Until despair itself grew strong,
And vengeance fed its torch from wrong?
Now, when the thunderbolt is speeding;
Now, when oppression's heart is bleeding;
Now, when the latent curse of Time
  Is raining down in fire and blood,
That curse which, through long years of crime,
  Has gathered, drop by drop, its flood, —
Why strikes he not, the foremost one,
Where murder's sternest deeds are done?

He stood the aged palms beneath,
  That shadowed o'er his humble door,
Listening, with half-suspended breath,

To the wild sounds of fear and death,
  Toussaint L'Ouverture!
What marvel that his heart beat high!
  The blow for freedom had been given,
And blood had answered to the cry
  Which Earth sent up to Heaven!
What marvel that a fierce delight
Smiled grimly o'er his brow of night,
As groan and shout and bursting flame
Told where the midnight tempest came,
With blood and fire along its van,
And death behind! he was a Man!

Yes, dark-souled chieftain! if the light
  Of mild Religion's heavenly ray
Unveiled not to thy mental sight
  The lowlier and the purer way,
In which the Holy Sufferer trod,
  Meekly amidst the sons of crime;
That calm reliance upon God
  For justice in His own good time;
That gentleness to which belongs
Forgiveness for its many wrongs,
Even as the primal martyr, kneeling
For mercy on the evil-dealing;
Let not the favored white man name
Thy stern appeal, with words of blame.
Has he not, with the light of heaven
  Broadly around him, made the same?
Yea, on his thousand war-fields striven,
  And gloried in his ghastly shame?
Kneeling amidst his brother's blood,
To offer mockery unto God,
As if the High and Holy One
Could smile on deeds of murder done!
As if a human sacrifice
Were purer in His holy eyes,
Though offered up by Christian hands,
Than the foul rites of Pagan lands!

. . . .

Sternly, amidst his household band,
His carbine grasped within his hand,
  The white man stood, prepared and still,

Waiting the shock of maddened men,
Unchained, and fierce as tigers, when
  The horn winds through their caverned hill.
And one was weeping in his sight,
  The sweetest flower of all the isle,
The bride who seemed but yesternight
  Love's fair embodied smile.
And, clinging to her trembling knee,
Looked up the form of infancy,
With tearful glance in either face
The secret of its fear to trace.

"Ha! stand or die!" The white man's eye
  His steady musket gleamed along,
As a tall Negro hastened nigh,
  With fearless step and strong.
"What ho, Toussaint!" A moment more,
His shadow crossed the lighted floor.
"Away!" he shouted; "fly with me,
The white man's bark is on the sea;
Her sails must catch the seaward wind,
For sudden vengeance sweeps behind.
Our brethren from their graves have spoken,
The yoke is spurned, the chain is broken;
On all the hills our fires are glowing,
Through all the vales red blood is flowing!
No more the mocking White shall rest
His foot upon the Negro's breast;
No more, at morn or eve, shall drip
The warm blood from the driver's whip:
Yet, though Toussaint has vengeance sworn
For all the wrongs his race have borne,
Though for each drop of Negro blood
The white man's veins shall pour a flood;
Not all alone the sense of ill
Around his heart is lingering still,
Nor deeper can the white man feel
The generous warmth of grateful zeal.
Friends of the Negro! fly with me,
The path is open to the sea:
Away, for life!" He spoke, and pressed
The young child to his manly breast,
As, headlong, through the cracking cane,
Down swept the dark insurgent train,

Drunken and grim, with shout and yell
Howled through the dark, like sounds from hell.

Far out, in peace, the white man's sail
Swayed free before the sunrise gale.
Cloud-like that island hung afar,
  Along the bright horizon's verge,
O'er which the curse of servile war
  Rolled its red torrent, surge on surge;
And he, the Negro champion, where
  In the fierce tumult struggled he?
Go trace him by the fiery glare
Of dwellings in the midnight air,
The yells of triumph and despair,
  The streams that crimson to the sea!

Sleep calmly in thy dungeon-tomb,
  Beneath Besançon's alien sky,
Dark Haytien! for the time shall come,
  Yea, even now is nigh,
When, everywhere, thy name shall be
Redeemed from color's infamy;
And men shall learn to speak of thee
As one of earth's great spirits, born
In servitude, and nursed in scorn,
Casting aside the weary weight
And fetters of its low estate,
In that strong majesty of soul
  Which knows no color, tongue, or clime,
Which still hath spurned the base control
  Of tyrants through all time!
Far other hands than mine may wreathe
The laurel round thy brow of death,
And speak thy praise, as one whose word
A thousand fiery spirits stirred,
Who crushed his foeman as a worm,
Whose step on human hearts fell firm:
Be mine the better task to find
A tribute for thy lofty mind,
Amidst whose gloomy vengeance shone
Some milder virtues all thine own,
Some gleams of feeling pure and warm,
Like sunshine on a sky of storm,
Proofs that the Negro's heart retains

TO FANEUIL HALL

Finish what your sires began!
Up, to Faneuil Hall!

Some nobleness amid its chains, —
That kindness to the wronged is never
Without its excellent reward,
Holy to human-kind and ever
Acceptable to God.

To Faneuil Hall

Men! if manhood still ye claim,
If the Northern pulse can thrill,
Roused by wrong or stung by shame,
Freely, strongly still;
Let the sounds of traffic die:
Shut the mill-gate, leave the stall,
Fling the axe and hammer by;
Throng to Faneuil Hall!

Wrongs which freemen never brooked,
Dangers grim and fierce as they,
Which, like couching lions, looked
On your fathers' way;
These your instant zeal demand,
Shaking with their earthquake-call
Every rood of Pilgrim land,
Ho, to Faneuil Hall!

From your capes and sandy bars,
From your mountain-ridges cold,
Through whose pines the westering stars
Stoop their crowns of gold;
Come, and with your footsteps wake
Echoes from that holy wall;
Once again, for Freedom's sake,
Rock your fathers' hall!

Up, and tread beneath your feet
Every cord by party spun:
Let your hearts together beat
As the heart of one.
Banks and tariffs, stocks and trade,
Let them rise or let them fall:
Freedom asks your common aid, —
Up, to Faneuil Hall!

Up, and let each voice that speaks
  Ring from thence to Southern plains,
Sharply as the blow which breaks
  Prison-bolts and chains!
Speak as well becomés the free:
  Dreaded more than steel or ball,
Shall your calmest utterance be,
  Heard from Faneuil Hall!

Have they wronged us? Let us then
  Render back nor threats nor prayers;
Have they chained our free-born men?
  Let us unchain theirs!
Up, your banner leads the van,
  Blazoned, "Liberty for all!"
Finish what your sires began!
  Up, to Faneuil Hall!

The Slave-Ships

"That fatal, that perfidious bark,
Built i' the eclipse, and rigged with curses dark."

MILTON'S *Lycidas.*

"The French ship Le Rodeur, with a crew of twenty-two men, and with one hundred and sixty Negro slaves, sailed from Bonny, in Africa, April, 1819. On approaching the line, a terrible malady broke out, — an obstinate disease of the eyes, — contagious, and altogether beyond the resources of medicine. It was aggravated by the scarcity of water among the slaves (only half a wine-glass per day being allowed to an individual), and by the extreme impurity of the air in which they breathed. By the advice of the physician, they were brought upon deck occasionally; but some of the poor wretches, locking themselves in each other's arms, leaped overboard, in the hope, which so universally prevails among them, of being swiftly transported to their own homes in Africa. To check this, the captain ordered several, who were stopped in the attempt, to be shot, or hanged, before their companions. The disease extended to the crew; and one after another were smitten with it, until only *one* remained unaffected. Yet even this dreadful condition did not preclude calculation: to save the expense of supporting slaves rendered unsalable, and to obtain grounds for a claim against the underwriters, *thirty-six of the Negroes, having become blind, were thrown into the sea and drowned!" — Speech of M. Benjamin Constant, in the French Chamber of Deputies,* June 17, 1820.

In the midst of their dreadful fears lest the solitary individual whose sight remained unaffected should also be seized with the malady, a sail was discovered. It was the Spanish slaver, Leon. The same disease had been there; and, horrible to tell, all the crew had become blind! Unable to assist each other, the vessels parted. The Spanish ship has never since been heard of. The Rodeur reach Guadaloupe on the 21st of June; the only man who had escaped the disease, and had thus been enabled to steer the slaver into port, caught it in three days after its arrival. — *Bibliothèque Ophthalmologique* for November, 1819.

"All ready?" cried the captain;
 "Ay, ay!" the seamen said;
"Heave up the worthless lubbers, —
 The dying and the dead."
Up from the slave-ship's prison
 Fierce, bearded heads were thrust;
"Now let the sharks look to it, —
 Toss up the dead ones first!"

Corpse after corpse came up, —
 Death had been busy there;
Where every blow is mercy,
 Why should the spoiler spare?
Corpse after corpse they cast
 Sullenly from the ship,
Yet bloody with the traces
 Of fetter-link and whip.

Gloomily stood the captain,
 With his arms upon his breast,
With his cold brow sternly knotted
 And his iron lip compressed.
"Are all the dead dogs over?"
 Growled through that matted lip;
"The blind ones are no better,
 Let's lighten the good ship."

Hark! from the ship's dark bosom,
 The very sounds of hell!
The ringing clank of iron,
 The maniac's short, sharp yell!
The hoarse, low curse, throat-stifled;
 The starving infant's moan,
The horror of a breaking heart
 Poured through a mother's groan.

Up from that loathsome prison
 The stricken blind ones came;
Below, had all been darkness,
 Above, was still the same.
Yet the holy breath of heaven
 Was sweetly breathing there,
And the heated brow of fever
 Cooled in the soft sea air.

"Overboard with them, shipmates!"
  Cutlass and dirk were plied;
Fettered and blind, one after one,
  Plunged down the vessel's side.
The sabre smote above,
  Beneath, the lean shark lay,
Waiting with wide and bloody jaw
  His quick and human prey.

God of the earth! what cries
  Rang upward unto thee?
Voices of agony and blood,
  From ship-deck and from sea.
The last dull plunge was heard,
  The last wave caught its stain,
And the unsated shark looked up
  For human hearts in vain.

Red glowed the western waters,
  The setting sun was there,
Scattering alike on wave and cloud
  His fiery mesh of hair.
Amidst a group in blindness,
  A solitary eye
Gazed, from the burdened slaver's deck,
  Into that burning sky.

"A storm," spoke out the gazer,
  "Is gathering and at hand;
Curse on't, I'd give my other eye
  For one firm rood of land."
And then he laughed, but only
  His echoed laugh replied,
For the blinded and the suffering
  Alone were at his side.

Night settled on the waters,
  And on a stormy heaven,
While fiercely on that lone ship's track
  The thunder-gust was driven.
"A sail! — thank God, a sail!"
  And as the helmsman spoke,
Up through the stormy murmur
  A shout of gladness broke.

Down came the stranger vessel,
Unheeding on her way,
So near that on the slaver's deck
Fell off her driven spray.
"Ho! for the love of mercy,
We're perishing and blind!"
A wail of utter agony
Came back upon the wind:

"Help us! for we are stricken
With blindness every one;
Ten days we've floated fearfully,
Unnoting star or sun.
Our ship's the slaver Leon, —
We've but a score on board;
Our slaves are all gone over, —
Help, for the love of God!"

On livid brows of agony
The broad red lightning shone;
But the roar of wind and thunder
Stifled the answering groan;
Wailed from the broken waters
A last despairing cry,
As, kindling in the stormy light,
The stranger ship went by.

In the sunny Guadaloupe
A dark-hulled vessel lay,
With a crew who noted never
The nightfall or the day.
The blossom of the orange
Was white by every stream,
And tropic leaf, and flower, and bird
Were in the warm sunbeam.

And the sky was bright as ever,
And the moonlight slept as well,
On the palm-trees by the hillside,
And the streamlet of the dell:
And the glances of the Creole
Were still as archly deep,
And her smiles as full as ever
Of passion and of sleep.

But vain were bird and blossom,
 The green earth and the sky,
And the smile of human faces,
 To the slaver's darkened eye;
At the breaking of the morning,
 At the star-lit evening time,
O'er a world of light and beauty
 Fell the blackness of his crime.

Expostulation

Our fellow-countrymen in chains!
 Slaves, in a land of light and law!
Slaves, crouching on the very plains
 Where rolled the storm of Freedom's war!
A groan from Eutaw's haunted wood,
 A wail where Camden's martyrs fell,
By every shrine of patriot blood,
 From Moultrie's wall and Jasper's well!

By storied hill and hallowed grot,
 By mossy wood and marshy glen,
Whence rang of old the rifle-shot,
 And hurrying shout of Marion's men!
The groan of breaking hearts is there,
 The falling lash, the fetter's clank!
Slaves, slaves are breathing in that air
 Which old De Kalb and Sumter drank!

What ho! our countrymen in chains!
 The whip on woman's shrinking flesh!
Our soil yet reddening with the stains
 Caught from her scourging, warm and fresh!
What! mothers from their children riven!
 What! God's own image bought and sold!
Americans to market driven,
 And bartered as the brute for gold!

Speak! shall their agony of prayer
 Come thrilling to our hearts in vain?
To us whose fathers scorned to bear
 The paltry menace of a chain;
To us, whose boast is loud and long

Of holy Liberty and Light;
Say, shall these writhing slaves of Wrong
Plead vainly for their plundered Right?

What! shall we send, with lavish breath,
Our sympathies across the wave,
Where Manhood, on the field of death,
Strikes for his freedom or a grave?
Shall prayers go up, and hymns be sung
For Greece, the Moslem fetter spurning,
And millions hail with pen and tongue
Our light on all her altars burning?

Shall Belgium feel, and gallant France,
By Vendome's pile and Schoenbrun's wall,
And Poland, gasping on her lance,
The impulse of our cheering call?
And shall the slave, beneath our eye,
Clank o'er our fields his hateful chain?
And toss his fettered arms on high,
And groan for Freedom's gift, in vain?

Oh, say, shall Prussia's banner be
A refuge for the stricken slave?
And shall the Russian serf go free
By Baikal's lake and Neva's wave?
And shall the wintry-bosomed Dane
Relax the iron hand of pride,
And bid his bondmen cast the chain
From fettered soul and limb aside?

Shall every flap of England's flag
Proclaim that all around are free,
From farthest Ind to each blue crag
That beetles o'er the Western Sea?
And shall we scoff at Europe's kings,
When Freedom's fire is dim with us,
And round our country's altar clings
The damning shade of Slavery's curse?

Go, let us ask of Constantine
To loose his grasp on Poland's throat;
And beg the lord of Mahmoud's line
To spare the struggling Suliote;

Will not the scorching answer come
From turbaned Turk, and scornful Russ:
"Go, loose your fettered slaves at home,
Then turn and ask the like of us!"

Just God! and shall we calmly rest,
The Christian's scorn, the heathen's mirth,
Content to live the lingering jest
And by-word of a mocking Earth?
Shall our own glorious land retain
That curse which Europe scorns to bear?
Shall our own brethren drag the chain
Which not even Russia's menials wear?

Up, then, in Freedom's manly part,
From graybeard eld to fiery youth,
And on the nation's naked heart
Scatter the living coals of Truth!
Up! while ye slumber, deeper yet
The shadow of our fame is growing!
Up! while ye pause, our sun may set
In blood around our altars flowing!

Oh! rouse ye, ere the storm comes forth,
The gathered wrath of God and man,
Like that which wasted Egypt's earth,
When hail and fire above it ran.
Hear ye no warnings in the air?
Feel ye no earthquake underneath?
Up, up! why will ye slumber where
The sleeper only wakes in death?

Rise now for Freedom! not in strife
Like that your sterner fathers saw,
The awful waste of human life,
The glory and the guilt of war:
But break the chain, the yoke remove,
And smite to earth Oppression's rod,
With those mild arms of Truth and Love,
Made mighty through the living God!

Down let the shrine of Moloch sink,
And leave no traces where it stood;
Nor longer let its idol drink
His daily cup of human blood;

But rear another altar there,
To Truth and Love and Mercy given,
And Freedom's gift, and Freedom's prayer,
Shall call an answer down from Heaven!

Hymn

O Thou, whose presence went before
Our fathers in their weary way,
As with Thy chosen moved of yore
The fire by night, the cloud by day!

When from each temple of the free,
A nation's song ascends to Heaven,
Most Holy Father! unto Thee
May not our humble prayer be given?

Thy children all, though hue and form
Are varied in Thine own good will,
With Thy own holy breathings warm,
And fashioned in Thine image still.

We thank Thee, Father! hill and plain
Around us wave their fruits once more,
And clustered vine and blossomed grain
Are bending round each cottage door.

And peace is here; and hope and love
Are round us as a mantle thrown,
And unto Thee, supreme above,
The knee of prayer is bowed alone.

But oh, for those this day can bring,
As unto us, no joyful thrill;
For those who, under Freedom's wing,
Are bound in Slavery's fetters still:

For those to whom Thy written word
Of light and love is never given;
For those whose ears have never heard
The promise and the hope of heaven!

For broken heart, and clouded mind,
Whereon no human mercies fall;
Oh, be Thy gracious love inclined,
Who, as a Father, pitiest all!

And grant, O Father! that the time
Of Earth's deliverance may be near,
When every land and tongue and clime
The message of Thy love shall hear;

When, smitten as with fire from heaven,
The captive's chain shall sink in dust,
And to his fettered soul be given
The glorious freedom of the just!

The Yankee Girl

She sings by her wheel at that low cottage-door,
Which the long evening shadow is stretching before,
With a music as sweet as the music which seems
Breathed softly and faint in the ear of our dreams!

How brilliant and mirthful the light of her eye,
Like a star glancing out from the blue of the sky!
And lightly and freely her dark tresses play
O'er a brow and a bosom as lovely as they!

Who comes in his pride to that low cottage-door,
The haughty and rich to the humble and poor?
'Tis the great Southern planter, the master who waves
His whip of dominion o'er hundreds of slaves.

"Nay, Ellen, for shame! Let those Yankee fools spin,
Who would pass for our slaves with a change of their skin;
Let them toil as they will at the loom or the wheel,
Too stupid for shame, and too vulgar to feel!

"But thou art too lovely and precious a gem
To be bound to their burdens and sullied by them;
For shame, Ellen, shame, cast thy bondage aside,
And away to the South, as my blessing and pride.

"Oh, come where no winter thy footsteps can wrong,
But where flowers are blossoming all the year long,
Where the shade of the palm-tree is over my home,
And the lemon and orange are white in their bloom!

"Oh, come to my home, where my servants shall all
Depart at thy bidding and come at thy call;

They shall heed thee as mistress with trembling and awe,
And each wish of thy heart shall be felt as a law."

Oh, could ye have seen her — that pride of our girls —
Arise and cast back the dark wealth of her curls,
With a scorn in her eye which the gazer could feel,
And a glance like the sunshine that flashes on steel!

"Go back, haughty Southron! thy treasures of gold
Are dim with the blood of the hearts thou hast sold;
Thy home may be lovely, but round it I hear
The crack of the whip and the footsteps of fear!

"And the sky of thy South may be brighter than ours,
And greener thy landscapes, and fairer thy flowers;
But dearer the blast round our mountains which raves,
Than the sweet summer zephyr which breathes over slaves!

"Full low at thy bidding thy Negroes may kneel,
With the iron of bondage on spirit and heel;
Yet know that the Yankee girl sooner would be
In fetters with them, than in freedom with thee!"

The Hunters of Men

Have ye heard of our hunting, o'er mountain and glen,
Through cane-brake and forest, — the hunting of men?
The lords of our land to this hunting have gone,
As the fox-hunter follows the sound of the horn;
Hark! the cheer and the hallo! the crack of the whip,
And the yell of the hound as he fastens his grip!
All blithe are our hunters, and noble their match,
Though hundreds are caught, there are millions to catch.
So speed to their hunting, o'er mountain and glen,
Through cane-brake and forest, — the hunting of men!

Gay luck to our hunters! how nobly they ride
In the glow of their zeal, and the strength of their pride!
The priest with his cassock flung back on the wind,
Just screening the politic statesman behind;
The saint and the sinner, with cursing and prayer,
The drunk and the sober, ride merrily there.
And woman, kind woman, wife, widow, and maid,

For the good of the hunted, is lending her aid:
Her foot's in the stirrup, her hand on the rein,
How blithely she rides to the hunting of men!

Oh, goodly and grand is our hunting to see,
In this "land of the brave and this home of the free."
Priest, warrior, and statesman, from Georgia to Maine,
All mounting the saddle, all grasping the rein;
Right merrily hunting the black man, whose sin
Is the curl of his hair and the hue of his skin!
Woe, now, to the hunted who turns him at bay!
Will our hunters be turned from their purpose and prey?
Will their hearts fail within them? their nerves tremble, when
All roughly they ride to the hunting of men?

Ho! alms for our hunters! all weary and faint,
Wax the curse of the sinner and prayer of the saint.
The horn is wound faintly, the echoes are still,
Over cane-brake and river, and forest and hill.
Haste, alms for our hunters! the hunted once more
Have turned from their flight with their backs to the shore:
What right have they here in the home of the white,
Shadowed o'er by our banner of Freedom and Right?
Ho! alms for the hunters! or never again
Will they ride in their pomp to the hunting of men!

Alms, alms for our hunters! why will ye delay,
When their pride and their glory are melting away?
The parson has turned; for, on charge of his own,
Who goeth a warfare, or hunting, alone?
The politic statesman looks back with a sigh,
There is doubt in his heart, there is fear in his eye.
Oh, haste, lest that doubting and fear shall prevail,
And the head of his steed take the place of the tail.
Oh, haste, ere he leave us! for who will ride then,
For pleasure or gain, to the hunting of men?

Stanzas for the Times

Is this the land our fathers loved,
  The freedom which they toiled to win?
Is this the soil whereon they moved?
  Are these the graves they slumber in?

Are we the sons by whom are borne
The mantles which the dead have worn?

And shall we crouch above these graves,
  With craven soul and fettered lip?
Yoke in with marked and branded slaves,
  And tremble at the driver's whip?
Bend to the earth our pliant knees,
And speak but as our masters please?

Shall outraged Nature cease to feel?
  Shall Mercy's tears no longer flow?
Shall ruffian threats of cord and steel,
  The dungeon's gloom, the assassin's blow,
Turn back the spirit roused to save
The Truth, our Country, and the slave?

Of human skulls that shrine was made,
  Round which the priests of Mexico
Before their loathsome idol prayed;
  Is Freedom's altar fashioned so?
And must we yield to Freedom's God,
As offering meet, the Negro's blood?

Shall tongue be mute, when deeds are wrought
  Which well might shame extremest hell?
Shall freemen lock the indignant thought?
  Shall Pity's bosom cease to swell?
Shall Honor bleed? — shall Truth succumb?
Shall pen, and press, and soul be dumb?

No; by each spot of haunted ground,
  Where Freedom weeps her children's fall;
By Plymouth's rock, and Bunker's mound;
  By Griswold's stained and shattered wall;
By Warren's ghost, by Langdon's shade;
By all the memories of our dead!

By their enlarging souls, which burst
  The bands and fetters round them set;
By the free Pilgrim spirit nursed
  Within our inmost bosoms, yet,
By all above, around, below,
Be ours the indignant answer, — No!

No; guided by our country's laws,
For truth, and right, and suffering man,
Be ours to strive in Freedom's cause,
As Christians may, as freemen can!
Still pouring on unwilling ears
That truth oppression only fears.

What! shall we guard our neighbor still,
While woman shrieks beneath his rod,
And while he tramples down at will
The image of a common God?
Shall watch and ward be round him set,
Of Northern nerve and bayonet?

And shall we know and share with him
The danger and the growing shame?
And see our Freedom's light grow dim,
Which should have filled the world with flame?
And, writhing, feel, where'er we turn,
A world's reproach around us burn?

Is't not enough that this is borne?
And asks our haughty neighbor more?
Must fetters which his slaves have worn
Clank round the Yankee farmer's door?
Must he be told, beside his plough,
What he must speak, and when, and how?

Must he be told his freedom stands
On Slavery's dark foundations strong;
On breaking hearts and fettered hands,
On robbery, and crime, and wrong?
That all his fathers taught is vain, —
That Freedom's emblem is the chain?

Its life, its soul, from slavery drawn!
False, foul, profane! Go, teach as well
Of holy Truth from Falsehood born!
Of Heaven refreshed by airs from Hell!
Of Virtue in the arms of Vice!
Of Demons planting Paradise!

Rail on, then, brethren of the South,
Ye shall not hear the truth the less;

No seal is on the Yankee's mouth,
No fetter on the Yankee's press!
From our Green Mountains to the sea,
One voice shall thunder, We are free!

Clerical Oppressors

In the report of the celebrated pro-slavery meeting in Charleston, S.C., on the 4th of the ninth month, 1835, published in the *Courier* of that city, it is stated: "The clergy of all denominations attended in a body, lending their sanction to the proceedings, and adding by their presence to the impressive character of the scene!"

Just God! and these are they
Who minister at thine altar, God of Right!
Men who their hands with prayer and blessing lay
On Israel's Ark of light!

What! preach, and kidnap men?
Give thanks, and rob thy own afflicted poor?
Talk of thy glorious liberty, and then
Bolt hard the captive's door?

What, servants of thy own
Merciful Son, who came to seek and save
The homeless and the outcast, fettering down
The tasked and plundered slave!

Pilate and Herod, friends!
Chief priests and rulers, as of old, combine!
Just God and holy! is that church, which lends
Strength to the spoiler, thine?

Paid hypocrites, who turn
Judgment aside, and rob the Holy Book
Of those high words of truth which search and burn
In warning and rebuke;

Feed fat, ye locusts, feed!
And, in your tasselled pulpits, thank the Lord
That, from the toiling bondman's utter need,
Ye pile your own full board.

How long, O Lord! how long
Shall such a priesthood barter truth away,

And in Thy name, for robbery and wrong
At Thy own altars pray?

Is not Thy hand stretched forth
Visibly in the heavens, to awe and smite?
Shall not the living God of all the earth,
And heaven above, do right?

Woe, then, to all who grind
Their brethren of a common Father down!
To all who plunder from the immortal mind
Its bright and glorious crown!

Woe to the priesthood! woe
To those whose hire is with the price of blood;
Perverting, darkening, changing, as they go,
The searching truths of God!

Their glory and their might
Shall perish; and their very names shall be
Vile before all the people, in the light
Of a world's liberty.

Oh, speed the moment on
When Wrong shall cease, and Liberty and Love
And Truth and Right throughout the earth be known
As in their home above.

The Moral Warfare

When Freedom, on her natal day,
Within her war-rocked cradle lay,
An iron race around her stood,
Baptized her infant brow in blood;
And, through the storm which round her swept,
Their constant ward and watching kept.

Then, where our quiet herds repose,
The roar of baleful battle rose,
And brethren of a common tongue
To mortal strife as tigers sprung,
And every gift on Freedom's shrine
Was man for beast, and blood for wine!

Our fathers to their graves have gone;
Their strife is past, their triumph won;
But sterner trials wait the race
Which rises in their honored place;
A moral warfare with the crime
And folly of an evil time.

So let it be. In God's own might
We gird us for the coming fight,
And, strong in Him whose cause is ours
In conflict with unholy powers,
We grasp the weapons He has given, —
The Light, and Truth, and Love of Heaven.

The Farewell OF A VIRGINIA SLAVE MOTHER TO HER DAUGHTERS SOLD INTO SOUTHERN BONDAGE

Gone, gone, — sold and gone,
To the rice-swamp dank and lone.
Where the slave-whip ceaseless swings,
Where the noisome insect stings,
Where the fever demon strews
Poison with the falling dews,
Where the sickly sunbeams glare
Through the hot and misty air;
Gone, gone, — sold and gone,
To the rice-swamp dank and lone,
From Virginia's hills and waters;
Woe is me, my stolen daughters!

Gone, gone, — sold and gone,
To the rice-swamp dank and lone.
There no mother's eye is near them,
There no mother's ear can hear them;
Never, when the torturing lash
Seams their back with many a gash,
Shall a mother's kindness bless them,
Or a mother's arms caress them.
Gone, gone, — sold and gone,
To the rice-swamp dank and lone,
From Virginia's hills and waters;
Woe is me, my stolen daughters!

Gone, gone, — sold and gone,
To the rice-swamp dank and lone.
Oh, when weary, sad, and slow,
From the fields at night they go,
Faint with toil, and racked with pain,
To their cheerless homes again,
There no brother's voice shall greet them;
There no father's welcome meet them.
Gone, gone, — sold and gone,
To the rice-swamp dank and lone,
From Virginia's hills and waters;
Woe is me, my stolen daughters!

Gone, gone, — sold and gone,
To the rice-swamp dank and lone.
From the tree whose shadow lay
On their childhood's place of play;
From the cool spring where they drank;
Rock, and hill, and rivulet bank;
From the solemn house of prayer,
And the holy counsels there;
Gone, gone, — sold and gone,
To the rice-swamp dank and lone,
From Virginia's hills and waters;
Woe is me, my stolen daughters!

Gone, gone, — sold and gone,
To the rice-swamp dank and lone;
Toiling through the weary day,
And at night the spoiler's prey.
Oh, that they had earlier died,
Sleeping calmly, side by side,
Where the tyrant's power is o'er,
And the fetter galls no more!
Gone, gone, — sold and gone,
To the rice-swamp dank and lone,
From Virginia's hills and waters;
Woe is me my stolen daughters!

Gone, gone, — sold and gone,
To the rice-swamp dank and lone.
By the holy love He beareth;
By the bruisëd reed He spareth;
Oh, may He, to whom alone

All their cruel wrongs are known,
Still their hope and refuge prove,
With a more than mother's love.
Gone, gone, — sold and gone,
To the rice-swamp dank and lone,
From Virginia's hills and waters;
Woe is me, my stolen daughters!

Pennsylvania Hall

Read at the dedication of Pennsylvania Hall, Philadelphia, May 15, 1838. The building was erected by an association of gentlemen, irrespective of sect or party, "that the citizens of Philadelphia should possess a room wherein the principles of Liberty, and Equality of Civil Rights, could be freely discussed, and the evils of slavery fearlessly portrayed." On the evening of the 17th it was burned by a mob, destroying the office of the *Pennsylvania Freeman,* of which I was editor, and with it my books and papers.

Not with the splendors of the days of old,
The spoil of nations, and barbaric gold;
No weapons wrested from the fields of blood,
Where dark and stern the unyielding Roman stood,
And the proud eagles of his cohorts saw
A world, war-wasted, crouching to his law;
Nor blazoned car, nor banners floating gay,
Like those which swept along the Appian Way,
When, to the welcome of imperial Rome,
The victor warrior came in triumph home,
And trumpet peal, and shoutings wild and high,
Stirred the blue quiet of the Italian sky;
But calm and grateful, prayerful and sincere,
As Christian freemen only, gathering here,
We dedicate our fair and lofty Hall,
Pillar and arch, entablature and wall,
As Virtue's shrine, as Liberty's abode,
Sacred to Freedom, and to Freedom's God!
Far statelier Halls, 'neath brighter skies than these,
Stood darkly mirrored in the Ægean seas,
Pillar and shrine, and life-like statues seen,
Graceful and pure, the marble shafts between;
Where glorious Athens from her rocky hill
Saw Art and Beauty subject to her will;
And the chaste temple, and the classic grove,
The hall of sages, and the bowers of love,
Arch, fane, and column, graced the shores, and gave

Their shadows to the blue Saronic wave;
And statelier rose on Tiber's winding side,
The Pantheon's dome, the Coliseum's pride,
The Capitol, whose arches backward flung
The deep, clear cadence of the Roman tongue,
Whence stern decrees, like words of fate, went forth
To the awed nations of a conquered earth,
Where the proud Cæsars in their glory came,
And Brutus lightened from his lips of flame!
Yet in the porches of Athena's halls,
And in the shadow of her stately walls,
Lurked the sad bondman, and his tears of woe
Wet the cold marble with unheeded flow;
And fetters clanked beneath the silver dome
Of the proud Pantheon of imperious Rome.
Oh, not for him, the chained and stricken slave,
By Tiber's shore, or blue Ægina's wave,
In the thronged forum, or the sages' seat,
The bold lip pleaded, and the warm heart beat;
No soul of sorrow melted at his pain,
No tear of pity rusted on his chain!

But this fair Hall to Truth and Freedom given,
Pledged to the Right before all Earth and Heaven,
A free arena for the strife of mind,
To caste, or sect, or color unconfined,
Shall thrill with echoes such as ne'er of old
From Roman hall or Grecian temple rolled;
Thoughts shall find utterance such as never yet
The Propylea or the Forum met.
Beneath its roof no gladiator's strife
Shall win applauses with the waste of life;
Nor lordly lictor urge the barbarous game,
No wanton Lais glory in her shame.
But here the tear of sympathy shall flow,
As the ear listens to the tale of woe;
Here in stern judgment of the oppressor's wrong
Shall strong rebukings thrill on Freedom's tongue,
No partial justice hold th' unequal scale,
No pride of caste a brother's rights assail,
No tyrant's mandates echo from this wall,
Holy to Freedom and the Rights of All!
But a fair field, where mind may close with mind,
Free as the sunshine and the chainless wind;

Where the high trust is fixed on Truth alone,
And bonds and fetters from the soul are thrown;
Where wealth, and rank, and worldly pomp, and might,
Yield to the presence of the True and Right.

And fitting is it that this Hall should stand
Where Pennsylvania's Founder led his band,
From thy blue waters, Delaware! — to press
The virgin verdure of the wilderness.
Here, where all Europe with amazement saw
The soul's high freedom trammelled by no law;
Here, where the fierce and warlike forestmen
Gathered, in peace, around the home of Penn,
Awed by the weapons Love alone had given
Drawn from the holy armory of Heaven;
Where Nature's voice against the bondman's wrong
First found an earnest and indignant tongue;
Where Lay's bold message to the proud was borne;
And Keith's rebuke, and Franklin's manly scorn!
Fitting it is that here, where Freedom first
From her fair feet shook off the Old World's dust,
Spread her white pinions to our Western blast,
And her free tresses to our sunshine cast,
One Hall should rise redeemed from Slavery's ban,
One Temple sacred to the Rights of Man!

Oh! if the spirits of the parted come,
Visiting angels, to their olden home;
If the dead fathers of the land look forth
From their fair dwellings, to the things of earth,
Is it a dream, that with their eyes of love,
They gaze now on us from the bowers above?
Lay's ardent soul, and Benezet the mild,
Steadfast in faith, yet gentle as a child,
Meek-hearted Woolman, and that brother-band,
The sorrowing exiles from their "Fatherland,"
Leaving their homes in Krieshiem's bowers of vine,
And the blue beauty of their glorious Rhine,
To seek amidst our solemn depths of wood
Freedom from man, and holy peace with God;
Who first of all their testimonial gave
Against the oppressor, for the outcast slave,
Is it a dream that such as these look down,
And with their blessing our rejoicings crown?

Let us rejoice, that while the pulpit's door
Is barred against the pleaders for the poor;
While the Church, wrangling upon points of faith,
Forgets her bondmen suffering unto death;
While crafty Traffic and the lust of Gain
Unite to forge Oppression's triple chain,
One door is open, and one Temple free,
As a resting-place for hunted Liberty!
Where men may speak, unshackled and unawed,
High words of Truth, for Freedom and for God.
And when that truth its perfect work hath done,
And rich with blessings o'er our land hath gone;
When not a slave beneath his yoke shall pine,
From broad Potomac to the far Sabine:
When unto angel lips at last is given
The silver trump of Jubilee in Heaven;
And from Virginia's plains, Kentucky's shades,
And through the dim Floridian everglades,
Rises, to meet that angel-trumpet's sound,
The voice of millions from their chains unbound;
Then, though this Hall be crumbling in decay,
Its strong walls blending with the common clay,
Yet round the ruins of its strength shall stand
The best and noblest of a ransomed land —
Pilgrims, like these who throng around the shrine
Of Mecca, or of holy Palestine!
A prouder glory shall that ruin own
Than that which lingers round the Parthenon.
Here shall the child of after years be taught
The works of Freedom which his fathers wrought;
Told of the trials of the present hour,
Our weary strife with prejudice and power;
How the high errand quickened woman's soul,
And touched her lip as with a living coal;
How Freedom's martyrs kept their lofty faith
True and unwavering, unto bonds and death;
The pencil's art shall sketch the ruined Hall,
The Muses' garland crown its aged wall,
And History's pen for after times record
Its consecration unto Freedom's God!

The Christian Slave

In a publication of L. F. Tasistro — *Random Shots and Southern Breezes* — is a description of a slave auction at New Orleans, at which the auctioneer recommended the woman on the stand as "a good Christian!" It was not uncommon to see advertisements of slaves for sale, in which they were described as pious or as members of the church. In one advertisement a slave was noted as "a Baptist preacher."

A Christian! going, gone!
Who bids for God's own image? for his grace,
Which that poor victim of the market-place,
Hath in her suffering won?

My God! can such things be?
Hast Thou not said that whatsoe'er is done
Unto Thy weakest and Thy humblest one
Is even done to Thee?

In that sad victim, then,
Child of Thy pitying love, I see Thee stand;
Once more the jest-word of a mocking band,
Bound, sold, and scourged again!

A Christian up for sale!
Wet with her blood your whips, o'ertask her frame,
Make her life loathsome with your wrong and shame,
Her patience shall not fail!

A heathen hand might deal
Back on your heads the gathered wrong of years:
But her low, broken prayer and nightly tears,
Ye neither heed nor feel.

Con well thy lesson o'er,
Thou prudent teacher, tell the toiling slave
No dangerous tale of Him who came to save
The outcast and the poor.

But wisely shut the ray
Of God's free Gospel from her simple heart,
And to her darkened mind alone impart
One stern command, Obey!

So shalt thou deftly raise
The market price of human flesh; and while
On thee, their pampered guest, the planters smile,
Thy church shall praise.

Grave, reverend men shall tell
From Northern pulpits how thy work was blest,
While in that vile South Sodom first and best,
Thy poor disciples sell.

Oh, shame! the Moslem thrall,
Who, with his master, to the Prophet kneels,
While turning to the sacred Kebla feels
His fetters break and fall.

Cheers for the turbaned Bey
Of robber-peopled Tunis! he hath torn
The dark slave-dungeons open, and hath borne
Their inmates into day:

But our poor slave in vain
Turns to the Christian shrine his aching eyes;
Its rites will only swell his market price,
And rivet on his chain.

God of all right! how long
Shall priestly robbers at Thine altar stand,
Lifting in prayer to Thee the bloody hand
And haughty brow of wrong?

Oh, from the fields of cane,
From the low rice-swamp, from the trader's cell;
From the black slave-ship's foul and loathsome hell,
And coffle's weary chain;

Hoarse, horrible, and strong,
Rises to Heaven that agonizing cry,
Filling the arches of the hollow sky,
How long, O God, how long?

To William Lloyd Garrison

Champion of those who groan beneath
Oppression's iron hand:
In view of penury, hate, and death,
I see thee fearless stand.
Still bearing up thy lofty brow,
In the steadfast strength of truth,
In manhood sealing well the vow
And promise of thy youth.

[TO WILLIAM LLOYD GARRISON]

Go on, for thou hast chosen well;
On in the strength of God!
Long as one human heart shall swell
Beneath the tyrant's rod.
Speak in a slumbering nation's ear,
As thou hast ever spoken,
Until the dead in sin shall hear,
The fetter's link be broken!

I love thee with a brother's love,
I feel my pulses thrill,
To mark thy spirit soar above
The cloud of human ill.
My heart hath leaped to answer thine,
And echo back thy words,
As leaps the warrior's at the shine
And flash of kindred swords!

They tell me thou art rash and vain,
A searcher after fame;
That thou art striving but to gain
A long-enduring name;
That thou hast nerved the Afric's hand
And steeled the Afric's heart,
To shake aloft his vengeful brand,
And rend his chain apart.

Have I not known thee well, and read
Thy mighty purpose long?
And watched the trials which have made
Thy human spirit strong?
And shall the slanderer's demon breath
Avail with one like me,
To dim the sunshine of my faith
And earnest trust in thee?

Go on, the dagger's point may glare
Amid thy pathway's gloom;
The fate which sternly threatens there
Is glorious martyrdom!
Then onward with a martyr's zeal;
And wait thy sure reward
When man to man no more shall kneel,
And God alone be Lord!

To Massachusetts

What though around thee blazes
No fiery rallying sign?
From all thy own high places,
Give heaven the light of thine!
What though unthrilled, unmoving,
The statesman stand apart,
And comes no warm approving
From Mammon's crowded mart?

Still let the land be shaken
By a summons of thine own!
By all save truth forsaken,
Stand fast with that alone!
Shrink not from strife unequal!
With the best is always hope;
And ever in the sequel
God holds the right side up!

But when, with thine uniting,
Come voices long and loud,
And far-off hills are writing
Thy fire-words on the cloud;
When from Penobscot's fountains
A deep response is heard,
And across the Western mountains
Rolls back thy rallying word;

Shall thy line of battle falter,
With its allies just in view?
Oh, by hearth and holy altar,
My fatherland, be true!
Fling abroad thy scrolls of Freedom!
Speed them onward far and fast!
Over hill and valley speed them,
Like the sibyl's on the blast!

Lo! the Empire State is shaking
The shackles from her hand;
With the rugged North is waking
The level sunset land!
On they come, the free battalions!
East and West and North they come,
And the heart-beat of the millions
Is the beat of Freedom's drum.

"To the tyrant's plot no favor!
No heed to place-fed knaves!
Bar and bolt the door forever
Against the land of slaves!"
Hear it, mother Earth, and hear it,
The heavens above us spread!
The land is roused, — its spirit
Was sleeping, but not dead!

New Hampshire

God bless New Hampshire! from her granite peaks
Once more the voice of Stark and Langdon speaks.
The long-bound vassal of the exulting South
For very shame her self-forged chain has broken;
Torn the black seal of slavery from her mouth,
And in the clear tones of her old time spoken!
Oh, all undreamed-of, all unhoped-for changes!
The tyrant's ally proves his sternest foe;
To all his biddings, from her mountain ranges,
New Hampshire thunders an indignant No!
Who is it now despairs? Oh, faint of heart,
Look upward to those Northern mountains cold,
Flouted by Freedom's victor-flag unrolled,
And gather strength to bear a manlier part!
All is not lost. The angel of God's blessing
Encamps with Freedom on the field of fight;
Still to her banner, day by day, are pressing
Unlooked-for allies, striking for the right!
Courage, then, Northern hearts! Be firm, be true:
What one brave State hath done, can ye not also do?

To a Southern Statesman

John C. Calhoun, who had strongly urged the extension of slave territory by the annexation of Texas, even if it should involve a war with England, was unwilling to promote the acquisition of Oregon, which would enlarge the Northern domain of freedom, and pleaded as an excuse the peril of foreign complications which he had defied when the interests of slavery were involved.

Is this thy voice whose treble notes of fear
Wail in the wind? And dost thou shake to hear,
Actæon-like, the bay of thine own hounds,

Spurning the leash, and leaping o'er their bounds?
Sore-baffled statesman! when thy eager hand,
With game afoot, unslipped the hungry pack,
To hunt down Freedom in her chosen land,
Hadst thou no fear, that, erelong, doubling back,
These dogs of thine might snuff on Slavery's track?
Where's now the boast, which even thy guarded tongue,
Cold, calm, and proud, in the teeth o' the Senate flung,
O'er the fulfilment of thy baleful plan,
Like Satan's triumph at the fall of man?
How stood'st thou then, thy feet on Freedom planting,
And pointing to the lurid heaven afar,
Whence all could see, through the south windows slanting,
Crimson as blood, the beams of that Lone Star!
The Fates are just; they give us but our own;
Nemesis ripens what our hands have sown.
There is an Eastern story, not unknown,
Doubtless, to thee, of one whose magic skill
Called demons up his water-jars to fill;
Deftly and silently, they did his will,
But, when the task was done, kept pouring still.
In vain with spell and charm the wizard wrought,
Faster and faster were the buckets brought,
Higher and higher rose the flood around,
Till the fiends clapped their hands above their master drowned!
So, Carolinian, it may prove with thee,
For God still overrules man's schemes, and takes
Craftiness in its self-set snare, and makes
The wrath of man to praise Him. It may be,
That the roused spirits of Democracy
May leave to freer States the same wide door
Through which thy slave-cursed Texas entered in,
From out the blood and fire, the wrong and sin,
Of the stormed city and the ghastly plain,
Beat by hot hail, and wet with bloody rain,
The myriad-handed pioneer may pour,
And the wild West with the roused North combine
And heave the engineer of evil with his mine.

To Delaware

Thrice welcome to thy sisters of the East,
  To the strong tillers of a rugged home,
With spray-wet locks to Northern winds released,
  And hardy feet o'erswept by ocean's foam;
And to the young nymphs of the golden West,
  Whose harvest mantles, fringed with prairie bloom,
Trail in the sunset, — O redeemed and blest,
  To the warm welcome of thy sisters come!
Broad Pennsylvania, down her sail-white bay
  Shall give thee joy, and Jersey from her plains,
And the great lakes, where echo, free alway,
  Moaned never shoreward with the clank of chains,
Shall weave new sun-bows in their tossing spray,
And all their waves keep grateful holiday.
And, smiling on thee through her mountain rains,
  Vermont shall bless thee; and the granite peaks,
And vast Katahdin o'er his woods, shall wear
Their snow-crowns brighter in the cold, keen air;
  And Massachusetts, with her rugged cheeks
O'errun with grateful tears, shall turn to thee,
  When, at thy bidding, the electric wire
  Shall tremble northward with its words of fire;
Glory and praise to God! another State is free!

The Lost Statesman

As they who, tossing midst the storm at night,
  While turning shoreward, where a beacon shone,
  Meet the walled blackness of the heaven alone,
So, on the turbulent waves of party tossed,
In gloom and tempest, men have seen thy light
  Quenched in the darkness. At thy hour of noon,
While life was pleasant to thy undimmed sight,
And, day by day, within thy spirit grew
A holier hope than young Ambition knew,
As through thy rural quiet, not in vain,
Pierced the sharp thrill of Freedom's cry of pain,
  Man of the millions, thou art lost too soon!
Portents at which the bravest stand aghast, —
The birth-throes of a Future, strange and vast,
  Alarm the land; yet thou, so wise and strong,
Suddenly summoned to the burial bed,
  Lapped in its slumbers deep and ever long,

Hear'st not the tumult surging overhead.
Who now shall rally Freedom's scattering host?
Who wear the mantle of the leader lost?
Who stay the march of slavery? He whose voice
  Hath called thee from thy task-field shall not lack
  Yet bolder champions, to beat bravely back
The wrong which, through his poor ones, reaches Him:
Yet firmer hands shall Freedom's torchlights trim,
  And wave them high across the abysmal black,
Till bound, dumb millions there shall see them and rejoice.

The Crisis

Across the Stony Mountains, o'er the desert's drouth and sand,
The circles of our empire touch the western ocean's strand;
From slumberous Timpanogos, to Gila, wild and free,
Flowing down from Nuevo-Leon to California's sea;
And from the mountains of the east, to Santa Rosa's shore,
The eagles of Mexitli shall beat the air no more.

O Vale of Rio Bravo! Let thy simple children weep;
Close watch about their holy fire let maids of Pecos keep;
Let Taos send her cry across Sierra Madre's pines,
And Santa Barbara toll her bells amidst her corn and vines;
For lo! the pale land-seekers come, with eager eyes of gain,
Wide scattering, like the bison herds on broad Salada's plain.

Let Sacramento's herdsmen heed what sound the winds bring down
Of footsteps on the crisping snow, from cold Nevada's crown!
Full hot and fast the Saxon rides, with rein of travel slack,
And, bending o'er his saddle, leaves the sunrise at his back;
By many a lonely river, and gorge of fir and pine,
On many a wintry hill-top, his nightly camp-fires shine.

O countrymen and brothers! that land of lake and plain,
Of salt wastes alternating with valleys fat with grain;
Of mountains white with winter, looking downward, cold, serene,
On their feet with spring-vines tangled and lapped in softest green;
Swift through whose black volcanic gates, o'er many a sunny vale,
Wind-like the Arapahoe sweeps the bison's dusty trail!

Great spaces yet untravelled, great lakes whose mystic shores
The Saxon rifle never heard, nor dip of Saxon oars;

Great herds that wander all unwatched, wild steeds that none have
tamed,
Strange fish in unknown streams, and birds the Saxon never named;
Deep mines, dark mountain crucibles, where Nature's chemic powers
Work out the Great Designer's will; all these ye say are ours!

Forever ours! for good or ill, on us the burden lies:
God's balance, watched by angels, is hung across the skies.
Shall Justice, Truth, and Freedom turn the poised and trembling scale?
Or shall the Evil triumph, and robber Wrong prevail?
Shall the broad land o'er which our flag in starry splendor waves,
Forego through us its freedom, and bear the tread of slaves?

The day is breaking in the East of which the prophets told,
And brightens up the sky of Time the Christian Age of Gold;
Old Might to Right is yielding, battle blade to clerkly pen,
Earth's monarchs are her peoples, and her serfs stand up as men;
The isles rejoice together, in a day are nations born,
And the slave walks free in Tunis, and by Stamboul's Golden Horn!

Is this, O countrymen of mine! a day for us to sow
The soil of new-gained empire with slavery's seeds of woe?
To feed with our fresh life-blood the Old World's cast-off crime,
Dropped, like some monstrous early birth, from the tired lap of Time?
To run anew the evil race the old lost nations ran,
And die like them of unbelief of God, and wrong of man?

Great Heaven! Is this our mission? End in this the prayers and tears,
The toil, the strife, the watchings of our younger, better years?
Still as the Old World rolls in light, shall ours in shadow turn,
A beamless Chaos, cursed of God, through outer darkness borne?
Where the far nations looked for light, a blackness in the air?
Where for words of hope they listened, the long wail of despair?

The Crisis presses on us; face to face with us it stands,
With solemn lips of question, like the Sphinx in Egypt's sands!
This day we fashion Destiny, our web of Fate we spin;
This day for all hereafter choose we holiness or sin;
Even now from starry Gerizim, or Ebal's cloudy crown,
We call the dews of blessing or the bolts of cursing down!

By all for which the martyrs bore their agony and shame;
By all the warning words of truth with which the prophets came;
By the Future which awaits us; by all the hopes which cast

Their faint and trembling beams across the blackness of the Past;
And by the blessed thought of Him who for Earth's freedom died,
O my people! O my brothers! let us choose the righteous side.

So shall the Northern pioneer go joyful on his way;
To wed Penobscot's waters to San Francisco's bay,
To make the rugged places smooth, and sow the vales with grain;
And bear, with Liberty and Law, the Bible in his train:
The mighty West shall bless the East, and sea shall answer sea,
And mountain unto mountain call, Praise God, for we are free!

A Sabbath Scene

This poem finds its justification in the readiness with which, even in the North, clergymen urged the prompt execution of the Fugitive Slave Law as a Christian duty, and defended the system of slavery as a Bible institution.

Scarce had the solemn Sabbath-bell
  Ceased quivering in the steeple,
Scarce had the parson to his desk
  Walked stately through his people,

When down the summer-shaded street
  A wasted female figure,
With dusky brow and naked feet,
  Came rushing wild and eager.

She saw the white spire through the trees,
  She heard the sweet hymn swelling:
O pitying Christ! a refuge give
  That poor one in Thy dwelling!

Like a scared fawn before the hounds,
  Right up the aisle she glided,
While close behind her, whip in hand,
  A lank-haired hunter strided.

She raised a keen and bitter cry,
  To Heaven and Earth appealing;
Were manhood's generous pulses dead?
  Had woman's heart no feeling?

A score of stout hands rose between
  The hunter and the flying:

Age clenched his staff, and maiden eyes
Flashed tearful, yet defying.

"Who dares profane this house and day?"
Cried out the angry pastor.
"Why, bless your soul, the wench's a slave,
And I'm her lord and master!

"I've law and gospel on my side,
And who shall dare refuse me?"
Down came the parson, bowing low,
"My good sir, pray excuse me!

"Of course I know your right divine
To own and work and whip her;
Quick, deacon, throw that Polyglott
Before the wench, and trip her!"

Plump dropped the holy tome, and o'er
Its sacred pages stumbling,
Bound hand and foot, a slave once more,
The hapless wretch lay trembling.

I saw the parson tie the knots,
The while his flock addressing,
The Scriptural claims of slavery
With text on text impressing.

"Although," said he, "on Sabbath day
All secular occupations
Are deadly sins, we must fulfil
Our moral obligations:

"And this commends itself as one
To every conscience tender;
As Paul sent back Onesimus,
My Christian friends, we send her!"

Shriek rose on shriek, — the Sabbath air
Her wild cries tore asunder;
I listened, with hushed breath, to hear
God answering with his thunder!

All still! the very altar's cloth
  Had smothered down her shrieking,
And, dumb, she turned from face to face,
  For human pity seeking!

I saw her dragged along the aisle,
  Her shackles harshly clanking;
I heard the parson, over all,
  The Lord devoutly thanking!

My brain took fire: "Is this," I cried,
  "The end of prayer and preaching?
Then down with pulpit, down with priest,
  And give us Nature's teaching!

"Foul shame and scorn be on ye all
  Who turn the good to evil,
And steal the Bible from the Lord,
  To give it to the Devil!

"Than garbled text or parchment law
  I own a statute higher;
And God is true, though every book
  And every man's a liar!"

Just then I felt the deacon's hand
  In wrath my coat-tail seize on;
I heard the priest cry, "Infidel!"
  The lawyer mutter, "Treason!"

I started up, — where now were church,
  Slave, master, priest, and people?
I only heard the supper-bell,
  Instead of clanging steeple.

But, on the open window's sill,
  O'er which the white blooms drifted,
The pages of a good old Book
  The wind of summer lifted,

And flower and vine, like angel wings
  Around the Holy Mother,
Waved softly there, as if God's truth
  And Mercy kissed each other.

And freely from the cherry-bough
Above the casement swinging,
With golden bosom to the sun,
The oriole was singing.

As bird and flower made plain of old
The lesson of the Teacher,
So now I heard the written Word
Interpreted by Nature!

For to my ear methought the breeze
Bore Freedom's blessed word on;
Thus saith the Lord: Break every yoke,
Undo the heavy burden!

The Rendition

On the 2d of June, 1854, Anthony Burns, a fugitive slave from Virginia, after being under arrest for ten days in the Boston Court House, was remanded to slavery under the Fugitive Slave Act, and taken down State Street to a steamer chartered by the United States Government, under guard of United States troops and artillery, Massachusetts militia and Boston police. Public excitement ran high, a futile attempt to rescue Burns having been made during his confinement, and the streets were crowded with tens of thousands of people, of whom many came from other towns and cities of the State to witness the humiliating spectacle.

I heard the train's shrill whistle call,
I saw an earnest look beseech,
And rather by that look than speech
My neighbor told me all.

And, as I thought of Liberty
Marched handcuffed down that sworded street,
The solid earth beneath my feet
Reeled fluid as the sea.

I felt a sense of bitter loss, —
Shame, tearless grief, and stifling wrath,
And loathing fear, as if my path
A serpent stretched across.

All love of home, all pride of place,
All generous confidence and trust,
Sank smothering in that deep disgust
And anguish of disgrace.

Down on my native hills of June,
And home's green quiet, hiding all,
Fell sudden darkness like the fall
Of midnight upon noon!

And Law, an unloosed maniac, strong,
Blood-drunken, through the blackness trod,
Hoarse-shouting in the ear of God
The blasphemy of wrong.

"O Mother, from thy memories proud,
Thy old renown, dear Commonwealth,
Lend this dead air a breeze of health,
And smite with stars this cloud.

"Mother of Freedom, wise and brave,
Rise awful in thy strength," I said;
Ah me! I spake but to the dead;
I stood upon her grave!

The Kansas Emigrants

This poem and the three following were called out by the popular movement of Free State men to occupy the territory of Kansas, and by the use of the great democratic weapon – an overpowering majority – to settle the conflict on that ground between Freedom and Slavery. The opponents of the movement used another kind of weapon.

We cross the prairie as of old
The Pilgrims crossed the sea,
To make the West, as they the East,
The homestead of the free!

We go to rear a wall of men
On Freedom's southern line,
And plant beside the cotton-tree
The rugged Northern pine!

We're flowing from our native hills
As our free rivers flow:
The blessing of our Mother-land
Is on us as we go.

We go to plant her common schools
On distant prairie swells,
And give the Sabbaths of the wild
The music of her bells.

Upbearing, like the Ark of old,
The Bible in our van,
We go to test the truth of God
Against the fraud of man.

No pause, nor rest, save where the streams
That feed the Kansas run,
Save where our Pilgrim gonfalon
Shall flout the setting sun!

We'll tread the prairie as of old
Our fathers sailed the sea,
And make the West, as they the East,
The homestead of the free!

For Righteousness' Sake

The age is dull and mean. Men creep,
Not walk; with blood too pale and tame
To pay the debt they owe to shame;
Buy cheap, sell dear; eat, drink, and sleep
Down-pillowed, deaf to moaning want;
Pay tithes for soul-insurance; keep
Six days to Mammon, one to Cant.

In such a time, give thanks to God,
That somewhat of the holy rage
With which the prophets in their age
On all its decent seemings trod,
Has set your feet upon the lie,
That man and ox and soul and clod
Are market stock to sell and buy!

The hot words from your lips, my own,
To caution trained, might not repeat;
But if some tares among the wheat
Of generous thought and deed were sown,
No common wrong provoked your zeal;

The silken gauntlet that is thrown
In such a quarrel rings like steel.

The brave old strife the fathers saw
For Freedom calls for men again
Like those who battled not in vain
For England's Charter, Alfred's law;
And right of speech and trial just
Wage in your name their ancient war
With venal courts and perjured trust.

God's ways seem dark, but, soon or late,
They touch the shining hills of day;
The evil cannot brook delay,
The good can well afford to wait.
Give ermined knaves their hour of crime:
Ye have the future grand and great,
The safe appeal of Truth to Time!

Le Marais du Cygne

The massacre of unarmed and unoffending men, in Southern Kansas, in May, 1858, took place near the Marais du Cygne of the French *voyageurs.*

A blush as of roses
Where rose never grew!
Great drops on the bunch-grass,
But not of the dew!
A taint in the sweet air
For wild bees to shun!
A stain that shall never
Bleach out in the sun!

Back, steed of the prairies!
Sweet song-bird, fly back!
Wheel hither, bald vulture!
Gray wolf, call thy pack!
The foul human vultures
Have feasted and fled;
The wolves of the Border
Have crept from the dead.

From the hearths of their cabins,
  The fields of their corn,
Unwarned and unweaponed,
  The victims were torn, —
By the whirlwind of murder
  Swooped up and swept on
To the low, reedy fen-lands,
  The Marsh of the Swan.

With a vain plea for mercy
  No stout knee was crooked;
In the mouths of the rifles
  Right manly they looked.
How paled the May sunshine,
  O Marais du Cygne!
On death for the strong life,
  On red grass for green!

In the homes of their rearing,
  Yet warm with their lives,
Ye wait the dead only,
  Poor children and wives!
Put out the red forge-fire,
  The smith shall not come;
Unyoke the brown oxen,
  The ploughman lies dumb.

Wind slow from the Swan's Marsh,
  O dreary death-train,
With pressed lips as bloodless
  As lips of the slain!
Kiss down the young eyelids,
  Smooth down the gray hairs;
Let tears quench the curses
  That burn through your prayers.

Strong man of the prairies,
  Mourn bitter and wild!
Wail, desolate woman!
  Weep, fatherless child!
But the grain of God springs up
  From ashes beneath,
And the crown of his harvest
  Is life out of death.

Not in vain on the dial
The shade moves along,
To point the great contrasts
Of right and of wrong:
Free homes and free altars,
Free prairie and flood, —
The reeds of the Swan's Marsh,
Whose bloom is of blood!

On the lintels of Kansas
That blood shall not dry;
Henceforth the Bad Angel
Shall harmless go by;
Henceforth to the sunset,
Unchecked on her way,
Shall Liberty follow
The march of the day.

Thy Will Be Done

We see not, know not; all our way
Is night, — with Thee alone is day:
From out the torrent's troubled drift,
Above the storm our prayers we lift,
Thy will be done!

The flesh may fail, the heart may faint,
But who are we to make complaint,
Or dare to plead, in times like these,
The weakness of our love of ease?
Thy will be done!

We take with solemn thankfulness
Our burden up, nor ask it less,
And count it joy that even we
May suffer, serve, or wait for Thee,
Whose will be done!

Though dim as yet in tint and line,
We trace Thy picture's wise design,
And thank Thee that our age supplies
Its dark relief of sacrifice.
Thy will be done!

And if, in our unworthiness,
Thy sacrificial wine we press;
If from Thy ordeal's heated bars
Our feet are seamed with crimson scars,
Thy will be done!

If, for the age to come, this hour
Of trial hath vicarious power,
And, blest by Thee, our present pain
Be Liberty's eternal gain,
Thy will be done!

Strike, Thou the Master, we Thy keys,
The anthem of the destinies!
The minor of Thy loftier strain,
Our hearts shall breathe the old refrain,
Thy will be done!

At Port Royal

In November, 1861, a Union force under Commodore Dupont and General Sherman captured Port Royal, and from this point as a basis of operations the neighboring islands between Charleston and Savannah were taken possession of. The early occupation of this district, where the Negro population was greatly in excess of the white, gave an opportunity which was at once seized upon, of practically emancipating the slaves and of beginning that work of civilization which was accepted as the grave responsibility of those who had labored for freedom.

The tent-lights glimmer on the land,
The ship-lights on the sea;
The night-wind smooths with drifting sand
Our track on lone Tybee.

At last our grating keels outslide,
Our good boats forward swing;
And while we ride the land-locked tide,
Our Negroes row and sing.

For dear the bondman holds his gifts
Of music and of song:
The gold that kindly Nature sifts
Among his sands of wrong;

The power to make his toiling days
 And poor home-comforts please;
The quaint relief of mirth that plays
 With sorrow's minor keys.

Another glow than sunset's fire
 Has filled the west with light,
Where field and garner, barn and byre,
 Are blazing through the night.

The land is wild with fear and hate,
 The rout runs mad and fast;
From hand to hand, from gate to gate
 The flaming brand is passed.

The lurid glow falls strong across
 Dark faces broad with smiles:
Not theirs the terror, hate, and loss
 That fire yon blazing piles.

With oar-strokes timing to their song,
 They weave in simple lays
The pathos of remembered wrong,
 The hope of better days, —

The triumph-note that Miriam sung,
 The joy of uncaged birds:
Softening with Afric's mellow tongue
 Their broken Saxon words.

SONG OF THE NEGRO BOATMEN

Oh, praise an' tanks! De Lord He come
 To set de people free;
An' massa tink it day ob doom,
 An' we ob jubilee.
De Lord dat heap de Red Sea waves
 He jus' as 'trong as den;
He say de word: we las' night slaves;
 To-day, de Lord's free men.
  De yam will grow, de cotton blow,
   We'll hab de rice an' corn;
  Oh nebber you fear, if nebber you hear
   De driver blow his horn!

Ole massa on he trabbels gone;
He leaf de land behind:
De Lord's breff blow him furder on,
Like corn-shuck in de wind.
We own de hoe, we own de plough,
We own de hands dat hold;
We sell de pig, we sell de cow,
But nebber chile be sold.
De yam will grow, de cotton blow,
We'll hab de rice an' corn;
Oh nebber you fear, if nebber you hear
De driver blow his horn!

We pray de Lord: He gib us signs
Dat some day we be free;
De norf-wind tell it to de pines,
De wild-duck to de sea;
We tink it when de church-bell ring,
We dream it in de dream;
De rice-bird mean it when he sing,
De eagle when he scream.
De yam will grow, de cotton blow,
We'll hab de rice an' corn;
Oh nebber you fear, if nebber you hear
De driver blow his horn!

We know de promise nebber fail,
An' nebber lie de word;
So, like de 'postles in de jail,
We waited for de Lord:
An' now He open ebery door,
An' trow away de key;
He tink we lub Him so before,
We lub Him better free.
De yam will grow, de cotton blow,
He'll gib de rice an' corn;
Oh nebber you fear, if nebber you hear
De driver blow his horn!

So sing our dusky gondoliers;
And with a secret pain,
And smiles that seem akin to tears,
We hear the wild refrain.

We dare not share the Negro's trust,
  Nor yet his hope deny;
We only know that God is just,
  And every wrong shall die.

Rude seems the song; each swarthy face,
  Flame-lighted, ruder still:
We start to think that hapless race
  Must shape our good or ill;

That laws of changeless justice bind
  Oppressor with oppressed;
And, close as sin and suffering joined,
  We march to Fate abreast.

Sing on, poor hearts! your chant shall be
  Our sign of blight or bloom,
The Vala-song of Liberty,
  Or death-rune of our doom!

Laus Deo!

On hearing the bells ring on the passage of the constitutional amendment abolishing slavery. The resolution was adopted by Congress, January 31, 1865. The ratification by the requisite number of States was announced December 18, 1865.

It is done!
  Clang of bell and roar of gun
Send the tidings up and down.
  How the belfries rock and reel!
  How the great guns, peal on peal,
Fling the joy from town to town!

Ring, O bells!
  Every stroke exulting tells
Of the burial hour of crime.
  Loud and long, that all may hear,
  Ring for every listening ear
Of Eternity and Time!

Let us kneel:
  God's own voice is in that peal,
And this spot is holy ground.

Lord, forgive us! What are we,
That our eyes this glory see,
That our ears have heard the sound!

For the Lord
On the whirlwind is abroad;
In the earthquake He has spoken;
He has smitten with His thunder
The iron walls asunder,
And the gates of brass are broken!

Loud and long
Lift the old exulting song;
Sing with Miriam by the sea,
He has cast the mighty down;
Horse and rider sink and drown;
"He hath triumphed gloriously!"

Did we dare,
In our agony of prayer,
Ask for more than He has done?
When was ever His right hand
Over any time or land
Stretched as now beneath the sun?

How they pale,
Ancient myth and song and tale,
In this wonder of our days,
When the cruel rod of war
Blossoms white with righteous law,
And the wrath of man is praise!

Blotted out!
All within and all about
Shall a fresher life begin;
Freer breathe the universe
As it rolls its heavy curse
On the dead and buried sin!

It is done!
In the circuit of the sun
Shall the sound thereof go forth.
It shall bid the sad rejoice,
It shall give the dumb a voice,
It shall belt with joy the earth!

Ring and swing,
Bells of joy! On morning's wing
Send the song of praise abroad!
With a sound of broken chains
Tell the nations that He reigns,
Who alone is Lord and God!

Hymn FOR THE CELEBRATION OF EMANCIPATION AT NEWBURYPORT

Not unto us who did but seek
The word that burned within to speak,
Not unto us this day belong
The triumph and exultant song.

Upon us fell in early youth
The burden of unwelcome truth,
And left us, weak and frail and few,
The censor's painful work to do.

Thenceforth our life a fight became,
The air we breathed was hot with blame;
For not with gauged and softened tone
We made the bondman's cause our own.

We bore, as Freedom's hope forlorn,
The private hate, the public scorn;
Yet held through all the paths we trod
Our faith in man and trust in God.

We prayed and hoped; but still, with awe,
The coming of the sword we saw;
We heard the nearing steps of doom,
We saw the shade of things to come.

In grief which they alone can feel
Who from a mother's wrong appeal,
With blended lines of fear and hope
We cast our country's horoscope.

For still within her house of life
We marked the lurid sign of strife,

And, poisoning and imbittering all,
We saw the star of Wormwood fall.

Deep as our love for her became
Our hate of all that wrought her shame,
And if, thereby, with tongue and pen
We erred, — we were but mortal men.

We hoped for peace; our eyes survey
The blood-red dawn of Freedom's day:
We prayed for love to loose the chain;
'Tis shorn by battle's axe in twain!

Nor skill nor strength nor zeal of ours
Has mined and heaved the hostile towers;
Not by our hands is turned the key
That sets the sighing captives free.

A redder sea than Egypt's wave
Is piled and parted for the slave;
A darker cloud moves on in light;
A fiercer fire is guide by night!

The praise, O Lord! is Thine alone,
In Thy own way Thy work is done!
Our poor gifts at Thy feet we cast,
To whom be glory, first and last!

The Hive at Gettysburg

In the old Hebrew myth the lion's frame,
So terrible alive,
Bleached by the desert's sun and wind, became
The wandering wild bees' hive;
And he who, lone and naked-handed, tore
Those jaws of death apart,
In after time drew forth their honeyed store
To strengthen his strong heart.

Dead seemed the legend: but it only slept
To wake beneath our sky;
Just on the spot whence ravening Treason crept
Back to its lair to die,

Bleeding and torn from Freedom's mountain bounds,
A stained and shattered drum
Is now the hive where, on their flowery rounds,
The wild bees go and come.

Unchallenged by a ghostly sentinel,
They wander wide and far,
Along green hillsides, sown with shot and shell,
Through vales once choked with war.
The low reveille of their battle-drum
Disturbs no morning prayer:
With deeper peace in summer noons their hum
Fills all the drowsy air.

And Samson's riddle is our own to-day,
Of sweetness from the strong,
Of union, peace, and freedom plucked away
From the rent jaws of wrong.
From Treason's death we draw a purer life,
As, from the beast he slew,
A sweetness sweeter for his bitter strife
The old-time athlete drew!

The Jubilee Singers

A number of students of Fisk University, under the direction of one of the officers, gave a series of concerts in the Northern States, for the purpose of establishing the college on a firmer financial foundation. Their hymns and songs, mostly in a minor key, touched the hearts of the people, and were received as peculiarly expressive of a race delivered from bondage.

Voice of a people suffering long,
The pathos of their mournful song,
The sorrow of their night of wrong!

Their cry like that which Israel gave,
A prayer for one to guide and save,
Like Moses by the Red Sea's wave!

The stern accord her timbrel lent
To Miriam's note of triumph sent
O'er Egypt's sunken armament!

The tramp that startled camp and town,
And shook the walls of slavery down,
The spectral march of old John Brown!

The storm that swept through battle-days,
The triumph after long delays,
The bondmen giving God the praise!

Voice of a ransomed race, sing on
Till Freedom's every right is won,
And slavery's every wrong undone!

The Poems of John Greenleaf Whittier

VI

REMINISCENCE AND REFORM

The Editor's Commentary

As Whittier grew in years the mood of reminiscence grew in depth. "The Barefoot Boy" was published in his fiftieth year; "In School-Days" in his sixty-third. Both poems recreate the poet's own boyhood; their unaffected artlessness, their retrospective simplicity have made them part of our household literature.

Whittier was fonder of "Memories," another expression of backward-longing reverie. He placed it at the head of his *Poems Subjective and Reminiscent*. Although the romance it embalmed was early and short-lived, it remained dear to the remembering blood; "I hardly knew whether to publish it," wrote Whittier, "it was so personal and near my heart."

Some of the "Songs of Labor" proceed from the author's crusading consciousness, and at least one of them ("The Shoemakers") was written from experience, a reminder of the time when the youth earned his tuition at Haverhill Academy by making carpet slippers.

The passion for reform did not die until Whittier was deep in his twilight. "Astræa" and "The Peace of Europe" are contrasting poems of despair and hope. Together they are as timely today as when they were written almost a hundred years ago.

The Barefoot Boy

Blessings on thee, little man,
Barefoot boy, with cheek of tan!
With thy turned-up pantaloons,
And thy merry whistled tunes;
With thy red lip, redder still
Kissed by strawberries on the hill;
With the sunshine on thy face,
Through thy torn brim's jaunty grace;
From my heart I give thee joy, —
I was once a barefoot boy!
Prince thou art, — the grown-up man
Only is republican.
Let the million-dollared ride!
Barefoot, trudging at his side,
Thou hast more than he can buy
In the reach of ear and eye, —
Outward sunshine, inward joy:
Blessings on thee, barefoot boy!

Oh for boyhood's painless play,
Sleep that wakes in laughing day,
Health that mocks the doctor's rules,
Knowledge never learned of schools,
Of the wild bee's morning chase,
Of the wild-flower's time and place,
Flight of fowl and habitude
Of the tenants of the wood;
How the tortoise bears his shell,
How the woodchuck digs his cell,
And the ground-mole sinks his well;
How the robin feeds her young,
How the oriole's nest is hung;
Where the whitest lilies blow,
Where the freshest berries grow,
Where the ground-nut trails its vine,
Where the wood-grape's clusters shine;
Of the black wasp's cunning way,
Mason of his walls of clay,
And the architectural plans
Of gray hornet artisans!
For, eschewing books and tasks,
Nature answers all he asks;
Hand in hand with her he walks,
Face to face with her he talks,

Part and parcel of her joy, —
Blessings on the barefoot boy!

Oh for boyhood's time of June,
Crowding years in one brief moon,
When all things I heard or saw,
Me, their master, waited for.
I was rich in flowers and trees,
Humming-birds and honey-bees;
For my sport the squirrel played,
Plied the snouted mole his spade;
For my taste the blackberry cone
Purpled over hedge and stone;
Laughed the brook for my delight
Through the day and through the night,
Whispering at the garden wall,
Talked with me from fall to fall;
Mine the sand-rimmed pickerel pond,
Mine the walnut slopes beyond,
Mine, on bending orchard trees,
Apples of Hesperides!
Still as my horizon grew,
Larger grew my riches too;
All the world I saw or knew
Seemed a complex Chinese toy,
Fashioned for a barefoot boy!

Oh for festal dainties spread,
Like my bowl of milk and bread;
Pewter spoon and bowl of wood,
On the door-stone, gray and rude!
O'er me, like a regal tent,
Cloudy-ribbed, the sunset bent,
Purple-curtained, fringed with gold,
Looped in many a wind-swung fold;
While for music came the play
Of the pied frogs' orchestra;
And, to light the noisy choir,
Lit the fly his lamp of fire.
I was monarch: pomp and joy
Waited on the barefoot boy!

Cheerily, then, my little man,
Live and laugh, as boyhood can!

Though the flinty slopes be hard,
Stubble-speared the new-mown sward,
Every morn shall lead thee through
Fresh baptisms of the dew;
Every evening from thy feet
Shall the cool wind kiss the heat:
All too soon these feet must hide
In the prison cells of pride,
Lose the freedom of the sod,
Like a colt's for work be shod,
Made to tread the mills of toil,
Up and down in ceaseless moil:
Happy if their track be found
Never on forbidden ground;
Happy if they sink not in
Quick and treacherous sands of sin.
Ah! that thou couldst know thy joy,
Ere it passes, barefoot boy!

In School-Days

Still sits the school-house by the road,
A ragged beggar sleeping;
Around it still the sumachs grow,
And blackberry-vines are creeping.

Within, the master's desk is seen,
Deep scarred by raps official;
The warping floor, the battered seats,
The jack-knife's carved initial;

The charcoal frescos on its wall;
Its door's worn sill, betraying
The feet that, creeping slow to school,
Went storming out to playing!

Long years ago a winter sun
Shone over it at setting;
Lit up its western window-panes,
And low eaves' icy fretting.

It touched the tangled golden curls,
And brown eyes full of grieving,

Of one who still her steps delayed
When all the school were leaving.

For near her stood the little boy
Her childish favor singled:
His cap pulled low upon a face
Where pride and shame were mingled.

Pushing with restless feet the snow
To right and left, he lingered; —
As restlessly her tiny hands
The blue-checked apron fingered.

He saw her lift her eyes; he felt
The soft hand's light caressing,
And heard the tremble of her voice,
As if a fault confessing.

"I'm sorry that I spelt the word:
I hate to go above you,
Because," — the brown eyes lower fell, —
"Because, you see, I love you!"

Still memory to a gray-haired man
That sweet child-face is showing.
Dear girl! the grasses on her grave
Have forty years been growing!

He lives to learn, in life's hard school,
How few who pass above him
Lament their triumph and his loss,
Like her, — because they love him.

Memories

A beautiful and happy girl,
With step as light as summer air,
Eyes glad with smiles, and brow of pearl,
Shadowed by many a careless curl
Of unconfined and flowing hair;
A seeming child in everything,
Save thoughtful brow and ripening charms,
As Nature wears the smile of Spring
When sinking into Summer's arms.

THE BAREFOOT BOY

Laughed the brook for my delight
Through the day and through the night

A mind rejoicing in the light
  Which melted through its graceful bower,
Leaf after leaf, dew-moist and bright,
And stainless in its holy white,
  Unfolding like a morning flower:
A heart, which, like a fine-toned lute,
  With every breath of feeling woke,
And, even when the tongue was mute,
  From eye and lip in music spoke.

How thrills once more the lengthening chain
  Of memory, at the thought of thee!
Old hopes which long in dust have lain,
Old dreams, come thronging back again,
  And boyhood lives again in me;
I feel its glow upon my cheek,
  Its fulness of the heart is mine,
As when I leaned to hear thee speak,
  Or raised my doubtful eye to thine.

I hear again thy low replies,
  I feel thy arm within my own,
And timidly again uprise
The fringëd lids of hazel eyes,
  With soft brown tresses overblown.
Ah! memories of sweet summer eves,
  Of moonlit wave and willowy way,
Of stars and flowers, and dewy leaves,
  And smiles and tones more dear than they!

Ere this, thy quiet eye hath smiled
  My picture of thy youth to see,
When, half a woman, half a child,
Thy very artlessness beguiled,
  And folly's self seemed wise in thee;
I too can smile, when o'er that hour
  The lights of memory backward stream,
Yet feel the while that manhood's power
  Is vainer than my boyhood's dream.

Years have passed on, and left their trace,
  Of graver care and deeper thought;
And unto me the calm, cold face
Of manhood, and to thee the grace

Of woman's pensive beauty brought.
More wide, perchance, for blame than praise,
The school-boy's humble name has flown;
Thine, in the green and quiet ways
Of unobtrusive goodness known.

And wider yet in thought and deed
Diverge our pathways, one in youth;
Thine the Genevan's sternest creed,
While answers to my spirit's need
The Derby dalesman's simple truth.
For thee, the priestly rite and prayer,
And holy day, and solemn psalm;
For me, the silent reverence where
My brethren gather, slow and calm.

Yet hath thy spirit left on me
An impress Time has worn not out,
And something of myself in thee,
A shadow from the past, I see,
Lingering, even yet, thy way about;
Not wholly can the heart unlearn
That lesson of its better hours,
Not yet has Time's dull footstep worn
To common dust that path of flowers.

Thus, while at times before our eyes
The shadows melt, and fall apart,
And, smiling through them, round us lies
The warm light of our morning skies, —
The Indian Summer of the heart!
In secret sympathies of mind,
In founts of feeling which retain
Their pure, fresh flow, we yet may find
Our early dreams not wholly vain!

The Pumpkin

Oh, greenly and fair in the lands of the sun,
The vines of the gourd and the rich melon run,
And the rock and the tree and the cottage enfold,
With broad leaves all greenness and blossoms all gold,
Like that which o'er Nineveh's prophet once grew,

While he waited to know that his warning was true,
And longed for the storm-cloud, and listened in vain
For the rush of the whirlwind and red fire-rain.

On the banks of the Xenil the dark Spanish maiden
Comes up with the fruit of the tangled vine laden;
And the Creole of Cuba laughs out to behold
Through orange-leaves shining the broad spheres of gold;
Yet with dearer delight from his home in the North,
On the fields of his harvest the Yankee looks forth,
Where crook-necks are coiling and yellow fruit shines,
And the sun of September melts down on his vines.

Ah! on Thanksgiving day, when from East and from West,
From North and from South come the pilgrim and guest,
When the gray-haired New Englander sees round his board
The old broken links of affection restored,
When the care-wearied man seeks his mother once more,
And the worn matron smiles where the girl smiled before,
What moistens the lip and what brightens the eye?
What calls back the past, like the rich Pumpkin pie?

Oh, fruit loved of boyhood! the old days recalling,
When wood-grapes were purpling and brown nuts were falling!
When wild, ugly faces we carved in its skin,
Glaring out through the dark with a candle within!
When we laughed round the corn-heap, with hearts all in tune,
Our chair a broad pumpkin, — our lantern the moon,
Telling tales of the fairy who travelled like steam,
In a pumpkin-shell coach, with two rats for her team!

Then thanks for thy present! none sweeter or better
E'er smoked from an oven or circled a platter!
Fairer hands never wrought at a pastry more fine,
Brighter eyes never watched o'er its baking, than thine!
And the prayer, which my mouth is too full to express,
Swells my heart that thy shadow may never be less,
That the days of thy lot may be lengthened below,
And the fame of thy worth like a pumpkin-vine grow,
And thy life be as sweet, and its last sunset sky
Golden-tinted and fair as thy own Pumpkin pie!

Forgiveness

My heart was heavy, for its trust had been
Abused, its kindness answered with foul wrong;
So, turning gloomily from my fellowmen,
One summer Sabbath day I strolled among
The green mounds of the village burial-place;
Where, pondering how all human love and hate
Find one sad level; and how, soon or late,
Wronged and wrongdoer, each with meekened face,
And cold hands folded over a still heart,
Pass the green threshold of our common grave,
Whither all footsteps tend, whence none depart,
Awed for myself, and pitying my race,
Our common sorrow, like a mighty wave,
Swept all my pride away, and trembling I forgave!

My Psalm

I mourn no more my vanished years:
Beneath a tender rain,
An April rain of smiles and tears,
My heart is young again.

The west-winds blow, and, singing low,
I hear the glad streams run;
The windows of my soul I throw
Wide open to the sun.

No longer forward nor behind
I look in hope or fear;
But, grateful, take the good I find,
The best of now and here.

I plough no more a desert land,
To harvest weed and tare;
The manna dropping from God's hand
Rebukes my painful care.

I break my pilgrim staff, I lay
Aside the toiling oar;
The angel sought so far away
I welcome at my door.

The airs of spring may never play
Among the ripening corn,

AN AUTOGRAPH

I write my name as one,
On sands by waves o'errun

Nor freshness of the flowers of May
Blow through the autumn morn;

Yet shall the blue-eyed gentian look
Through fringëd lids to heaven,
And the pale aster in the brook
Shall see its image given; —

The woods shall wear their robes of praise,
The south-wind softly sigh,
And sweet, calm days in golden haze
Melt down the amber sky.

Not less shall manly deed and word
Rebuke an age of wrong;
The graven flowers that wreathe the sword
Make not the blade less strong.

But smiting hands shall learn to heal, —
To build as to destroy;
Nor less my heart for others feel
That I the more enjoy.

All as God wills, who wisely heeds
To give or to withhold,
And knoweth more of all my needs
Than all my prayers have told!

Enough that blessings undeserved
Have marked my erring track;
That whereso'er my feet have swerved,
His chastening turned me back;

That more and more a Providence
Of love is understood,
Making the springs of time and sense
Sweet with eternal good; —

That death seems but a covered way
Which opens into light,
Wherein no blinded child can stray
Beyond the Father's sight;

That care and trial seem at last,
Through Memory's sunset air,
Like mountain-ranges overpast,
In purple distance fair;

That all the jarring notes of life
Seem blending in a psalm,
And all the angles of its strife
Slow rounding into calm.

And so the shadows fall apart,
And so the west-winds play;
And all the windows of my heart
I open to the day.

The Waiting

I wait and watch: before my eyes
Methinks the night grows thin and gray;
I wait and watch the eastern skies
To see the golden spears uprise
Beneath the oriflamme of day!

Like one whose limbs are bound in trance
I hear the day-sounds swell and grow,
And see across the twilight glance,
Troop after troop, in swift advance,
The shining ones with plumes of snow!

I know the errand of their feet,
I know what mighty work is theirs;
I can but lift up hands unmeet
The threshing-floors of God to beat,
And speed them with unworthy prayers.

I will not dream in vain despair
The steps of progress wait for me:
The puny leverage of a hair
The planet's impulse well may spare,
A drop of dew the tided sea.

The loss, if loss there be, is mine,
And yet not mine if understood;

For one shall grasp and one resign,
One drink life's rue, and one its wine,
And God shall make the balance good.

Oh power to do! Oh baffled will!
Oh prayer and action! ye are one.
Who may not strive, may yet fulfil
The harder task of standing still,
And good but wished with God is done!

My Birthday

Beneath the moonlight and the snow
Lies dead my latest year;
The winter winds are wailing low
Its dirges in my ear.

I grieve not with the moaning wind
As if a loss befell;
Before me, even as behind,
God is, and all is well!

His light shines on me from above,
His low voice speaks within, —
The patience of immortal love
Outwearying mortal sin.

Not mindless of the growing years
Of care and loss and pain,
My eyes are wet with thankful tears
For blessings which remain.

If dim the gold of life has grown,
I will not count it dross,
Nor turn from treasures still my own
To sigh for lack and loss.

The years no charm from Nature take;
As sweet her voices call,
As beautiful her mornings break,
As fair her evenings fall.

Love watches o'er my quiet ways,
Kind voices speak my name,

And lips that find it hard to praise
Are slow, at least, to blame.

How softly ebb the tides of will!
How fields, once lost or won,
Now lie behind me green and still
Beneath a level sun!

How hushed the hiss of party hate,
The clamor of the throng!
How old, harsh voices of debate
Flow into rhythmic song!

Methinks the spirit's temper grows
Too soft in this still air;
Somewhat the restful heart foregoes
Of needed watch and prayer.

The bark by tempest vainly tossed
May founder in the calm,
And he who braved the polar frost
Faint by the isles of balm.

Better than self-indulgent years
The outflung heart of youth,
Than pleasant songs in idle ears
The tumult of the truth.

Rest for the weary hands is good,
And love for hearts that pine,
But let the manly habitude
Of upright souls be mine.

Let winds that blow from heaven refresh,
Dear Lord, the languid air;
And let the weakness of the flesh
Thy strength of spirit share.

And, if the eye must fail of light,
The ear forget to hear,
Make clearer still the spirit's sight,
More fine the inward ear!

Be near me in mine hours of need
To soothe, or cheer, or warn,
And down these slopes of sunset lead
As up the hills of morn!

At Eventide

Poor and inadequate the shadow-play
Of gain and loss, of waking and of dream,
Against life's solemn background needs must seem
At this late hour. Yet, not unthankfully,
I call to mind the fountains by the way,
The breath of flowers, the bird-song on the spray,
Dear friends, sweet human loves, the joy of giving
And of receiving, the great boon of living
In grand historic years when Liberty
Had need of word and work, quick sympathies
For all who fail and suffer, song's relief,
Nature's uncloying loveliness; and chief,
The kind restraining hand of Providence,
The inward witness, the assuring sense
Of an Eternal Good which overlies
The sorrow of the world, Love which outlives
All sin and wrong, Compassion which forgives
To the uttermost, and Justice whose clear eyes
Through lapse and failure look to the intent,
And judge our frailty by the life we meant.

Greeting

I spread a scanty board too late;
The old-time guests for whom I wait
Come few and slow, methinks, to-day.
Ah! who could hear my messages
Across the dim unsounded seas
On which so many have sailed away!

Come, then, old friends, who linger yet,
And let us meet, as we have met,
Once more beneath this low sunshine;
And grateful for the good we've known,
The riddles solved, the ills outgrown,
Shake hands upon the border line.

The favor, asked too oft before,
From your indulgent ears, once more
  I crave, and, if belated lays
To slower, feebler measures move,
The silent sympathy of love
  To me is dearer now than praise.

And ye, O younger friends, for whom
My hearth and heart keep open room,
  Come smiling through the shadows long,
Be with me while the sun goes down,
And with your cheerful voices drown
  The minor of my even-song.

For, equal through the day and night,
The wise Eternal oversight
  And love and power and righteous will
Remain: the law of destiny,
The best for each and all must be,
  And life its promise shall fulfil.

An Autograph

I write my name as one,
On sands by waves o'errun
Or winter's frosted pane,
Traces a record vain.

Oblivion's blankness claims
Wiser and better names,
And well my own may pass
As from the strand or glass.

Wash on, O waves of time!
Melt, noons, the frosty rime!
Welcome the shadow vast,
The silence that shall last!

When I and all who know
And love me vanish so,
What harm to them or me
Will the lost memory be?

If any words of mine,
Through right of life divine,
Remain, what matters it
Whose hand the message writ?

Why should the "crowner's quest"
Sit on my worst or best?
Why should the showman claim
The poor ghost of my name?

Yet, as when dies a sound
Its spectre lingers round,
Haply my spent life will
Leave some faint echo still.

A whisper giving breath
Of praise or blame to death,
Soothing or saddening such
As loved the living much.

Therefore with yearnings vain
And fond I still would fain
A kindly judgment seek,
A tender thought bespeak.

And, while my words are read,
Let this at least be said:
"Whate'er his life's defeatures,
He loved his fellow-creatures.

"If, of the Law's stone table,
To hold he scarce was able
The first great precept fast,
He kept for man the last.

"Through mortal lapse and dulness
What lacks the Eternal Fulness,
If still our weakness can
Love Him in loving man?

"Age brought him no despairing
Of the world's future faring;
In human nature still
He found more good than ill.

"To all who dumbly suffered,
His tongue and pen he offered;
His life was not his own,
Nor lived for self alone.

"Hater of din and riot
He lived in days unquiet;
And, lover of all beauty,
Trod the hard ways of duty.

"He meant no wrong to any,
He sought the good of many,
Yet knew both sin and folly,—
May God forgive him wholly!"

Abram Morrison

'Midst the men and things which will
Haunt an old man's memory still,
Drollest, quaintest of them all,
With a boy's laugh I recall
Good old Abram Morrison.

When the Grist and Rolling Mill
Ground and rumbled by Po Hill,
And the old red school-house stood
Midway in the Powow's flood,
Here dwelt Abram Morrison.

From the Beach to far beyond
Bear-Hill, Lion's Mouth and Pond,
Marvellous to our tough old stock,
Chips o' the Anglo-Saxon block,
Seemed the Celtic Morrison.

Mudknock, Balmawhistle, all
Only knew the Yankee drawl,
Never brogue was heard till when,
Foremost of his countrymen,
Hither came Friend Morrison;

Yankee born, of alien blood,
Kin of his had well withstood

ABRAM MORRISON

Underneath his hat's broad brim
Peered the queer old face of him

Pope and King with pike and ball
Under Derry's leaguered wall,
As became the Morrisons.

Wandering down from Nutfield woods
With his household and his goods,
Never was it clearly told
How within our quiet fold
Came to be a Morrison.

Once a soldier, blame him not
That the Quaker he forgot,
When, to think of battles won,
And the red-coats on the run,
Laughed aloud Friend Morrison.

From gray Lewis over sea
Bore his sires their family tree,
On the rugged boughs of it
Grafting Irish mirth and wit,
And the brogue of Morrison.

Half a genius, quick to plan,
Blundering like an Irishman,
But with canny shrewdness lent
By his far-off Scotch descent,
Such was Abram Morrison.

Back and forth to daily meals,
Rode his cherished pig on wheels,
And to all who came to see,
"Aisier for the pig an' me,
Sure it is," said Morrison.

Simple-hearted, boy o'ergrown,
With a humor quite his own,
Of our sober-stepping ways,
Speech and look and cautious phrase,
Slow to learn was Morrison.

Much we loved his stories told
Of a country strange and old,
Where the fairies danced till dawn,
And the goblin Leprecaun
Looked, we thought, like Morrison.

Or wild tales of feud and fight,
Witch and troll and second sight
Whispered still where Stornoway
Looks across its stormy bay,
    Once the home of Morrisons.

First was he to sing the praise
Of the Powow's winding ways;
And our straggling village took
City grandeur to the look
    Of its poet Morrison.

All his words have perished. Shame
On the saddle-bags of Fame,
That they bring not to our time
One poor couplet of the rhyme
    Made by Abram Morrison!

When, on calm and fair First Days,
Rattled down our one-horse chaise,
Through the blossomed apple-boughs
To the old brown meeting-house,
    There was Abram Morrison.

Underneath his hat's broad brim
Peered the queer old face of him;
And with Irish jauntiness
Swung the coat-tails of the dress
    Worn by Abram Morrison.

Still, in memory, on his feet,
Leaning o'er the elders' seat,
Mingling with a solemn drone,
Celtic accents all his own,
    Rises Abram Morrison.

"Don't," he's pleading, "don't ye go,
Dear young friends, to sight and show;
Don't run after elephants,
Learned pigs and presidents
    And the likes!" said Morrison.

On his well-worn theme intent,
Simple, child-like, innocent,

Heaven forgive the half-checked smile
Of our careless boyhood, while
Listening to Friend Morrison!

We have learned in latter days
Truth may speak in simplest phrase;
That the man is not the less
For quaint ways and home-spun dress,
Thanks to Abram Morrison!

Not to pander nor to please
Come the needed homilies,
With no lofty argument
Is the fitting message sent,
Through such lips as Morrison's.

Dead and gone! But while its track
Powow keeps to Merrimac,
While Po Hill is still on guard,
Looking land and ocean ward,
They shall tell of Morrison!

After half a century's lapse,
We are wiser now, perhaps,
But we miss our streets amid
Something which the past has hid,
Lost with Abram Morrison.

Gone forever with the queer
Characters of that old year!
Now the many are as one;
Broken is the mould that run
Men like Abram Morrison.

The Quaker of the Olden Time

The Quaker of the olden time!
How calm and firm and true,
Unspotted by its wrong and crime,
He walked the dark earth through.
The lust of power, the love of gain,
The thousand lures of sin
Around him, had no power to stain
The purity within.

With that deep insight which detects
All great things in the small,
And knows how each man's life affects
The spiritual life of all,
He walked by faith and not by sight,
By love and not by law;
The presence of the wrong or right
He rather felt than saw.

He felt that wrong with wrong partakes,
That nothing stands alone,
That whoso gives the motive, makes
His brother's sin his own.
And, pausing not for doubtful choice
Of evils great or small,
He listened to that inward voice
Which called away from all.

O Spirit of that early day,
So pure and strong and true,
Be with us in the narrow way
Our faithful fathers knew.
Give strength the evil to forsake,
The cross of Truth to bear,
And love and reverent fear to make
Our daily lives a prayer!

Democracy

All things whatsoever ye would that men should do to you, do ye even so to them.
– *Matthew* vii. 12.

Bearer of Freedom's holy light,
Breaker of Slavery's chain and rod,
The foe of all which pains the sight,
Or wounds the generous ear of God!

Beautiful yet thy temples rise,
Though there profaning gifts are thrown;
And fires unkindled of the skies
Are glaring round thy altar-stone.

FORGIVENESS

One summer Sabbath day I strolled among
The green mounds of the village burial-place

Still sacred, though thy name be breathed
By those whose hearts thy truth deride;
And garlands, plucked from thee, are wreathed
Around the haughty brows of Pride.

Oh, ideal of my boyhood's time!
The faith in which my father stood,
Even when the sons of Lust and Crime
Had stained thy peaceful courts with blood!

Still to those courts my footsteps turn,
For through the mists which darken there
I see the flame of Freedom burn, —
The Kebla of the patriot's prayer!

The generous feeling, pure and warm,
Which owns the right of all divine;
The pitying heart, the helping arm,
The prompt self-sacrifice, are thine.

Beneath thy broad, impartial eye,
How fade the lines of caste and birth!
How equal in their suffering lie
The groaning multitudes of earth!

Still to a stricken brother true,
Whatever clime hath nurtured him;
As stooped to heal the wounded Jew
The worshipper of Gerizim.

By misery unrepelled, unawed
By pomp or power, thou seest a Man
In prince or peasant, slave or lord,
Pale priest, or swarthy artisan.

Through all disguise, form, place, or name,
Beneath the flaunting robes of sin,
Through poverty and squalid shame,
Thou lookest on the man within.

On man, as man, retaining yet,
Howe'er debased, and soiled, and dim,
The crown upon his forehead set,
The immortal gift of God to him.

And there is reverence in thy look;
  For that frail form which mortals wear
The Spirit of the Holiest took,
  And veiled His perfect brightness there.

Not from the shallow babbling fount
  Of vain philosophy thou art;
He who of old on Syria's Mount
  Thrilled, warmed, by turns, the listener's heart,

In holy words which cannot die,
  In thoughts which angels leaned to know,
Proclaimed thy message from on high,
  Thy mission to a world of woe.

That voice's echo hath not died!
  From the blue lake of Galilee,
And Tabor's lonely mountain-side,
  It calls a struggling world to thee.

Thy name and watchword o'er this land
  I hear in every breeze that stirs,
And round a thousand altars stand
  Thy banded party worshippers.

Not to these altars of a day,
  At party's call, my gift I bring;
But on thy olden shrine I lay
  A freeman's dearest offering:

The voiceless utterance of his will, —
  His pledge to Freedom and to Truth,
That manhood's heart remembers still
  The homage of his generous youth.

The Shoemakers

Ho! workers of the old time styled
The Gentle Craft of Leather!
Young brothers of the ancient guild,
Stand forth once more together!
Call out again your long array,
In the olden merry manner!
Once more, on gay St. Crispin's day,
Fling out your blazoned banner!

Rap, rap! upon the well-worn stone
How falls the polished hammer!
Rap, rap! the measured sound has grown
A quick and merry clamor.
Now shape the sole! now deftly curl
The glossy vamp around it,
And bless the while the bright-eyed girl
Whose gentle fingers bound it!

For you, along the Spanish main
A hundred keels are ploughing;
For you, the Indian on the plain
His lasso-coil is throwing;
For you, deep glens with hemlock dark
The woodman's fire is lighting;
For you, upon the oak's gray bark,
The woodman's axe is smiting.

For you, from Carolina's pine
The rosin-gum is stealing;
For you, the dark-eyed Florentine
Her silken skein is reeling;
For you, the dizzy goatherd roams
His rugged Alpine ledges;
For you, round all her shepherd homes,
Bloom England's thorny hedges.

The foremost still, by day or night,
On moated mound or heather,
Where'er the need of trampled right
Brought toiling men together;
Where the free burghers from the wall
Defied the mail-clad master,
Than yours, at Freedom's trumpet-call,
No craftsmen rallied faster.

Let foplings sneer, let fools deride,
Ye heed no idle scorner;
Free hands and hearts are still your pride,
And duty done your honor.
Ye dare to trust, for honest fame,
The jury Time empanels,
And leave to truth each noble name
Which glorifies your annals.

Thy songs, Hans Sachs, are living yet,
In strong and hearty German;
And Bloomfield's lay, and Gifford's wit,
And patriot fame of Sherman;
Still from his book, a mystic seer,
The soul of Behmen teaches,
And England's priestcraft shakes to hear
Of Fox's leathern breeches.

The foot is yours; where'er it falls,
It treads your well-wrought leather,
On earthen floor, in marble halls,
On carpet, or on heather.
Still there the sweetest charm is found
Of matron grace or vestal's,
As Hebe's foot bore nectar round
Among the old celestials!

Rap, rap! — your stout and bluff brogan,
With footsteps slow and weary,
May wander where the sky's blue span
Shuts down upon the prairie.
On Beauty's foot your slippers glance,
By Saratoga's fountains,
Or twinkle down the summer dance
Beneath the Crystal Mountains!

The red brick to the mason's hand,
The brown earth to the tiller's,
The shoe in yours shall wealth command,
Like fairy Cinderella's!
As they who shunned the household maid
Beheld the crown upon her,
So all shall see your toil repaid
With hearth and home and honor.

Then let the toast be freely quaffed,
  In water cool and brimming, —
"All honor to the good old Craft,
  Its merry men and women!"
Call out again your long array,
  In the old time's pleasant manner:
Once more, on gay St. Crispin's day,
  Fling out his blazoned banner!

The Fishermen

Hurrah! the seaward breezes
  Sweep down the bay amain;
Heave up, my lads, the anchor!
  Run up the sail again!
Leave to the lubber landsmen
  The rail-car and the steed;
The stars of heaven shall guide us,
  The breath of heaven shall speed.

From the hill-top looks the steeple,
  And the lighthouse from the sand;
And the scattered pines are waving
  Their farewell from the land.
One glance, my lads, behind us,
  For the homes we leave one sigh,
Ere we take the change and chances
  Of the ocean and the sky.

Now, brothers, for the icebergs
  Of frozen Labrador,
Floating spectral in the moonshine,
  Along the low, black shore!
Where like snow the gannet's feathers
  On Brador's rocks are shed,
And the noisy murr are flying,
  Like black scuds, overhead;

Where in mist the rock is hiding,
  And the sharp reef lurks below,
And the white squall smites in summer,
  And the autumn tempests blow;
Where, through gray and rolling vapor,

From evening unto morn,
A thousand boats are hailing,
Horn answering unto horn.

Hurrah! for the Red Island,
With the white cross on its crown!
Hurrah! for Meccatina,
And its mountains bare and brown!
Where the Caribou's tall antlers
O'er the dwarf-wood freely toss,
And the footstep of the Mickmack
Has no sound upon the moss.

There we'll drop our lines, and gather
Old Ocean's treasures in,
Where'er the mottled mackerel
Turns up a steel-dark fin.
The sea's our field of harvest,
Its scaly tribes our grain;
We'll reap the teeming waters
As at home they reap the plain!

Our wet hands spread the carpet,
And light the hearth of home;
From our fish, as in the old time,
The silver coin shall come.
As the demon fled the chamber
Where the fish of Tobit lay,
So ours from all our dwellings
Shall frighten Want away.

Though the mist upon our jackets
In the bitter air congeals,
And our lines wind stiff and slowly
From off the frozen reels;
Though the fog be dark around us,
And the storm blow high and loud,
We will whistle down the wild wind,
And laugh beneath the cloud!

In the darkness as in daylight,
On the water as on land,
God's eye is looking on us,
And beneath us is His hand!

Death will find us soon or later,
  On the deck or in the cot;
And we cannot meet him better
  Than in working out our lot.

Hurrah! hurrah! the west-wind
  Comes freshening down the bay,
The rising sails are filling;
  Give way, my lads, give way!
Leave the coward landsman clinging
  To the dull earth, like a weed;
The stars of heaven shall guide us,
  The breath of heaven shall speed!

The Lumbermen

Wildly round our woodland quarters
  Sad-voiced Autumn grieves;
Thickly down these swelling waters
  Float his fallen leaves.
Through the tall and naked timber,
  Column-like and old,
Gleam the sunsets of November,
  From their skies of gold.

O'er us, to the southland heading,
  Screams the gray wild-goose;
On the night-frost sounds the treading
  Of the brindled moose.
Noiseless creeping, while we're sleeping,
  Frost his task-work plies;
Soon, his icy bridges heaping,
  Shall our log-piles rise.

When, with sounds of smothered thunder,
  On some night of rain,
Lake and river break asunder
  Winter's weakened chain,
Down the wild March flood shall bear them
  To the saw-mill's wheel,
Or where Steam, the slave, shall tear them
  With his teeth of steel.

Keep who will the city's alleys,
  Take the smooth-shorn plain;
Give to us the cedarn valleys,
  Rocks and hills of Maine!
In our North-land, wild and woody,
  Let us still have part:
Rugged nurse and mother sturdy,
  Hold us to thy heart!

Oh, our free hearts beat the warmer
  For thy breath of snow;
And our tread is all the firmer
  For thy rocks below.
Freedom, hand in hand with labor,
  Walketh strong and brave;
On the forehead of his neighbor
  No man writeth Slave!

Lo, the day breaks! old Katahdin's
  Pine-trees show its fires,
While from these dim forest gardens
  Rise their blackened spires.
Up, my comrades! up and doing!
  Manhood's rugged play
Still renewing, bravely hewing
  Through the world our way!

The Ship-Builders

The sky is ruddy in the east,
  The earth is gray below,
And, spectral in the river-mist,
  The ship's white timbers show.
Then let the sounds of measured stroke
  And grating saw begin;
The broad-axe to the gnarlëd oak,
  The mallet to the pin!

Hark! roars the bellows, blast on blast,
  The sooty smithy jars,
And fire-sparks, rising far and fast,
  Are fading with the stars.
All day for us the smith shall stand

THE SHIP-BUILDERS

From far-off hills, the panting team
For us is toiling near

Beside that flashing forge;
All day for us his heavy hand
The groaning anvil scourge.

From far-off hills, the panting team
For us is toiling near;
For us the raftsmen down the stream
Their island barges steer.
Rings out for us the axe-man's stroke
In forests old and still;
For us the century-circled oak
Falls crashing down his hill.

Up! up! in nobler toil than ours
No craftsmen bear a part:
We make of Nature's giant powers
The slaves of human Art.
Lay rib to rib and beam to beam,
And drive the treenails free;
Nor faithless joint nor yawning seam
Shall tempt the searching sea!

Where'er the keel of our good ship
The sea's rough field shall plough;
Where'er her tossing spars shall drip
With salt-spray caught below;
That ship must heed her master's beck,
Her helm obey his hand,
And seamen tread her reeling deck
As if they trod the land.

Her oaken ribs the vulture-beak
Of Northern ice may peel;
The sunken rock and coral peak
May grate along her keel;
And know we well the painted shell
We give to wind and wave,
Must float, the sailor's citadel,
Or sink, the sailor's grave!

Ho! strike away the bars and blocks,
And set the good ship free!
Why lingers on these dusty rocks
The young bride of the sea?

Look! how she moves adown the grooves,
In graceful beauty now!
How lowly on the breast she loves
Sinks down her virgin prow!

God bless her! wheresoe'er the breeze
Her snowy wing shall fan,
Aside the frozen Hebrides,
Or sultry Hindostan!
Where'er, in mart or on the main,
With peaceful flag unfurled,
She helps to wind the silken chain
Of commerce round the world!

Speed on the ship! But let her bear
No merchandise of sin,
No groaning cargo of despair
Her roomy hold within;
No Lethean drug for Eastern lands,
Nor poison-draught for ours;
But honest fruits of toiling hands
And Nature's sun and showers.

Be hers the Prairie's golden grain,
The Desert's golden sand,
The clustered fruits of sunny Spain,
The spice of Morning-land!
Her pathway on the open main
May blessings follow free,
And glad hearts welcome back again
Her white sails from the sea!

The Huskers

It was late in mild October, and the long autumnal rain
Had left the summer harvest-fields all green with grass again;
The first sharp frosts had fallen, leaving all the woodlands gay
With the hues of summer's rainbow, or the meadow-flowers of May.

Through a thin, dry mist, that morning, the sun rose broad and red,
At first a rayless disk of fire, he brightened as he sped;
Yet even his noontide glory fell chastened and subdued,
On the cornfields and the orchards and softly pictured wood.

And all that quiet afternoon, slow sloping to the night,
He wove with golden shuttle the haze with yellow light;
Slanting through the painted beeches, he glorified the hill;
And, beneath it, pond and meadow lay brighter, greener still.

And shouting boys in woodland haunts caught glimpses of that sky,
Flecked by the many-tinted leaves, and laughed, they knew not why;
And school-girls, gay with aster-flowers, beside the meadow brooks,
Mingled the glow of autumn with the sunshine of sweet looks.

From spire and barn looked westerly the patient weathercocks;
But even the birches on the hill stood motionless as rocks.
No sound was in the woodlands, save the squirrel's dropping shell,
And the yellow leaves among the boughs, low rustling as they fell.

The summer grains were harvested; the stubble-fields lay dry,
Where June winds rolled, in light and shade, the green waves of rye;
But still, on gentle hill-slopes, in valleys fringed with wood,
Ungathered, bleaching in the sun, the heavy corn crop stood.

Bent low, by autumn's wind and rain, through husks that, dry and sere,
Unfolded from their ripened charge, shone out the yellow ear;
Beneath, the turnip lay concealed, in many a verdant fold,
And glistened in the slanting light the pumpkin's sphere of gold.

There wrought the busy harvesters; and many a creaking wain
Bore slowly to the long barn-floor its load of husk and grain;
Till broad and red, as when he rose, the sun sank down, at last,
And like a merry guest's farewell, the day in brightness passed.

And lo! as through the western pines, on meadow, stream, and pond,
Flamed the red radiance of a sky, set all afire beyond,
Slowly o'er the eastern sea-bluffs a milder glory shone,
And the sunset and the moonrise were mingled into one!

As thus into the quiet night the twilight lapsed away,
And deeper in the brightening moon the tranquil shadows lay;
From many a brown old farm-house, and hamlet without name,
Their milking and their home-tasks done, the merry huskers came.

Swung o'er the heaped-up harvest, from pitchforks in the mow,
Shone dimly down the lanterns on the pleasant scene below;
The growing pile of husks behind, the golden ears before,
And laughing eyes and busy hands and brown cheeks glimmering o'er.

Half hidden, in a quiet nook, serene of look and heart,
Talking their old times over, the old men sat apart;
While up and down the unhusked pile, or nestling in its shade,
At hide-and-seek, with laugh and shout, the happy children played.

Urged by the good host's daughter, a maiden young and fair,
Lifting to light her sweet blue eyes and pride of soft brown hair,
The master of the village school, sleek of hair and smooth of tongue,
To the quaint tune of some old psalm, a husking-ballad sung.

THE CORN-SONG

Heap high the farmer's wintry hoard!
 Heap high the golden corn!
No richer gift has Autumn poured
 From out her lavish horn!

Let other lands, exulting, glean
 The apple from the pine,
The orange from its glossy green,
 The cluster from the vine;

We better love the hardy gift
 Our rugged vales bestow,
To cheer us when the storm shall drift
 Our harvest-fields with snow.

Through vales of grass and meads of flowers
 Our ploughs their furrows made,
While on the hills the sun and showers
 Of changeful April played.

We dropped the seed o'er hill and plain
 Beneath the sun of May,
And frightened from our sprouting grain
 The robber crows away.

All through the long, bright days of June
 Its leaves grew green and fair,
And waved in hot midsummer's noon
 Its soft and yellow hair.

And now, with autumn's moonlit eves,
 Its harvest-time has come,

OUR STATE

Yet, on her rocks, and on her sands,
And wintry hills, the school-house stands

We pluck away the frosted leaves,
And bear the treasure home.

There, when the snows about us drift,
And winter winds are cold,
Fair hands the broken grain shall sift,
And knead its meal of gold.

Let vapid idlers loll in silk
Around their costly board;
Give us the bowl of samp and milk,
By homespun beauty poured!

Where'er the wide old kitchen hearth
Sends up its smoky curls,
Who will not thank the kindly earth,
And bless our farmers girls!

Then shame on all the proud and vain,
Whose folly laughs to scorn
The blessing of our hardy grain,
Our wealth of golden corn!

Let earth withhold her goodly root,
Let mildew blight the rye,
Give to the worm the orchard's fruit,
The wheat-field to the fly:

But let the good old crop adorn
The hills our fathers trod;
Still let us, for His golden corn,
Send up our thanks to God!

Our State

The South-land boasts its teeming cane,
The prairied West its heavy grain,
And sunset's radiant gates unfold
On rising marts and sands of gold!

Rough, bleak, and hard, our little State
Is scant of soil, of limits strait;
Her yellow sands are sands alone,
Her only mines are ice and stone!

From Autumn frost to April rain,
Too long her winter woods complain;
From budding flower to falling leaf,
Her summer time is all too brief.

Yet, on her rocks, and on her sands,
And wintry hills, the school-house stands,
And what her rugged soil denies,
The harvest of the mind supplies.

The riches of the Commonwealth
Are free, strong minds, and hearts of health;
And more to her than gold or grain,
The cunning hand and cultured brain.

For well she keeps her ancient stock,
The stubborn strength of Pilgrim Rock;
And still maintains, with milder laws,
And clearer light, the Good Old Cause!

Nor heeds the skeptic's puny hands,
While near her school the church-spire stands;
Nor fears the blinded bigot's rule,
While near her church-spire stands the school.

The Peace of Europe

"Great peace in Europe! Order reigns
From Tiber's hills to Danube's plains!"
So say her kings and priests; so say
The lying prophets of our day.

Go lay to earth a listening ear;
The tramp of measured marches hear;
The rolling of the cannon's wheel,
The shotted musket's murderous peal,
The night alarm, the sentry's call,
The quick-eared spy in hut and hall!
From Polar sea and tropic fen
The dying-groans of exiled men!
The bolted cell, the galley's chains,
The scaffold smoking with its stains!

Order, the hush of brooding slaves!
Peace, in the dungeon-vaults and graves!

O Fisher! of the world-wide net,
With meshes in all waters set,
Whose fabled keys of heaven and hell
Bolt hard the patriot's prison-cell,
And open wide the banquet-hall,
Where kings and priests hold carnival!
Weak vassal tricked in royal guise,
Boy Kaiser with thy lip of lies;
Base gambler for Napoleon's crown,
Barnacle on his dead renown!
Thou, Bourbon Neapolitan,
Crowned scandal, loathed of God and man;
And thou, fell Spider of the North!
Stretching thy giant feelers forth,
Within whose web the freedom dies
Of nations eaten up like flies!
Speak, Prince and Kaiser, Priest and Czar!
If this be Peace, pray what is War?

White Angel of the Lord! unmeet
That soil accursed for thy pure feet.
Never in Slavery's desert flows
The fountain of thy charmed repose;
No tyrant's hand thy chaplet weaves
Of lilies and of olive-leaves;
Not with the wicked shalt thou dwell,
Thus saith the Eternal Oracle;
Thy home is with the pure and free!
Stern herald of thy better day,
Before thee, to prepare thy way,
The Baptist Shade of Liberty,
Gray, scarred and hairy-robed, must press
With bleeding feet the wilderness!
Oh that its voice might pierce the ear
Of princes, trembling while they hear
A cry as of the Hebrew seer:
Repent! God's kingdom draweth near!

Astræa

"Jove means to settle
Astræa in her seat again,
And let down from his golden chain
An age of better metal."
BEN JONSON, 1615.

O poet rare and old!
Thy words are prophecies;
Forward the age of gold,
The new Saturnian lies.

The universal prayer
And hope are not in vain;
Rise, brothers! and prepare
The way for Saturn's reign.

Perish shall all which takes
From labor's board and can;
Perish shall all which makes
A spaniel of the man!

Free from its bonds the mind,
The body from the rod;
Broken all chains that bind
The image of our God.

Just men no longer pine
Behind their prison-bars;
Through the rent dungeon shine
The free sun and the stars.

Earth own, at last, untrod
By sect, or caste, or clan,
The fatherhood of God,
The brotherhood of man!

Fraud fail, craft perish, forth
The money-changers driven,
And God's will done on earth,
As now in heaven!

The Poor Voter on Election Day

The proudest now is but my peer,
  The highest not more high;
To-day, of all the weary year,
  A king of men am I.
To-day alike are great and small,
  The nameless and the known;
My palace is the people's hall,
  The ballot-box my throne!

Who serves to-day upon the list
  Beside the served shall stand;
Alike the brown and wrinkled fist,
  The gloved and dainty hand!
The rich is level with the poor,
  The weak is strong to-day;
And sleekest broadcloth counts no more
  Than homespun frock of gray.

To-day let pomp and vain pretence
  My stubborn right abide;
I set a plain man's common sense
  Against the pedant's pride.
To-day shall simple manhood try
  The strength of gold and land;
The wide world has not wealth to buy
  The power in my right hand!

While there's a grief to seek redress,
  Or balance to adjust,
Where weighs our living manhood less
  Than Mammon's vilest dust, —
While there's a right to need my vote,
  A wrong to sweep away,
Up! clouted knee and ragged coat!
  A man's a man to-day!

The Poems of John Greenleaf Whittier

VII

THE ETERNAL GOODNESS

The Editor's Commentary

More than most poets', Whittier's life is reflected in his work: a slow progression from conflict to peace, from struggle to serenity. Even the devotional poems show the progress of an increasingly spiritual nature.

Whittier's religion was never the repetition of a narrow creed. It was too broad, too benignant, to preach dogmas or accept a Hell. The poet was firmly rooted in the belief that God is Good; he maintained it in the face of a hostile and heretical world; he made it his credo. "Requirement" is the keynote of Whittier's religious poems; "The Brewing of Soma" is the amplification; "The Eternal Goodness" is the fulfilment; "At Last" is the pure distillation.

The later poetry is a set of variations on an organ-point of faith. It is a faith that discards sectarian claims and becomes steadily less self-righteous and more abstruse. "We live by Faith," says Whittier with a confidence that is beyond argument; it is not "the slave of text and legend"; it is:

> . . . the calm beauty of an ordered life
> Whose very breathing is unuttered praise.

Whittier was seventy-five when he wrote "At Last." He was to live another ten years; but he was never to utter a nobler expression of his creed. It was so simple and so final that it was recited by one of a little group of relatives standing at the poet's bedside as the end drew near. As the last lines were murmured, the poet lifted his eyes to the light and was gathered to the Eternal Goodness.

The Star of Bethlehem

Where Time the measure of his hours
By changeful bud and blossom keeps,
And, like a young bride crowned with flowers,
Fair Shiraz in her garden sleeps;

Where, to her poet's turban stone,
The Spring her gift of flowers imparts,
Less sweet than those his thoughts have sown
In the warm soil of Persian hearts:

There sat the stranger, where the shade
Of scattered date-trees thinly lay,
While in the hot clear heaven delayed
The long and still and weary day.

Strange trees and fruits above him hung,
Strange odors filled the sultry air,
Strange birds upon the branches swung,
Strange insect voices murmured there.

And strange bright blossoms shone around,
Turned sunward from the shadowy bowers,
As if the Gheber's soul had found
A fitting home in Iran's flowers.

Whate'er he saw, whate'er he heard,
Awakened feelings new and sad,—
No Christian garb, nor Christian word,
Nor church with Sabbath-bell chimes glad,

But Moslem graves, with turban stones,
And mosque-spires gleaming white, in view,
And graybeard Mollahs in low tones
Chanting their Koran service through.

The flowers which smiled on either hand,
Like tempting fiends, were such as they
Which once, o'er all that Eastern land,
As gifts on demon altars lay.

As if the burning eye of Baal
The servant of his Conqueror knew,
From skies which knew no cloudy veil,
The Sun's hot glances smote him through.

"Ah me!" the lonely stranger said,
"The hope which led my footsteps on,
And light from heaven around them shed,
O'er weary wave and waste, is gone!

"Where are the harvest fields all white,
For Truth to thrust her sickle in?
Where flock the souls, like doves in flight,
From the dark hiding-place of sin?

"A silent horror broods o'er all, —
The burden of a hateful spell, —
The very flowers around recall
The hoary Magi's rites of hell!

"And what am I, o'er such a land
The banner of the Cross to bear?
Dear Lord, uphold me with Thy hand,
Thy strength with human weakness share!"

He ceased; for at his very feet
In mild rebuke a floweret smiled;
How thrilled his sinking heart to greet
The Star-flower of the Virgin's child!

Sown by some wandering Frank, it drew
Its life from alien air and earth,
And told to Paynim sun and dew
The story of the Saviour's birth.

From scorching beams, in kindly mood,
The Persian plants its beauty screened,
And on its pagan sisterhood,
In love, the Christian floweret leaned.

With tears of joy the wanderer felt
The darkness of his long despair
Before that hallowed symbol melt,
Which God's dear love had nurtured there.

From Nature's face, that simple flower
The lines of sin and sadness swept;
And Magian pile and Paynim bower
In peace like that of Eden slept.

Each Moslem tomb, and cypress old,
  Looked holy through the sunset air;
And, angel-like, the Muezzin told
  From tower and mosque the hour of prayer.

With cheerful steps, the morrow's dawn
  From Shiraz saw the stranger part;
The Star-flower of the Virgin-Born
  Still blooming in his hopeful heart!

The Cities of the Plain

"Get ye up from the wrath of God's terrible day!
Ungirded, unsandalled, arise and away!
'Tis the vintage of blood, 'tis the fulness of time,
And vengeance shall gather the harvest of crime!"

The warning was spoken — the righteous had gone,
And the proud ones of Sodom were feasting alone;
All gay was the banquet — the revel was long,
With the pouring of wine and the breathing of song.

'Twas an evening of beauty; the air was perfume,
The earth was all greenness, the trees were all bloom;
And softly the delicate viol was heard,
Like the murmur of love or the notes of a bird.

And beautiful maidens moved down in the dance,
With the magic of motion and sunshine of glance;
And white arms wreathed lightly, and tresses fell free
As the plumage of birds in some tropical tree.

Where the shrines of foul idols were lighted on high,
And wantonness tempted the lust of the eye;
Midst rites of obsceneness, strange, loathsome, abhorred,
The blasphemer scoffed at the name of the Lord.

Hark! the growl of the thunder, — the quaking of earth!
Woe, woe to the worship, and woe to the mirth!
The black sky has opened; there's flame in the air;
The red arm of vengeance is lifted and bare!

Then the shriek of the dying rose wild where the song
And the low tone of love had been whispered along;
For the fierce flames went lightly o'er palace and bower,
Like the red tongues of demons, to blast and devour!

Down, down on the fallen the red ruin rained,
And the reveller sank with his wine-cup undrained;
The foot of the dancer, the music's loved thrill,
And the shout and the laughter grew suddenly still.

The last throb of anguish was fearfully given;
The last eye glared forth in its madness on Heaven!
The last groan of horror rose wildly and vain,
And death brooded over the pride of the Plain!

The Call of the Christian

Not always as the whirlwind's rush
  On Horeb's mount of fear,
Not always as the burning bush
  To Midian's shepherd seer,
Nor as the awful voice which came
  To Israel's prophet bards,
Nor as the tongues of cloven flame,
  Nor gift of fearful words, —

Not always thus, with outward sign
  Of fire or voice from Heaven,
The message of a truth divine,
  The call of God is given!
Awaking in the human heart
  Love for the true and right, —
Zeal for the Christian's better part,
  Strength for the Christian's fight.

Nor unto manhood's heart alone
  The holy influence steals:
Warm with a rapture not its own,
  The heart of woman feels!
As she who by Samaria's wall
  The Saviour's errand sought, —
As those who with the fervent Paul
  And meek Aquila wrought:

THE POOR VOTER ON ELECTION DAY

My palace is the people's hall,
The ballot-box my throne!

Or those meek ones whose martyrdom
  Rome's gathered grandeur saw:
Or those who in their Alpine home
  Braved the Crusader's war,
When the green Vaudois, trembling, heard,
  Through all its vales of death,
The martyr's song of triumph poured
  From woman's failing breath.

And gently, by a thousand things
  Which o'er our spirits pass,
Like breezes o'er the harp's fine strings,
  Or vapors o'er a glass,
Leaving their token strange and new
  Of music or of shade,
The summons to the right and true
  And merciful is made.

Oh, then, if gleams of truth and light
  Flash o'er thy waiting mind,
Unfolding to thy mental sight
  The wants of human-kind;
If, brooding over human grief,
  The earnest wish is known
To soothe and gladden with relief
  An anguish not thine own;

Though heralded with naught of fear,
  Or outward sign or show;
Though only to the inward ear
  It whispers soft and low;
Though dropping, as the manna fell,
  Unseen, yet from above,
Noiseless as dew-fall, heed it well, —
  Thy Father's call of love!

The Crucifixion

Sunlight upon Judæa's hills!
  And on the waves of Galilee;
On Jordan's stream, and on the rills
  That feed the dead and sleeping sea!
Most freshly from the green wood springs

The light breeze on its scented wings;
And gayly quiver in the sun
The cedar tops of Lebanon!

A few more hours, — a change hath come!
  The sky is dark without a cloud!
The shouts of wrath and joy are dumb,
  And proud knees unto earth are bowed.
A change is on the hill of Death,
The helmëd watchers pant for breath,
And turn with wild and maniac eyes
From the dark scene of sacrifice!

That Sacrifice! — the death of Him, —
  The Christ of God, the holy One!
Well may the conscious Heaven grow dim,
  And blacken the beholding Sun.
The wonted light hath fled away,
Night settles on the middle day,
And earthquake from his caverned bed
Is waking with a thrill of dread!

The dead are waking underneath!
  Their prison door is rent away!
And, ghastly with the seal of death
  They wander in the eye of day!
The temple of the Cherubim,
The House of God is cold and dim;
A curse is on its trembling walls,
Its mighty veil asunder falls!

Well may the cavern-depths of Earth
  Be shaken, and her mountains nod;
Well may the sheeted dead come forth
  To see the suffering Son of God!
Well may the temple-shrine grow dim,
And shadows veil the Cherubim,
When He, the chosen one of Heaven,
A sacrifice for guilt is given!

And shall the sinful heart, alone,
  Behold unmoved the fearful hour,
When Nature trembled on her throne,
  And Death resigned his iron power?

Oh, shall the heart — whose sinfulness
Gave keenness to His sore distress,
And added to His tears of blood —
Refuse its trembling gratitude?

My Soul and I

Stand still, my soul, in the silent dark
I would question thee,
Alone in the shadow drear and stark
With God and me!

What, my soul, was thy errand here?
Was it mirth or ease,
Or heaping up dust from year to year?
"Nay, none of these!"

Speak, soul, aright in His holy sight
Whose eye looks still
And steadily on thee through the night:
"To do His will!"

What hast thou done, O soul of mine,
That thou tremblest so?
Hast thou wrought His task, and kept the line
He bade thee go?

What, silent all! art sad of cheer?
Art fearful now?
When God seemed far and men were near,
How brave wert thou!

Aha! thou tremblest! — well I see
Thou'rt craven grown.
Is it so hard with God and me
To stand alone?

Summon thy sunshine bravery back,
O wretched sprite!
Let me hear thy voice through this deep and black
Abysmal night.

What hast thou wrought for Right and Truth,
For God and Man,

From the golden hours of bright-eyed youth
To life's mid span?

Ah, soul of mine, thy tones I hear,
But weak and low,
Like far sad murmurs on my ear
They come and go.

"I have wrestled stoutly with the Wrong,
And borne the Right
From beneath the footfall of the throng
To life and light.

"Wherever Freedom shivered a chain,
God speed, quoth I;
To Error amidst her shouting train
I gave the lie."

Ah, soul of mine! ah, soul of mine!
Thy deeds are well:
Were they wrought for Truth's sake or for thine?
My soul, pray tell.

"Of all the work my hand hath wrought
Beneath the sky,
Save a place in kindly human thought,
No gain have I."

Go to, go to! for thy very self
Thy deeds were done:
Thou for fame, the miser for pelf,
Your end is one!

And where art thou going, soul of mine?
Canst see the end?
And whither this troubled life of thine
Evermore doth tend?

What daunts thee now? what shakes thee so?
My sad soul, say.
"I see a cloud like a curtain low
Hang o'er my way.

"Whither I go I cannot tell:
That cloud hangs black,
High as the heaven and deep as hell
Across my track.

"I see its shadow coldly enwrap
The souls before.
Sadly they enter it, step by step,
To return no more.

"They shrink, they shudder, dear God! they kneel
To Thee in prayer.
They shut their eyes on the cloud, but feel
That it still is there.

"In vain they turn from the dread Before
To the Known and Gone;
For while gazing behind them evermore
Their feet glide on.

"Yet, at times, I see upon sweet pale faces
A light begin
To tremble, as if from holy places
And shrines within.

"And at times methinks their cold lips move
With hymn and prayer,
As if somewhat of awe, but more of love
And hope were there.

"I call on the souls who have left the light
To reveal their lot;
I bend mine ear to that wall of night,
And they answer not.

"But I hear around me sighs of pain
And the cry of fear,
And a sound like the slow sad dropping of rain,
Each drop a tear!

"Ah, the cloud is dark, and day by day
I am moving thither:
I must pass beneath it on my way —
God pity me! — whither?"

Ah, soul of mine! so brave and wise
In the life-storm loud,
Fronting so calmly all human eyes
In the sunlit crowd!

Now standing apart with God and me
Thou art weakness all,
Gazing vainly after the things to be
Through Death's dread wall.

But never for this, never for this
Was thy being lent;
For the craven's fear is but selfishness,
Like his merriment.

Folly and Fear are sisters twain:
One closing her eyes,
The other peopling the dark inane
With spectral lies.

Know well, my soul, God's hand controls
Whate'er thou fearest;
Round Him in calmest music rolls
Whate'er thou hearest.

What to thee is shadow, to Him is day,
And the end He knoweth,
And not on a blind and aimless way
The spirit goeth.

Man sees no future, — a phantom show
Is alone before him;
Past Time is dead, and the grasses grow,
And flowers bloom o'er him.

Nothing before, nothing behind;
The steps of Faith
Fall on the seeming void, and find
The rock beneath.

The Present, the Present is all thou hast
For thy sure possessing;
Like the patriarch's angel hold it fast
Till it gives its blessing.

Why fear the night? why shrink from Death,
That phantom wan?
There is nothing in heaven or earth beneath
Save God and man.

Peopling the shadows we turn from Him
And from one another;
All is spectral and vague and dim
Save God and our brother!

Like warp and woof all destinies
Are woven fast,
Linked in sympathy like the keys
Of an organ vast.

Pluck one thread, and the web ye mar;
Break but one
Of a thousand keys, and the paining jar
Through all will run.

O restless spirit! wherefore strain
Beyond thy sphere?
Heaven and hell, with their joy and pain,
Are now and here.

Back to thyself is measured well
All thou hast given;
Thy neighbor's wrong is thy present hell,
His bliss, thy heaven.

And in life, in death, in dark and light,
All are in God's care:
Sound the black abyss, pierce the deep of night,
And He is there!

All which is real now remaineth,
And fadeth never:
The hand which upholds it now sustaineth
The soul forever.

Leaning on Him, make with reverent meekness
His own thy will,
And with strength from Him shall thy utter weakness
Life's task fulfil;

And that cloud itself, which now before thee
    Lies dark in view,
Shall with beams of light from the inner glory
    Be stricken through.

And like meadow mist through autumn's dawn
    Uprolling thin,
Its thickest folds when about thee drawn
    Let sunlight in.

Then of what is to be, and of what is done,
    Why queriest thou?
The past and the time to be are one,
    And both are now!

Worship

Pure religion and undefiled before God and the Father is this, To visit the fatherless and widows in their affliction, and to keep himself unspotted from the world. — *James* i. 27.

The Pagan's myths through marble lips are spoken,
    And ghosts of old Beliefs still flit and moan
Round fane and altar overthrown and broken,
    O'er tree-grown barrow and gray ring of stone.

Blind Faith had martyrs in those old high places,
    The Syrian hill grove and the Druid's wood,
With mothers offering, to the Fiend's embraces,
    Bone of their bone, and blood of their own blood.

Red altars, kindling through that night of error,
    Smoked with warm blood beneath the cruel eye
Of lawless Power and sanguinary Terror,
    Throned on the circle of a pitiless sky;

Beneath whose baleful shadow, overcasting
    All heaven above, and blighting earth below,
The scourge grew red, the lip grew pale with fasting,
    And man's oblation was his fear and woe!

Then through great temples swelled the dismal moaning
    Of dirge-like music and sepulchral prayer;

WORSHIP

To worship rightly is to love each other,
Each smile a hymn, each kindly deed a prayer

Pale wizard priests, o'er occult symbols droning,
Swung their white censers in the burdened air:

As if the pomp of rituals, and the savor
Of gums and spices could the Unseen One please;
As if His ear could bend, with childish favor,
To the poor flattery of the organ keys!

Feet red from war-fields trod the church aisles holy,
With trembling reverence: and the oppressor there,
Kneeling before his priest, abased and lowly,
Crushed human hearts beneath his knee of prayer.

Not such the service the benignant Father
Requireth at His earthly children's hands:
Not the poor offering of vain rites, but rather
The simple duty man from man demands.

For Earth He asks it: the full joy of heaven
Knoweth no change of waning or increase;
The great heart of the Infinite beats even,
Untroubled flows the river of His peace.

He asks no taper lights, on high surrounding
The priestly altar and the saintly grave,
No dolorous chant nor organ music sounding,
Nor incense clouding up the twilight nave.

For he whom Jesus loved hath truly spoken:
The holier worship which He deigns to bless
Restores the lost, and binds the spirit broken,
And feeds the widow and the fatherless!

Types of our human weakness and our sorrow!
Who lives unhaunted by his loved ones dead?
Who, with vain longing, seeketh not to borrow
From stranger eyes the home lights which have fled?

O brother man! fold to thy heart thy brother;
Where pity dwells, the peace of God is there;
To worship rightly is to love each other,
Each smile a hymn, each kindly deed a prayer.

Follow with reverent steps the great example
Of Him whose holy work was "doing good";
So shall the wide earth seem our Father's temple,
Each loving life a psalm of gratitude.

Then shall all shackles fall; the stormy clangor
Of wild war music o'er the earth shall cease;
Love shall tread out the baleful fire of anger,
And in its ashes plant the tree of peace!

The Wish of To-day

I ask not now for gold to gild
With mocking shine a weary frame;
The yearning of the mind is stilled,
I ask not now for Fame.

A rose-cloud, dimly seen above,
Melting in heaven's blue depths away;
Oh, sweet, fond dream of human Love!
For thee I may not pray.

But, bowed in lowliness of mind,
I make my humble wishes known;
I only ask a will resigned,
O Father, to Thine own!

To-day, beneath Thy chastening eye
I crave alone for peace and rest,
Submissive in Thy hand to lie,
And feel that it is best.

A marvel seems the Universe,
A miracle our Life and Death;
A mystery which I cannot pierce,
Around, above, beneath.

In vain I task my aching brain,
In vain the sage's thought I scan,
I only feel how weak and vain,
How poor and blind, is man.

And now my spirit sighs for home,
And longs for light whereby to see,
And, like a weary child, would come,
O Father, unto Thee!

Though oft, like letters traced on sand,
My weak resolves have passed away,
In mercy lend Thy helping hand
Unto my prayer to-day!

Invocation

Through Thy clear spaces, Lord, of old,
Formless and void the dead earth rolled;
Deaf to Thy heaven's sweet music, blind
To the great lights which o'er it shined;
No sound, no ray, no warmth, no breath, —
A dumb despair, a wandering death.

To that dark, weltering horror came
Thy spirit, like a subtle flame, —
A breath of life electrical,
Awakening and transforming all,
Till beat and thrilled in every part
The pulses of a living heart.

Then knew their bounds the land and sea;
Then smiled the bloom of mead and tree;
From flower to moth, from beast to man,
The quick creative impulse ran;
And earth, with life from Thee renewed,
Was in Thy holy eyesight good.

As lost and void, as dark and cold
And formless as that earth of old;
A wandering waste of storm and night,
Midst spheres of song and realms of light;
A blot upon Thy holy sky,
Untouched, unwarmed of Thee, am I.

O Thou who movest on the deep
Of spirits, wake my own from sleep!
Its darkness melt, its coldness warm,

The lost restore, the ill transform,
That flower and fruit henceforth may be
Its grateful offering, worthy Thee.

Trust

The same old baffling questions! O my friend,
I cannot answer them. In vain I send
My soul into the dark, where never burn
The lamps of science, nor the natural light
Of Reason's sun and stars! I cannot learn
Their great and solemn meanings, nor discern
The awful secrets of the eyes which turn
Evermore on us through the day and night
With silent challenge and a dumb demand,
Proffering the riddles of the dread unknown,
Like the calm Sphinxes, with their eyes of stone,
Questioning the centuries from their veils of sand!
I have no answer for myself or thee,
Save that I learned beside my mother's knee;
"All is of God that is, and is to be;
And God is good." Let this suffice us still,
Resting in childlike trust upon His will
Who moves to His great ends unthwarted by the ill.

The Eternal Goodness

O friends! with whom my feet have trod
The quiet aisles of prayer,
Glad witness to your zeal for God
And love of man I bear.

I trace your lines of argument;
Your logic linked and strong
I weigh as one who dreads dissent,
And fears a doubt as wrong.

But still my human hands are weak
To hold your iron creeds:
Against the words ye bid me speak
My heart within me pleads.

Who fathoms the Eternal Thought?
Who talks of scheme and plan?
The Lord is God! He needeth not
The poor device of man.

I walk with bare, hushed feet the ground
Ye tread with boldness shod;
I dare not fix with mete and bound
The love and power of God.

Ye praise His justice; even such
His pitying love I deem:
Ye seek a king; I fain would touch
The robe that hath no seam.

Ye see the curse which overbroods
A world of pain and loss;
I hear our Lord's beatitudes
And prayer upon the cross.

More than your schoolmen teach, within
Myself, alas! I know:
Too dark ye cannot paint the sin,
Too small the merit show.

I bow my forehead to the dust,
I veil mine eyes for shame,
And urge, in trembling self-distrust,
A prayer without a claim.

I see the wrong that round me lies,
I feel the guilt within;
I hear, with groan and travail-cries,
The world confess its sin.

Yet, in the maddening maze of things,
And tossed by storm and flood,
To one fixed trust my spirit clings;
I know that God is good!

Not mine to look where cherubim
And seraphs may not see,
But nothing can be good in Him
Which evil is in me.

The wrong that pains my soul below
  I dare not throne above,
I know not of His hate, — I know
  His goodness and His love.

I dimly guess from blessings known
  Of greater out of sight,
And, with the chastened Psalmist, own
  His judgments too are right.

I long for household voices gone,
  For vanished smiles I long,
But God hath led my dear ones on,
  And He can do no wrong.

I know not what the future hath
  Of marvel or surprise,
Assured alone that life and death
  His mercy underlies.

And if my heart and flesh are weak
  To bear an untried pain,
The bruisëd reed He will not break,
  But strengthen and sustain.

No offering of my own I have,
  Nor works my faith to prove;
I can but give the gifts He gave,
  And plead His love for love.

And so beside the Silent Sea
  I wait the muffled oar;
No harm from Him can come to me
  On ocean or on shore.

I know not where His islands lift
  Their fronded palms in air;
I only know I cannot drift
  Beyond His love and care.

O brothers! if my faith is vain,
  If hopes like these betray,
Pray for me that my feet may gain
  The sure and safer way.

ALL'S WELL

The clouds, which rise with thunder, slake
Our thirsty souls with rain

And Thou, O Lord! by whom are seen
Thy creatures as they be,
Forgive me if too close I lean
My human heart on Thee!

All's Well

The clouds, which rise with thunder, slake
Our thirsty souls with rain;
The blow most dreaded falls to break
From off our limbs a chain;
And wrongs of man to man but make
The love of God more plain.
As through the shadowy lens of even
The eye looks farthest into heaven
On gleams of star and depths of blue
The glaring sunshine never knew!

The Clear Vision

I did but dream. I never knew
What charms our sternest season wore.
Was never yet the sky so blue,
Was never earth so white before.
Till now I never saw the glow
Of sunset on yon hills of snow,
And never learned the bough's designs
Of beauty in its leafless lines.

Did ever such a morning break
As that my eastern windows see?
Did ever such a moonlight take
Weird photographs of shrub and tree?
Rang ever bells so wild and fleet
The music of the winter street?
Was ever yet a sound by half
So merry as yon school-boy's laugh?

O Earth! with gladness overfraught,
No added charm thy face hath found;
Within my heart the change is wrought,
My footsteps make enchanted ground.

From couch of pain and curtained room
Forth to thy light and air I come,
To find in all that meets my eyes
The freshness of a glad surprise.

Fair seem these winter days, and soon
  Shall blow the warm west-winds of spring,
To set the unbound rills in tune
  And hither urge the bluebird's wing.
The vales shall laugh in flowers, the woods
Grow misty green with leafing buds,
And violets and wind-flowers sway
Against the throbbing heart of May.

Break forth, my lips, in praise, and own
  The wiser love severely kind;
Since, richer for its chastening grown,
  I see, whereas I once was blind.
The world, O Father! hath not wronged
With loss the life by Thee prolonged;
But still, with every added year,
More beautiful Thy works appear!

As Thou hast made Thy world without,
  Make Thou more fair my world within;
Shine through its lingering clouds of doubt;
  Rebuke its haunting shapes of sin;
Fill, brief or long, my granted span
Of life with love to Thee and man;
Strike when Thou wilt the hour of rest,
But let my last days be my best!

Divine Compassion

Long since, a dream of heaven I had,
  And still the vision haunts me oft;
I see the saints in white robes clad,
  The martyrs with their palms aloft;
But hearing still, in middle song,
  The ceaseless dissonance of wrong;
And shrinking, with hid faces, from the strain
Of sad, beseeching eyes, full of remorse and pain.

The glad song falters to a wail,
The harping sinks to low lament;
Before the still unlifted veil
I see the crownëd foreheads bent,
Making more sweet the heavenly air
With breathings of unselfish prayer;
And a Voice saith: "O Pity which is pain,
O Love that weeps, fill up my sufferings which remain!

"Shall souls redeemed by me refuse
To share my sorrow in their turn?
Or, sin-forgiven, my gift abuse
Of peace with selfish unconcern?
Has saintly ease no pitying care?
Has faith no work, and love no prayer?
While sin remains, and souls in darkness dwell,
Can heaven itself be heaven, and look unmoved on hell?"

Then through the Gates of Pain, I dream,
A wind of heaven blows coolly in;
Fainter the awful discords seem,
The smoke of torment grows more thin,
Tears quench the burning soil, and thence
Spring sweet, pale flowers of penitence:
And through the dreary realm of man's despair,
Star-crowned an angel walks, and lo! God's hope is there!

Is it a dream? Is heaven so high
That pity cannot breathe its air?
Its happy eyes forever dry,
Its holy lips without a prayer!
My God! my God! if thither led
By Thy free grace unmerited,
No crown nor palm be mine, but let me keep
A heart that still can feel, and eyes that still can weep.

The Brewing of Soma

"These libations mixed with milk have been prepared for Indra; offer Soma to the drinker of Soma." – *Vashista,* translated by MAX MÜLLER.

The fagots blazed, the caldron's smoke
Up through the green wood curled;
"Bring honey from the hollow oak,
Bring milky sap," the brewers spoke,
In the childhood of the world.

And brewed they well or brewed they ill,
The priests thrust in their rods,
First tasted, and then drank their fill,
And shouted, with one voice and will,
"Behold the drink of gods!"

They drank, and lo! in heart and brain
A new, glad life began;
The gray of hair grew young again,
The sick man laughed away his pain,
The cripple leaped and ran.

"Drink, mortals, what the gods have sent,
Forget your long annoy."
So sang the priests. From tent to tent
The Soma's sacred madness went,
A storm of drunken joy.

Then knew each rapt inebriate
A winged and glorious birth,
Soared upward, with strange joy elate,
Beat, with dazed head, Varuna's gate,
And, sobered, sank to earth.

The land with Soma's praises rang;
On Gihon's banks of shade
Its hymns the dusky maidens sang;
In joy of life or mortal pang
All men to Soma prayed.

The morning twilight of the race
Sends down these matin psalms;
And still with wondering eyes we trace
The simple prayers to Soma's grace,
That Vedic verse embalms.

As in that child-world's early year,
Each after age has striven
By music, incense, vigils drear,
And trance, to bring the skies more near,
Or lift men up to heaven!

Some fever of the blood and brain,
Some self-exalting spell,
The scourger's keen delight of pain,
The Dervish dance, the Orphic strain,
The wild-haired Bacchant's yell, —

The desert's hair-grown hermit sunk
The saner brute below;
The naked Santon, hashish-drunk,
The cloister madness of the monk,
The fakir's torture-show!

And yet the past comes round again,
And new doth old fulfil;
In sensual transports wild as vain
We brew in many a Christian fane
The heathen Soma still!

Dear Lord and Father of mankind,
Forgive our foolish ways!
Reclothe us in our rightful mind,
In purer lives Thy service find,
In deeper reverence, praise.

In simple trust like theirs who heard
Beside the Syrian sea
The gracious calling of the Lord,
Let us, like them, without a word,
Rise up and follow Thee.

O Sabbath rest by Galilee!
O calm of hills above,
Where Jesus knelt to share with Thee
The silence of eternity
Interpreted by love!

With that deep hush subduing all
  Our words and works that drown
The tender whisper of Thy call,
As noiseless let Thy blessing fall
  As fell Thy manna down.

Drop Thy still dews of quietness,
  Till all our strivings cease;
Take from our souls the strain and stress,
And let our ordered lives confess
  The beauty of Thy peace.

Breathe through the heats of our desire
  Thy coolness and Thy balm;
Let sense be dumb, let flesh retire;
Speak through the earthquake, wind, and fire,
  O still, small voice of calm!

Vesta

O Christ of God! whose life and death
  Our own have reconciled,
Most quietly, most tenderly
  Take home Thy star-named child!

Thy grace is in her patient eyes,
  Thy words are on her tongue;
The very silence round her seems
  As if the angels sung.

Her smile is as a listening child's
  Who hears its mother call;
The lilies of Thy perfect peace
  About her pillow fall.

She leans from out our clinging arms
  To rest herself in Thine;
Alone to Thee, dear Lord, can we
  Our well-beloved resign!

Oh, less for her than for ourselves
  We bow our heads and pray;
Her setting star, like Bethlehem's,
  To Thee shall point the way!

Still linger in our noon of time
And on our Saxon tongue
The echoes of the home-born hymns
The Aryan mothers sung.

And childhood had its litanies
In every age and clime;
The earliest cradles of the race
Were rocked to poet's rhyme.

Nor sky, nor wave, nor tree, nor flower,
Nor green earth's virgin sod,
So moved the singer's heart of old
As these small ones of God.

The mystery of unfolding life
Was more than dawning morn,
Than opening flower or crescent moon
The human soul new-born!

And still to childhood's sweet appeal
The heart of genius turns,
And more than all the sages teach
From lisping voices learns, —

The voices loved of him who sang,
Where Tweed and Teviot glide,
That sound to-day on all the winds
That blow from Rydal-side, —

Heard in the Teuton's household songs,
And folk-lore of the Finn,
Where'er to holy Christmas hearths
The Christ-child enters in!

Before life's sweetest mystery still
The heart in reverence kneels;
The wonder of the primal birth
The latest mother feels.

We need love's tender lessons taught
As only weakness can;
God hath His small interpreters;
The child must teach the man.

We wander wide through evil years,
Our eyes of faith grow dim;
But he is freshest from His hands
And nearest unto Him!

And haply, pleading long with Him
For sin-sick hearts and cold,
The angels of our childhood still
The Father's face behold.

Of such the kingdom! — Teach Thou us,
O Master most divine,
To feel the deep significance
Of these wise words of Thine!

The haughty eye shall seek in vain
What innocence beholds;
No cunning finds the key of heaven,
No strength its gate unfolds.

Alone to guilelessness and love
That gate shall open fall;
The mind of pride is nothingness,
The childlike heart is all!

Overruled

The threads our hands in blindness spin
No self-determined plan weaves in;
The shuttle of the unseen powers
Works out a pattern not as ours.

Ah! small the choice of him who sings
What sound shall leave the smitten strings;
Fate holds and guides the hand of art;
The singer's is the servant's part.

The wind-harp chooses not the tone
That through its trembling threads is blown;
The patient organ cannot guess
What hand its passive keys shall press.

Through wish, resolve, and act, our will
Is moved by undreamed forces still;
And no man measures in advance
His strength with untried circumstance.

As streams take hue from shade and sun,
As runs the life the song must run;
But, glad or sad, to His good end
God grant the varying notes may tend!

By Their Works

Call him not heretic whose works attest
His faith in goodness by no creed confessed.
Whatever in love's name is truly done
To free the bound and lift the fallen one
Is done to Christ. Whoso in deed and word
Is not against Him labors for our Lord.
When He, who, sad and weary, longing sore
For love's sweet service, sought the sisters' door,
One saw the heavenly, one the human guest,
But who shall say which loved the Master best?

The Word

Voice of the Holy Spirit, making known
Man to himself, a witness swift and sure,
Warning, approving, true and wise and pure,
Counsel and guidance that misleadeth none!
By thee the mystery of life is read;
The picture-writing of the world's gray seers,
The myths and parables of the primal years,
Whose letter kills, by thee interpreted
Take healthful meanings fitted to our needs,
And in the soul's vernacular express
The common law of simple righteousness.
Hatred of cant and doubt of human creeds
May well be felt: the unpardonable sin
Is to deny the Word of God within!

The Book

Gallery of sacred pictures manifold,
A minster rich in holy effigies,
And bearing on entablature and frieze
The hieroglyphic oracles of old.
Along its transept aureoled martyrs sit;
And the low chancel side-lights half acquaint
The eye with shrines of prophet, bard, and saint,
Their age-dimmed tablets traced in doubtful writ!

But only when on form and word obscure
Falls from above the white supernal light
We read the mystic characters aright,
And life informs the silent portraiture,
Until we pause at last, awe-held, before
The One ineffable Face, love, wonder, and adore.

Requirement

We live by Faith; but Faith is not the slave
Of text and legend. Reason's voice and God's,
Nature's and Duty's, never are at odds.
What asks our Father of His children, save
Justice and mercy and humility,
A reasonable service of good deeds,
Pure living, tenderness to human needs,
Reverence and trust, and prayer for light to see
The Master's footprints in our daily ways?
No knotted scourge nor sacrificial knife,
But the calm beauty of an ordered life
Whose very breathing is unworded praise! —
A life that stands as all true lives have stood,
Firm-rooted in the faith that God is Good.

At Last

When on my day of life the night is falling,
And, in the winds from unsunned spaces blown,
I hear far voices out of darkness calling
My feet to paths unknown,

Thou who hast made my home of life so pleasant,
Leave not its tenant when its walls decay;

O Love Divine, O Helper ever present,
Be Thou my strength and stay!

Be near me when all else is from me drifting;
Earth, sky, home's pictures, days of shade and shine,
And kindly faces to my own uplifting
The love which answers mine.

I have but Thee, my Father! let Thy spirit
Be with me then to comfort and uphold;
No gate of pearl, no branch of palm I merit,
Nor street of shining gold.

Suffice it if — my good and ill unreckoned,
And both forgiven through Thy abounding grace —
I find myself by hands familiar beckoned
Unto my fitting place.

Some humble door among Thy many mansions,
Some sheltering shade where sin and striving cease,
And flows forever through heaven's green expansions
The river of Thy peace.

There, from the music round about me stealing,
I fain would learn the new and holy song,
And find at last, beneath Thy trees of healing,
The life for which I long.